T0353387

# Challenges and Applications for Implementing Machine Learning in Computer Vision

Ramgopal Kashyap
*Amity University, Raipur, India*

A.V. Senthil Kumar
*Hindusthan College of Arts and Science, India*

A volume in the Advances
in Computer and Electrical
Engineering (ACEE) Book Series

Published in the United States of America by
　　　IGI Global
　　　Engineering Science Reference (an imprint of IGI Global)
　　　701 E. Chocolate Avenue
　　　Hershey PA, USA 17033
　　　Tel: 717-533-8845
　　　Fax: 717-533-8661
　　　E-mail: cust@igi-global.com
　　　Web site: http://www.igi-global.com

Library of Congress Cataloging-in-Publication Data

Names: Kashyap, Ramgopal, 1984- editor. | Kumar, A. V. Senthil, 1966-
　　editor.
Title: Challenges and applications for implementing machine learning in
　　computer vision / Ramgopal Kashyap and A.V. Senthil Kumar, editors.
Description: Hershey, PA : Engineering Science Reference, an imprint of IGI
　　Global, [2020] | Includes bibliographical references. | Summary: "This
　　book examines the latest advances and trends in computer vision and
　　machine learning algorithms for various applications"-- Provided by
　　publisher.
Identifiers: LCCN 2019018175 | ISBN 9781799801825 (hardcover) | ISBN
　　9781799801832 (paperback) | ISBN 9781799801849 (ebook)
Subjects: LCSH: Computer vision. | Machine learning.
Classification: LCC TA1634 .C44 2020 | DDC 006.3/7--dc23
LC record available at https://lccn.loc.gov/2019018175

This book is published in the IGI Global book series Advances in Computer and Electrical Engineering (ACEE) (ISSN: 2327-039X; eISSN: 2327-0403)

British Cataloguing in Publication Data
A Cataloguing in Publication record for this book is available from the British Library.

All work contributed to this book is new, previously-unpublished material.
The views expressed in this book are those of the authors, but not necessarily of the publisher.

For electronic access to this publication, please contact: eresources@igi-global.com.

# Advances in Computer and Electrical Engineering (ACEE) Book Series

Srikanta Patnaik
SOA University, India

ISSN:2327-039X
EISSN:2327-0403

## MISSION

The fields of computer engineering and electrical engineering encompass a broad range of interdisciplinary topics allowing for expansive research developments across multiple fields. Research in these areas continues to develop and become increasingly important as computer and electrical systems have become an integral part of everyday life.

The **Advances in Computer and Electrical Engineering (ACEE) Book Series** aims to publish research on diverse topics pertaining to computer engineering and electrical engineering. **ACEE** encourages scholarly discourse on the latest applications, tools, and methodologies being implemented in the field for the design and development of computer and electrical systems.

## COVERAGE

- Programming
- Circuit Analysis
- Computer Architecture
- Applied Electromagnetics
- Digital Electronics
- Computer Hardware
- VLSI Fabrication
- Algorithms
- Power Electronics
- Analog Electronics

IGI Global is currently accepting manuscripts for publication within this series. To submit a proposal for a volume in this series, please contact our Acquisition Editors at Acquisitions@igi-global.com or visit: http://www.igi-global.com/publish/.

# Titles in this Series

*For a list of additional titles in this series, please visit:*
*https://www.igi-global.com/book-series/advances-computer-electrical-engineering/73675*

### *Novel Practices and Trends in Grid and Cloud Computing*
Pethuru Raj (Reliance Jio Infocomm Ltd. (RJIL), India) and S. Koteeswaran (Vel Tech, India)
Engineering Science Reference • © 2019 • 374pp • H/C (ISBN: 9781522590231) • US $255.00

### *Blockchain Technology for Global Social Change*
Jane Thomason (University College London, UK) Sonja Bernhardt (ThoughtWare, Australia) Tia Kansara (Replenish Earth Ltd, UK) and Nichola Cooper (Blockchain Quantum Impact, Australia)
Engineering Science Reference • © 2019 • 243pp • H/C (ISBN: 9781522595786) • US $195.00

### *Contemporary Developments in High-Frequency Photonic Devices*
Siddhartha Bhattacharyya (RCC Institute of Information Technology, India) Pampa Debnath (RCC Institute of Information Technology, India) Arpan Deyasi (RCC Institute of Information Technology, India) and Nilanjan Dey (Techno India College of Technology, India)
Engineering Science Reference • © 2019 • 369pp • H/C (ISBN: 9781522585312) • US $225.00

### *Applying Integration Techniques and Methods in Distributed Systems and Technologies*
Gabor Kecskemeti (Liverpool John Moores University, UK)
Engineering Science Reference • © 2019 • 351pp • H/C (ISBN: 9781522582953) • US $245.00

### *Handbook of Research on Cloud Computing and Big Data Applications in IoT*
B. B. Gupta (National Institute of Technology Kurukshetra, India) and Dharma P. Agrawal (University of Cincinnati, USA)
Engineering Science Reference • © 2019 • 609pp • H/C (ISBN: 9781522584070) • US $295.00

701 East Chocolate Avenue, Hershey, PA 17033, USA
Tel: 717-533-8845 x100 • Fax: 717-533-8661
E-Mail: cust@igi-global.com • www.igi-global.com

# Editorial Advisory Board

# Table of Contents

**Chapter 1**
Development of Class Attendance System Using Face Recognition for
Faculty of Mechanical and Manufacturing Engineering, Universiti Tun
Hussein Onn Malaysia ................................................................................. 1
> *Pauline Ong, Universiti Tun Hussein Onn Malaysia, Malaysia*
> *Tze Wei Chong, Universiti Tun Hussein Onn Malaysia, Malaysia*
> *Woon Kiow Lee, Universiti Tun Hussein Onn Malaysia, Malaysia*

**Chapter 2**
Deep Learning in Computational Neuroscience .......................................... 43
> *Sanjay Saxena, Department of Computer Science and Engineering, IIIT*
> *Bhubaneswar, Bhubaneswar, India*
> *Sudip Paul, North-Eastern Hill University, India*
> *Adhesh Garg, Department of Computer Science and Engineering, IIIT*
> *Bhubaneswar, Bhubaneswar, India*
> *Angana Saikia, North-Eastern Hill University, India*
> *Amitava Datta, The University of Western Australia, Australia*

**Chapter 3**
Advanced Diagnosis Techniques in Medical Imaging ................................. 64
> *Ramgopal Kashyap, Amity School of Engineering and Technology,*
> *Amity University, Raipur, India*

# Detailed Table of Contents

## Chapter 1
Development of Class Attendance System Using Face Recognition for
Faculty of Mechanical and Manufacturing Engineering, Universiti Tun
Hussein Onn Malaysia ................................................................................. 1

*Pauline Ong, Universiti Tun Hussein Onn Malaysia, Malaysia*
*Tze Wei Chong, Universiti Tun Hussein Onn Malaysia, Malaysia*
*Woon Kiow Lee, Universiti Tun Hussein Onn Malaysia, Malaysia*

The traditional approach of student attendance monitoring system in Universiti Tun
Hussein Onn Malaysia is slow and disruptive. As a solution, biometric verification
based on face recognition for student attendance monitoring was presented. The face
recognition system consisted of five main stages. Firstly, face images under various
conditions were acquired. Next, face detection was performed using the Viola Jones
algorithm to detect the face in the original image. The original image was minimized
and transformed into grayscale for faster computation. Histogram techniques of
oriented gradients was applied to extract the features from the grayscale images,
followed by the principal component analysis (PCA) in dimension reduction stage.
Face recognition, the last stage of the entire system, using support vector machine
(SVM) as classifier. The development of a graphical user interface for student
attendance monitoring was also involved. The highest face recognition accuracy of
62% was achieved. The obtained results are less promising which warrants further
analysis and improvement.

*Sanjay Saxena, Department of Computer Science and Engineering, IIIT*
*Bhubaneswar, Bhubaneswar, India*
*Sudip Paul, North-Eastern Hill University, India*
*Adhesh Garg, Department of Computer Science and Engineering, IIIT*
*Bhubaneswar, Bhubaneswar, India*
*Angana Saikia, North-Eastern Hill University, India*
*Amitava Datta, The University of Western Australia, Australia*

Computational neuroscience is inspired by the mechanism of the human brain. Neural networks have reformed machine learning and artificial intelligence. Deep learning is a type of machine learning that teaches computers to do what comes naturally to individuals: acquire by example. It is inspired by biological brains and became the essential class of models in the field of machine learning. Deep learning involves several layers of computation. In the current scenario, researchers and scientists around the world are focusing on the implementation of different deep models and architectures. This chapter consists the information about major architectures of deep network. That will give the information about convolutional neural network, recurrent neural network, multilayer perceptron, and many more. Further, it discusses CNN (convolutional neural network) and its different pretrained models due to its major requirements in visual imaginary. This chapter also deliberates about the similarity of deep model and architectures with the human brain.

*Ramgopal Kashyap, Amity School of Engineering and Technology,*
*Amity University, Raipur, India*

The Boltzmann distribution was derived in this chapter. The Boltzmann equation was explained next to the main difficulty of this equation, the integral of the collision operator, which was solved by the BGK-approximation where a long-term substitute is essential. The discretization of the Boltzmann comparison with the BGK-approximation was introduced along with the lattice and the different lattice configurations to define the lattice framework where the method is applied. Also, in this framework, the algorithm of the process was described. The boundary conditions were summarised, where one can see that they represent macroscopic conditions acting locally in every node.

## Chapter 4
*Amit Kumar Tyagi, School of Computing Science and Engineering,*
*Vellore Institute of Technology, Chennai, India*
*G. Rekha, Department of Computer Science and Engineering, Koneru*
*Lakshmaiah Educational Foundation, Hyderabad, India*

Due to development in technology, millions of devices (internet of things: IoTs) are generating a large amount of data (which is called as big data). This data is required for analysis processes or analytics tools or techniques. In the past several decades, a lot of research has been using data mining, machine learning, and deep learning techniques. Here, machine learning is a subset of artificial intelligence and deep learning is a subset of machine leaning. Deep learning is more efficient than machine learning technique (in terms of providing result accurate) because in this, it uses perceptron and neuron or back propagation method (i.e., in these techniques, solve a problem by learning by itself [with being programmed by a human being]). In several applications like healthcare, retails, etc. (or any real-world problems), deep learning is used. But, using deep learning techniques in such applications creates several problems and raises several critical issues and challenges, which are need to be overcome to determine accurate results.

## Chapter 5
*Hiral R. Patel, Ganpat University, India*
*Ajay M Patel, AMPICS, India*
*Satyen M. Parikh, FCA, India*

The chapter introduces machine learning and why it is important. Machine learning is generally used to find knowledge from unknown data. There are many approaches and algorithms available for performing machine learning. Different kinds of algorithms are available to find different patterns from the data. This chapter focuses on different approaches with different usage.

## Chapter 6
*Ramgopal Kashyap, Amity School of Engineering and Technology,*
*Amity University, Raipur, India*

In the medical image resolution, automatic segmentation is a challenging task, and it's still an unsolved problem for most medical applications due to the wide variety connected with image modalities, encoding parameters, and organic variability. In this chapter, a review and critique of medical image segmentation using clustering, compression, histogram, edge detection, parametric, variational model. and level set-based methods is presented. Modes of segmentation like manual, semi-automatic, interactive, and automatic are also discussed. To present current challenges, aim and motivation for doing fast, interactive and correct segmentation, the medical image modalities X-ray, CT, MRI, and PET are discussed in this chapter.

# Chapter 7

This chapter presents the relevance of picture handling to distinguish different sorts of harm. For areal-type harm, 1) edge extraction, 2) unsupervised arrangement, 3) texture examination, and 4) edge improvement are suitable to distinguish harmed zone. For liner-type harm, it is hard to improve the permeability of harm partition by picture preparing. Likewise, the impact of overlaying office information to help staff to discover harm at an extraction is described.

# Chapter 8

With the recent development in technologies and integration of millions of internet of things devices, a lot of data is being generated every day (known as Big Data). This is required to improve the growth of several organizations or in applications like e-healthcare, etc. Also, we are entering into an era of smart world, where robotics is going to take place in most of the applications (to solve the world's problems). Implementing robotics in applications like medical, automobile, etc. is an aim/goal of computer vision. Computer vision (CV) is fulfilled by several components like artificial intelligence (AI), machine learning (ML), and deep learning (DL). Here, machine learning and deep learning techniques/algorithms are used to analyze Big Data. Today's various organizations like Google, Facebook, etc. are using ML techniques to search particular data or recommend any post. Hence, the requirement of a computer vision is fulfilled through these three terms: AI, ML, and DL.

Content-based image retrieval is a promising technique to access visual data. With the huge development of computer storage, networking, and the transmission technology now it becomes possible to retrieve the image data beside the text. In the traditional way, we find the content of image by the tagged image with some indexed text. With the development of machine learning technique in the domain of artificial intelligence, the feature extraction techniques become easier for CBIR. The medical images are continuously increasing day by day where each image holds some specific and unique information about some specific disease. The objectives of using CBIR in medical diagnosis are to provide correct and effective information to the specialist for the quality and efficient diagnosis of the disease. Medical image content requires different types of CBIR technique for different medical image acquisition techniques such as MRI, CT, PET Scan, USG, MRS, etc. So, in this concern, each CBIR technique has its unique feature extraction algorithm for each acquisition technique.

## Chapter 10

*Muralikrishna Iyyanki, Independent Researcher, India*
*Prisilla Jayanthi, Administrative Staff College of India, India*

At present, public health and population health are the key areas of major concern, and the current study highlights the significant challenges through a few case studies of application of machine learning for health data with focus on regression. Four types of machine learning methods found to be significant are supervised learning, unsupervised learning, semi-supervised learning, and reinforcement learning. In light of the case studies reported as part of the literature survey and specific exercises carried out for this chapter, it is possible to say that machine learning provides new opportunities for automatic learning in expressive models. Regression models including multiple and multivariate regression are suitable for modeling air pollution and heart disease prediction. The applicability of STATA and R packages for multiple linear regression and predictive modelling for crude birth rate and crude mortality rate is well established in the study as carried out using the data from data.gov.in. Decision tree as a class of very powerful machine learning models is applied for brain tumors. In simple terms, machine learning and data mining techniques go hand-in-hand for prediction, data modelling, and decision making. The health analytics and unpredictable growth of health databases require integration of the conventional data analysis to be paired with methods for efficient computer-assisted analysis. In the second case study, confidence interval is evaluated. Here, the statistical parameter CI is used to indicate the true range of the mean of the crude birth rate and crude mortality rate computed from the observed data.

# Foreword

The fields of software engineering have given us a lot to think and work with Machine Learning (ML), and Computer Vision probably won't have fulfilled all its development, yet instead, it had an unusually active job in animating idea about what learning can and can't illustrate. The entire book committed to Machine learning and computer vision. I think this book gives enough data and essential parts of the issues above. Looking into the substance of this book, I am struck by the extraordinary and different nature of the field just as how much combination and cognisance has developed in such a brief span. This book makes sense of with each part of the area without transforming into an enormous clumsy black box of a thing focused on information, data, learning and everything else under the sun. It is intriguing to see exactly how much understanding there exists among specialists and professionals about what information investigation, security and mining are. This book is a not too lousy walk in that heading. The present top organisations experience the most critical change since industrialisation. Human-made reasoning upsets enterprises, how we work, think, connect. Gartner predicts that by 2020, Artificial Intelligence (AI) will make 2.3 million employments while taking out 1.8 million. AI is the thing that drives AI. Specialists in this area are uncommon, bosses battle for the ML-gifted ability. With this book, you will figure out how Machine Learning functions. A hundred pages from now, you will be prepared to manufacture complex AI frameworks, pass a meeting or go into business. AI is one of the quickest developing territories of software engineering, with sweeping applications. The point of this course reading is to present AI, and the algorithmic standards it offers, in a principled way. The book gives a broad hypothetical record of machine learning and computer vision. Following an introduction of the fundamentals of the field, the book covers an extensive exhibit of focal points that have not been tended to by past course readings.

*Satyanarayan Kashyap*
*Independent Researcher, India*

# Preface

Participation is prime significant for both the educator and understudy of an instructive association. So it is imperative to keep a record of the involvement. The issue emerges when we consider the conventional procedure of gauging participation in study hall. Calling name or move number of the understudy isn't just an issue of time utilization yet; also, it needs vitality. So a programmed participation framework can tackle every single above problem. There are some programmed attendances making framework which are as of now utilised by much organisation. One such structure is a biometric procedure. Even though it is processed and a stage in front of customary strategy, it neglects to meet the time requirement. The understudy needs to sit tight in line for giving participation, which is time taking. This task presents an automatic participation stamping framework, without any obstruction with the ordinary instructing strategy. The structure can be additionally actualised during test sessions or in other instructing exercises where participation is profoundly essential. This framework disposes of old-style understudy recognisable proof, for example, calling the name of the understudy, or checking individual ID cards of the understudy, which can meddle with the progressing showing process, yet additionally can be distressing for understudies during assessment sessions.

The objective of computational neuroscience is to discover unthinking clarifications of how the sensory system forms data to offer ascent to intellectual capacity and conduct. At the core of the field are its models, for example, numerical and computational depictions of the framework examined, which guide tangible improvements to neural reactions as well as neural to social responses. These models run from easy to complex. As of late, deep neural systems (DNNs) have come to rule a few spaces of Artificial Intelligence (AI). Current DNNs disregard numerous subtleties of organic neural systems. These improvements add to their computational proficiency, empowering them to perform complex accomplishments of knowledge, extending from perceptual (for example visual article and sound-related discourse acknowledgement) to individual assignments (for example machine interpretation), and on to engine control (for instance, playing computer games or controlling a robot arm). Notwithstanding their capacity to demonstrate sophisticated shrewd practices,

DNNs exceed expectations at anticipating neural reactions to novel tactile boosts with exactnesses well past some other as of now accessible model sort. DNNs can have a considerable number of parameters, which are required to catch the space information required for fruitful undertaking execution. In spite of the instinct that this renders them into impervious secret elements, the computational properties of the system units are the aftereffect of four straightforwardly manipulable components: input measurements, arrange structure, useful target, and learning calculation. With full access to the action and availability everything being equal, propelled perception systems, and logical instruments for organizing portrayals to neural information, DNNs speak to a fantastic structure for structure task-performing models and will drive significant bits of knowledge in computational neuroscience.

Restorative Imaging Techniques are non-intrusive strategies for peering inside the body without opening up the shape precisely. It used to help determination or treatment of various ailments. There are numerous therapeutic imaging methods; each system has multiple dangers and advantages. This paper introduces an audit of these methods; ideas, favourable circumstances, disservices, and applications. The concerning systems are; X-ray radiography, X-ray Computed Tomography (CT), Magnetic Resonance Imaging (MRI), ultrasonography, Elastography, optical imaging, Radionuclide imaging incorporates (Scintigraphy, Positron Emission Tomography (PET) and Single Photon Emission Computed Tomography (SPECT)), thermography, and Terahertz imaging. The ideas, advantages, dangers and uses of these systems will give subtleties. An examination between these strategies from perspective, picture quality (spatial goals and complexity), security (impact of ionising radiation, and warming effect of pollution on the body), and framework accessibility (continuous data and cost) will exhibit.

The ascent of human-made brainpower as of late is grounded in the achievement of profound learning. Three noteworthy drivers caused the performance of (intelligent) neural systems: the accessibility of immense measures of preparing information, incredible computational foundation, and advances in the scholarly community. In this way, profound learning frameworks begin to beat old-style techniques, yet also personal benchmarks in different assignments like picture arrangement or face acknowledgement. It makes the potential for some, problematic new organisations utilising profound figuring out how to take care of genuine issues.

Computer vision innovation is exceptionally flexible and can adjust to numerous enterprises in altogether different ways. Some utilisation cases off-camera, while others are increasingly obvious. No doubt, you have officially utilised items or administrations improved by computer vision. Tesla has finished the absolute most popular uses of computer vision with their Autopilot work. The automaker propelled its driver-help framework in 2014 with just a couple of highlights, for example, path focusing and self-cleaving. However it's set to achieve completely self-driving autos at some point in 2018. Highlights like Tesla's Autopilot are conceivable gratitude to new businesses, for example, Mighty AI, which offers a stage to produce exact and different comments on the datasets to prepare, approve, and test calculations identified with independent vehicles. Computer vision has made a sprinkle in the retail business also. Amazon Go store opened up its ways to clients on January 22 this year. It's a mostly mechanised store that has no checkout stations or clerks. By using computer vision, profound learning, and sensor combination clients can necessarily leave their preferred store with results and get charged for their buys through their Amazon account. The innovation isn't 100% impeccable yet, as a few authority trials of the store's change demonstrated that a few things were let alone for the last bill. Notwithstanding, it's a fantastic positive development.

While computers won't supplant medicinal services workforce, there is a decent probability of supplementing routine diagnostics that require a great deal of time and skill of human doctors yet don't contribute altogether to the last conclusion. Like these computers fill in as a helping apparatus for the social insurance workforce. For instance, Gauss Surgical is creating a continuous blood screen that takes care of the issue of wrong blood misfortune estimation during wounds and medical procedures. The screen accompanies a straightforward application that uses a calculation that investigates images of careful wipes to precisely foresee how much blood lost during a therapeutic process. This innovation can spare around $10 billion in unnecessary blood transfusions consistently. One of the primary difficulties the medicinal services framework is encountering is the measure of information that is being delivered by patients. Today, we as patients depend on the information bank of the restorative workforce to break down every one of that information and produce the right analysis. It can be troublesome on occasion. Microsoft's venture InnerEye is chipping away at tackling portions of that issue by building up an instrument that utilizations AI to investigate three-dimensional radiological images. The innovation possibly can make the procedure multiple times snappier and recommend the best medications. As shown above, computer vision has made some fantastic progress as far as what it can accomplish for various ventures. Be that as it may, this field is still moderately youthful and inclined to difficulties. One unique angle that is by all accounts the foundation for the vast majority of the problems is the way that computer vision is as yet not similar to the human visual framework, which is the thing that it attempts to emulate. Computer vision calculations can be very weak. A computer can perform undertakings it was prepared to execute and misses the mark when acquainted with new errands that require an alternate arrangement of information — for instance, encouraging a computer what an idea is hard yet it essential with the end goal for it to learn independently from anyone else. A genuine model is the idea of a book. As children, we realise what a book is and inevitably can recognise a book, a magazine or a comic while understanding that they have a place with a similar generally speaking classification of things. For a computer, that learning is significantly more troublesome. The issue is raised further when we add digital books and book recordings to the condition. As people, we comprehend that each one of those things falls under a similar idea of a book, while for a computer the parameters of writing and a book recording are too unique even to consider being put into related gatherings of things.

To beat such deterrents and capacity ideally, computer vision calculations today require social inclusion. Information researchers need to pick the right design for the information type with the goal that the system can naturally learn highlights. Engineering that isn't ideal may deliver results that have no incentive for the venture. At times, a yield of a computer vision calculation can upgrade with different sorts of information, for example, sound and content, to deliver exceedingly exact outcomes. As such, computer vision still does not have the abnormal state of precision that is required to work in a whole, a different world ideally. As the advancement of this innovation is still in progress, much resilience for mix-ups needed from the information science groups taking a shot at it. Neural systems utilised for computer vision applications are more straightforward to prepare than any time in recent memory yet that requires a great deal of excellent information. It implies the calculations need a ton of information that explicitly identified with the undertaking to create unique outcomes. Regardless of the way that images are accessible online in more significant amounts than any time in recent memory, the answer for some real issues calls for brilliant marked preparing information. That can get rather costly because an individual must finish the naming. How about we take the case of Microsoft's undertaking InnerEye, a device uses computer vision to dissect radiological images. The calculation behind this undoubtedly requires well-commented on models where several physical oddities of the human body are named. Given that around 4-5 images can dissect every hour, and a satisfactory informational collection could contain a considerable number of them, appropriate marking of images can get over the top expensive. Information researchers now and again use pre-prepared neural systems that initially prepared on a massive number of images as a base model. Without great information, it's a sufficient method to show signs of improvement results. Be that as it may, the calculations can find out about new articles just by "looking" at this present reality information. Pharmaceutical and therapeutic gadget producers are attempting to get genuine, and controllers are empowering them. That is because randomised clinical preliminaries, the highest quality level for testing treatment viability and security, may give an inappropriate thought regarding how well medications work in regular day to day existence. That, alongside expense and effectiveness concerns, is driving energy for more prominent utilisation of information assembled outside of clinical preliminaries. Genuine information originates from numerous sources, for example, electronic medicinal records, libraries of patients with a specific condition and social insurance claims data. It can emerge out of patients, as well, including through their versatile applications or wearable wellbeing trackers. A geographic information system (GIS), or geospatial data framework is any framework that catches, stores, examines, oversees, and exhibits information that connects to the location(s). GIS is the converging of cartography, measurable examination, and database innovation, ordinary asset the board, exactness horticulture, photogrammetric, urban arranging, a crisis the board, route, ethereal video, and limited hunt engines. Today the idea of GIS is generally utilised in various territories of research and humanity.

The catastrophe the board frameworks are most founded on GIS today, and the centre thought of those frameworks is the past seismic tremor encounters. Remote detecting picture preparing can enable the government to evaluate tremor harm rapidly. Taking this innovation coordinated with the quondam structure can improve the appraisal's accuracy of this sort of framework. It talks about a technique which quickly assesses the tremor harm. Right off the bat, we talk about various cases and snappy assessment of seismic tremor harm by methods for GIS-based framework. Besides, breaks down the outcome by brisk evaluation. Thirdly, coordinating the picture handling module with the old structure to get the new framework, in which the evaluation's accuracy can improve. Computer-based intelligence innovations will keep upsetting in 2019 and will turn out to be much more generally accessible because of reasonably distributed computing and enormous information blast. I don't review some other tech area right now that pulls in such vast numbers of brilliant individuals and huge assets from both the open-source/producer network and the most significant ventures simultaneously. What is the distinction between Artificial Intelligence (AI), Machine Learning (ML) and Deep Learning (DL)? While individuals frequently utilise these terms reciprocally, I think underneath is a decent applied delineation to separate these three terms. Simulated intelligence is remarkably a broad term, and to some degree this likewise makes each organisation guarantee their item has AI nowadays then ML is a subset of AI and comprises of the further developed systems and models that empower computers to make sense of things from the information and convey AI applications. ML is the study of getting computers to act without being unequivocally Content-Based Image Retrieval (CBIR) is one of the extraordinary zones in Computer Vision and Image Processing. Content-Based Image Retrieval frameworks recover images from that database, which are like the question picture. It is finished by really coordinating the substance of the question picture with the images in the database. Picture database can be an embrace, containing many thousands or a considerable number of images. In like manner case, those just listed by catchphrases entered in database frameworks by human administrators. Images Content of a picture can be portrayed regarding shading, shape and surface of a picture. CBIR in radiology has been a subject of research enthusiasm for about ten years. Substance Based Image Retrieval in restorative is one of the conspicuous zones in Computer Vision and Image Processing. CBIR can be utilised to find radiology images in massive radiology picture databases. The primary objective of CBIR in restorative is to recover images that are outwardly like a question proficiently. Examination of enormous information by AI offers excellent focal points for digestion and assessment of a lot of complex social insurance information. Be that as it may, to successfully utilise AI instruments in human services, a few impediments must tend to and key issues considered, for example, its clinical usage and morals in social insurance conveyance. Preferences of AI incorporate adaptability and versatility contrasted and conventional biostatistical techniques, which makes it deployable for some undertakings.

The objective of the proposed book is to introduce the reader to the Challenges and Applications for Implementing Machine Learning in Computer Vision. In particular, the book looks into the use of Machine Learning techniques and Artificial Intelligence to model various technical problems of the real world. This book organized in ten chapters; it includes essential chapters written by researchers from prestigious laboratories/ educational institution. A brief description of each of the chapters in this section given below:

Chapter 1 presents an approach of student attendance monitoring system in Universiti Tun Hussein Onn Malaysia is slow and disruptive. As a solution, biometric verification based on face recognition for student attendance monitoring presented. The face recognition system consisted of five main stages. Firstly, face images under various conditions were acquired. Next, face detection was performed using the Viola-Jones algorithm to detect the face in the original image. The original image was minimised, and transformed into grayscale for faster computation. Histogram techniques of oriented gradients were applied to extract the features from the grayscale images, followed by the principal component analysis (PCA) in dimension reduction stage. Face recognition, the last stage of the entire system, using a support vector machine (SVM) as a classifier. The development of a graphical user interface for student attendance monitoring was also involved. The highest face recognition accuracy of 62% achieved. The obtained results are less promising, which warrants further analysis and improvement.

Chapter 2 addresses the Computational neuroscience is inspired by the mechanism of the human brain. Neural networks have reformed machine learning and artificial intelligence. Deep learning, it is a type of machine learning method that teaches computers to do that comes indeed to individuals: acquire by example. It inspired by biological brains and became the essential class of models in the field of machine learning. Deep Learning involves several layers of computation. In the current scenario, researchers and scientists around the world are focusing on the implementation of different deep models and architectures. This chapter consists the information about significant structures of the deep network. That will give the information about Convolutional neural network, recurrent neural network, multilayer perceptron and many more. Further, it discusses CNN (Convolutional Neural Network) and its different pre-trained models due to its significant requirements in visual imaginary. This chapter also deliberates about the similarity of deep model and architectures with the human brain.

Chapter 3 evaluates the Boltzmann distribution, which is the distribution that holds the statistical treatment of the method. The Boltzmann equation explained next to the main difficulty of this equation, the integral of the collision operator solved by the BGK-Approximation where a long term substitutes this essential. The discretisation of the Boltzmann comparison with the BGK-Approximation introduced, all along with the lattice and the different lattice configurations, to define the lattice framework where the method is applied. Also, in this framework, the algorithm of the process was described. The boundary conditions summarized in this chapter, where one can see that they represent macroscopic conditions acting locally in every node.

Chapter 4 reviews big data is required to analysis process or analytics tools or techniques. For that, in the past several decades, a lot of research has been using data mining, machine learning and deep learning techniques. Here, machine learning is a subset of artificial intelligence, and deep learning is a subset of machine learning. Deep learning is much efficient than machine learning technique because, in this, it use perceptron and neuron or back propagation method, i.e., in these techniques, solve a problem by learning by itself. Todays in several applications like healthcare, retails, etc., deep learning used everywhere. But, using deep learning techniques in such applications creates several problems or raised several critical issue and challenges which are highly needed to overcome to determine accurate results.

Chapter 5 aims to the current growth in the market insist on adopting machine learning the smart technology utilised by our nation widely. The proposed chapter focuses on deep introductory of Machine learning. Why is it Important? Machine learning generally used to find out knowledge from unknown data. There are many approaches and algorithms are available for performing machine learning. The different kind of algorithms is possible to find out a different type of patterns from the data. This chapter focuses on different approaches and usage.

Chapter 6 analyses the medical image resolution, automatic segmentation is a challenging task, and it's still an unsolved problem for most medical applications due to the wide variety connected with image modalities, encoding parameters and organic variability. In this chapter, medical image segmentation using clustering, compression, histogram, edge detection, parametric, variational model and level set-based methods. Here also discuss modes of segmentation like manual, semi-automatic, interactive and automatic. Aim and motivation for doing fast, interactive and correct segmentation, the medical image modalities X-ray, CT, MRI and PET discussed in this chapter.

Chapter 7 reviews a genuine seismic tremor; it sets aside more extended effort to handle harm, regardless of whether substantial damages concentrated in such a circumstance, remote detecting innovation can assume significant jobs. Since the time has come devouring to recognize the harm by human eyes, it is successful in applying picture Handling. This paper presents the relevance of picture handling to distinguish different sorts of Harm. For areal-type harm, 1) edge extraction, 2) unsupervised arrangement, 3) texture examination, and 4) edge improvement is Suitable to distinguish harmed zone. For liner-type harm, it is hard to improve the permeability of harm partition by picture preparing the impact of overlaying office information to help staff to discover damage at extraction by human described.

Chapter 8 considers the recent development in technologies and integration of millions of internet of thing's devices; a lot of data generated every day. It required to analysis for improving the growth of several organizations or in applications like e-healthcare, etc. Also, we are entering into an era of smart world, where Robotics is going to take place in most of the applications (to solve the world's problems). Implementing Robotics in applications like medical, automobile, etc., is an aim/ goal of computer vision. Computer Vision (CV) objective fulfilled by several components like Artificial Intelligence (AI), Machine Learning (ML) and Deep Learning (DL). Here, Machine Learning and Deep learning techniques/ algorithms used to analysis Big Data. Today's various organizations, like Google, Facebook, etc., are using ML techniques to search particular data or recommend any post. Hence, the requirement of a computer vision is fulfilled these three terms AI, ML, and DL.

Chapter 9 considers the Content-Based Image Retrieval is a promising technique to access visual data. With the massive development of computer storage, networking, and the transmission technology now it becomes possible to retrieve the image data besides the text. Traditionally we use to find the content of the image by the tagged model with some indexed text. In the development of a machine learning technique in the domain of Artificial Intelligence, the feature extraction techniques become easier for CBIR. The medical images are continuously increasing day by day, where each image holds some specific and unique information about some particular disease. The objectives of using CBIR in medical diagnosis are to provide correct and useful information to the specialist for the quality and efficient diagnosis of the disease. In the medical image, content required different types of CBIR technique for different medical image acquisition technique such as MRI, CT, PET scan, USG, MRS etc. So in this concern the each CBIR technique have its unique feature extraction algorithm for each acquisition technique.

Chapter 10 presents machine learning that is most ever-growing subfield in health data analytics. At present, public health and population health are a primary concern and the study highlights the significant challenges through a few case studies of the application of machine learning for health data analytics to focus on regression four categories of machine learning methods meaningful supervised, unsupervised, semi-supervised and reinforcement learning. Machine learning provides new opportunities for automatically learning inexpressive models. Regression Models, including Multiple and Multivariate Regression techniques, are suitable for modelling Air Pollution and heart disease prediction. The applicability of STATA and R packages for multiple linear regression and predictive modelling for Crude Birth Rate and Crude Mortality Rate is well established in this study. Decision Tree is a class of Machine Learning model and applied for Brain Tumor. In predictive modelling, the measurement of the uncertain estimated model is the confidence interval. The confidence interval evaluated as a case study.

The prospective audience of this book will be on one side undergraduate students, postgraduate students, and researchers who are interested in the emerging area of machine learning, computer vision and on the other side industry people who are working in the mentioned areas. The potential use of this book could be course supplement for upper-level courses; library reference for students' projects; resource for researchers in machine learning, Challenges and Applications for Implementing Machine Learning in Computer Vision area. As the book will give an overview of both major domains together with their current research progress, issues and ideas; reference for the industry field, as essential research issues could address in the real-world environment.

The *Challenges and Applications for Implementing Machine Learning in Computer Vision* book is published by IGI Global (formerly Idea Group Inc.), publisher of the "Information Science Reference" (formerly Idea Group Reference), "Medical Information Science Reference," "Business Science Reference," and "Engineering Science Reference" imprints. For additional information regarding the publisher, please visit www.igi-global.com.

The editors wish you a pleasant reading.

# Acknowledgment

As nothing can be accomplished by oneself, this work is also not an exception. Though only our name appears on the cover, a great many people have contributed to this work. We would like to have some space to acknowledge some of them that frequently fade into the background. It is a matter of great pleasure to express our sincere gratitude to Prof.(Dr.) Surendra Rahamatkar, Professor and Dean Faculty of Engineering and Technology, Director Amity School of Engineering and Technology, Amity University Chhattisgarh, Raipur, India, who encouraged us all the time to face the problems during my book publication. We want to express our deepest gratitude for providing us with the necessary facility. We have been amazingly fortunate to have a mentor who gave me the freedom to explore on my own and at the same time, the guidance to recover when my steps faltered.

We humbly extend my thanks to Prof. Basant Tiwari, Faculty of Informatics, Hawassa University, Ethiopia for his encouraging timely help, continual counsel and cooperation. We are also profoundly grateful and sincerely thank Dr. Vivek Tiwari, IIIT Naya Raipur for their inspiration, support and valuable comments to improve the quality of my research.

We are the most blessed one to have the helping hands of faculty members and staff of the Amity University Chhattisgarh for their timely help and suggestions. We are also thankful to all friends and colleagues whose significant contributions were evident in this book publication in accumulating information and discussion on various issues related to the subject under study. They have been very supportive and have encouraged us throughout every step of the way. We want to extend our heartfelt thanks for their friendship, empathy and a great sense of humour that needed for the completion of this book.

I Ramgopal Kashyap want to mention my father Mr. Satyanarayan Kashyap and mother Mrs. Meena Kashyap deserve the special thanks for their inseparable support, eternal love and prayers. This work is possible because of their moral support. I will be failing in my duty if I do not express my thanks to my better half Tulsi and my

## Acknowledgment

son Atharv for his continuous support and encouragement. I thank my Brother Shiv Kashyap, Sisters Mrs. Shashi Kaushik, Mrs. Savita and Kavita for their love. Last but not least, all praises to Almighty GOD, who is the source of knowledge. I give thanks to God for his eternal love and giving me this opportunity to edit this book. Without him, I can't do anything. Finally, our heartfelt thanks go to all the people who have supported us to complete this book directly or indirectly.

Chapter 1

# Development of Class Attendance System Using Face Recognition for Faculty of Mechanical and Manufacturing Engineering, Universiti Tun Hussein Onn Malaysia

**Pauline Ong**
*Universiti Tun Hussein Onn Malaysia, Malaysia*

**Tze Wei Chong**
*Universiti Tun Hussein Onn Malaysia, Malaysia*

**Woon Kiow Lee**
*Universiti Tun Hussein Onn Malaysia, Malaysia*

## ABSTRACT

*The traditional approach of student attendance monitoring system in Universiti Tun Hussein Onn Malaysia is slow and disruptive. As a solution, biometric verification based on face recognition for student attendance monitoring was presented. The face recognition system consisted of five main stages. Firstly, face images under various conditions were acquired. Next, face detection was performed using the Viola Jones algorithm to detect the face in the original image. The original image was minimized and transformed into grayscale for faster computation. Histogram techniques of oriented gradients was applied to extract the features from the grayscale images,*

DOI: 10.4018/978-1-7998-0182-5.ch001

*followed by the principal component analysis (PCA) in dimension reduction stage. Face recognition, the last stage of the entire system, using support vector machine (SVM) as classifier. The development of a graphical user interface for student attendance monitoring was also involved. The highest face recognition accuracy of 62% was achieved. The obtained results are less promising which warrants further analysis and improvement.*

## INTRODUCTION

Nowadays, biometric applications are widely applied across industries, institutions and government establishments. Biometric verification means that a person can be uniquely identified by evaluating one or more distinguishing biological traits (Zhang, 2013). Unique identifiers include fingerprints, face and hand geometry, retina and iris patterns, voice waves, DNA, and signatures. Every human has unique fingerprint, which is constructed by numerous ridges and valley on the surface of finger (Jain, Ross, & Prabhakar, 2004). Voice recognition is a technology that transforms the sound and words of human into electrical signals. These signals will then be converted into code design (Baumann, 1993). Iris recognition is one of the most accurate biometric verification techniques. The digital camera is used to take the impression of an iris, and then, the iris will be evaluated in the stored version (Saini & Rana, 2014). For hand geometry recognition, the shape, size of palm, and the lengths and width of the fingers are taken from the human hand based on a number of measurements (Jain, Flynn, & Ross, 2007).

Face recognition involves an analysis of facial features. Typically, it involves a computer system which determines or verifies an individual automatically from a digital image or video framework. The selected facial features from the image are then compared against the available features in facial database to identify the individual (Saini & Rana, 2014). Face recognition, in general, consists of three principal phases, specifically, face detection – detection of a human face from within the image phase for further scrutinization, feature extraction – extracting the distinguishable features from faces using the techniques of segmentation, image rendering and scaling, and face identification - applying the mathematical models or artificial intelligence methods to identify the face based on the features extracted from the facial area within an image.

Face recognition has been widely used in numerous applications, for instance, surveillance system (Zafar et al., 2019), photo album organization (Oh, Benenson, Fritz, & Schiele, 2018), identity verification in financial services (Szczuko, Czyżewski, Hoffmann, Bratoszewski, & Lech, 2019) and airport (Carlos-Roca, Torres, & Tena, 2018), and owner verification of mobile phone (Mahbub, Sarkar, & Chellappa,

2019). Using face recognition to monitor student attendance in universities is another potential application area to pursue. This is due to universities are using class attendance as a marker of student engagement for reasons including admission to the final examination. Most standard attendance monitoring methods, in fact, require trade-off between the effort spent to record the attendance and the aspect of accuracy (Joseph & Zacharia, 2013). For instance, lecturers take the student attendance at the expense of the available teaching time. This approach can be disruptive, imagine the case where the attendance list is passed around from attendee to attendee during an important part of the lecture (Alia, Tamimi, & Al-Allaf, 2013). Hence, utilization of biometric verification based on face recognition for student attendance seems to be a viable solution. Moreover, attendance monitoring using face recognition does not require any action from students. Student just simply let the camera or webcam to scan his/her face, and the attendance would be recorded automatically. Face recognition performs massive identification which usually other biometric systems could not do (Klokova, 2010). Taking the attendance based on face recognition helps to avoid attendance fraud on one hand, and reduces human mistake on another hand. Moreover, the paper-less attendance monitoring system contributes to a cleaner environment (Saini & Rana, 2014). The most important thing is that facial recognition technology can be easily programmed into real-time attendance monitoring system.

As such, an automated student attendance system based on biometric verification, particularly, face recognition used in this study, is proposed as an alternative solution to the traditional attendance sheet. Using face recognition as a system to monitor the student attendance does not only prevent fraud attendance, it reduces human mistake as all students have unique biometric.

The objectives of this study are:

1. To develop an automated student attendance system using face recognition technique
2. To develop a graphical user interface (GUI) in order to improve the efficiency of managing students' attendance.

## THEORETICAL FRAMEWORKS

Face recognition has become more popular due to the advancement in computer vision and machine learning. This section reviews some publicly available databases of face images, feature extraction methods, classifiers used in face recognition, and some prior work in attendance monitoring.

# PUBLICLY AVAILABLE DATABASES OF FACE IMAGES

## AR Database

AR database was collected at the Computer Vision Center in Barcelona, Spain in 1998 (Martinez, 1998). This database has 116 images (63 men and 53 women). The recording conditions (camera parameters, lighting setting, and camera distance) are controlled carefully and always checked to make sure that settings are identical across subjects. The images are in 768 x 576 pixels in size. Various facial expressions, illumination and occlusion were captured during each session. Table 1 summarizes the recording condition of AR database while Figure 1 shows an example for each condition.

## BANCA Database

The BANCA database was collected as part of the European BANCA project. This project develops and implements a secure system with improved authentication, identification, and access control schemes for applications over the internet (Bailly-

*Table 1. Record condition of AR database*

| No of subject | Conditions | | Image Resolution | No of Images |
|---|---|---|---|---|
| 116 | Facial expressions | 4 | 768 x 576 | 3288 |
| | Illumination | 4 | | |
| | Occlusion | 2 | | |
| | Time | 2 | | |

*Figure 1. AR database with different condition (Gross, 2005)*

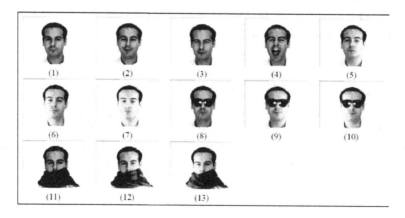

Bailliére et al., 2003). Data were collected for 52 individuals (26 men and 26 women). In a period of 3 months, 12 different sessions are recorded for each subject. Table 2 summarizes the recording conditions of BANCA database. Images from three recording conditions are shown in Figure 2. Controlled and adverse conditions was recorded by a high quality digital camera. The image of the degraded was taken by a low quality digital camera.

## CAS-PEAL Database

The CAS-PEAL database was collected at the Chinese Academy of Sciences (CAS) from August 2002 to April 2003. Data were collected for 1040 subjects (595 men and 445 women). The collected data fall in 7 categories, which are pose, expression, accessory, lighting, background, distance and time (Gao et al., 2004). Nine cameras were set in a semicircle around the individual for the pose subset. Images were recorded within a short time period (2 seconds). In addition, subjects were required to look up and look down each time by roughly 30° for additional recordings. Table

*Table 2. Record condition of BANCA database*

| No of Subject | Conditions | | Image Resolution |
|---|---|---|---|
| 208 | Image quality | 3 | 720 x 576 |
| | Time | 12 | |

*Figure 2. BANCA database (Gross, 2005)*

Controlled            Degraded            Adverse

3 summarizes the recording conditions of CAS-PEAL database while Figure 3 shows the example of the images. To record the face under varying lighting conditions, the light were set at (-90°, -45°, 0°, 45°, 90°) azimuth and (-45°, 0°, 45°) elevation. Figure 4 shows the image for all illumination conditions. For the expression conditions, the subjects were required to smile, to look surprise, to close their eyes, to frown, and to open their mouth. Some of the subjects were recorded wearing 3 type of glasses and hats. Subjects were also recorded with five plain colored background, which were blue, white, black, red, and yellow. Furthermore, images were obtained at 1.2 and 1.4 meters distances from camera. Lastly, small number of subjects were required to come back after 6 months for additional recordings. To simplify database distribution, the released images were stored as cropped gray-scale images of size 360 × 480. Figure 5 shows the currently distributed images.

*Table 3. Record condition of CAS-PEAL database*

| No of Subjects | Conditions | | Image Resolution | No of Image |
|---|---|---|---|---|
| 1040 | Pose | 21 | | |
| 377 | Facial expressions | 6 | | |
| 438 | Accessory | 6 | | |
| 233 | Illumination | 9 – 15 | 360 x 480 | 30900 |
| 297 | Background | 2 – 4 | | |
| 269 | Distance | 1 – 2 | | |
| 66 | Time | 2 | | |

*Figure 3. Pose variation in the CAS-PEAL database (Gross, 2005)*

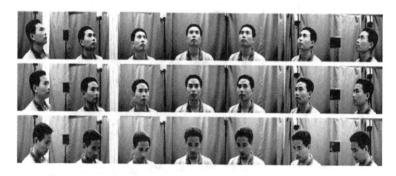

*Figure 4. Illumination variation in the CAS-PEAL database (Gross, 2005)*

*Figure 5. Released image of the pose in grayscale and 360x480 size (Gross, 2005)*

## FERET Database

The Facial Recognition Technology (FERET) database was collected at George Mason University and the US Army Research Laboratory facilities, sponsored by the US Department of Defense Counterdrug Technology Development Program (Phillips, Moon, Rizvi, & Rauss, 2000; Phillips, Wechsler, Huang, & Rauss, 1998). The FERET database has 24 facial image categories. Fifteen recording sessions were conducted from August 1993 until July 1996. The 35 mm camera was used to record the image. The captured images were digitized after that and then transformed to 8-bit grayscale images. The images were 256 × 384 pixels in size. Table 4 summarizes the recording condition of the FERET database while five frontal images are displayed in Figure 6.

*Table 4. Record condition of FERET database*

| No of Subjects | Conditions | | Image Resolution | No of Images |
|---|---|---|---|---|
| 1199 | Facial expression | 2 | 256 x 384 | 14051 |
| | Illumination | 2 | | |
| | Pose | 9 – 20 | | |
| | Time | 2 | | |

The *ia* and *ib* images were obtained in close succession. The subjects were required to show other facial expressions for the *ib* image. The changes in facial expression were switched between neutral and smiling. The image with a different camera and under different lighting conditions were categorized in the *ic* image. Some of the subjects were required to return at later date for another shot. For the images in duplicate I, at least 0 to 1031 days gap was in between two consequent recordings sessions. For the images in duplicate II, at least 18 months gap was in between two separate recording sessions.

The remaining image categories were set for pose variation. Figure 7 shows categories *ba* to *bi*. The subjects were asked to rotate the head and body when recording and the pose angles were ranged from +60° to −60°. Two hundred subjects were available for these pose data.

Diverse set of images are presented in Figure 8. These images were collected by using different head aspects: right and left face (labeled pr and pl), right and left half face (hr, hl), and right and left quarter face (qr, ql). There were three categories, specifically, right and left profile, right and left half profile and last is right and left quarter profile. There were 508 to 908 subjects recorded in these categories.

*Figure 6. Frontal image categories used for FERET evaluations (Gross, 2005)*

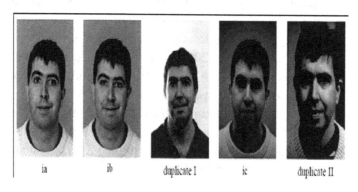

ia          ib          duplicate I          ic          duplicate II

*Figure 7. Pose variation in the FERET database (Gross, 2005)*

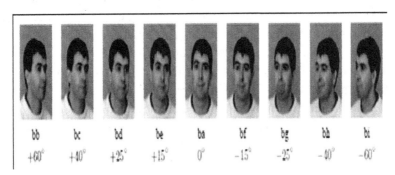

*Figure 8. Additional set of pose images from the FERET database (Gross, 2005)*

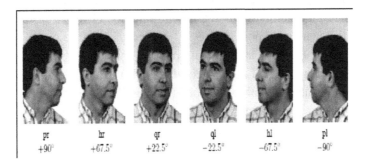

From the literature review of publicly available face recognition database, it can be seen that the factors of pose, illumination condition, facial expression and recording period are the main considered features, as summarized in Table 5.

## Feature Extraction for Face Recognition

The aim of feature extraction is to extract a compact set of interpersonal discriminating geometrical or/and photometrical features of the face. Feature extraction starts from

*Table 5. Summary of the record condition for the database*

| Database | No of Subject | Pose | Illumination | Facial Expressions | Time |
|---|---|---|---|---|---|
| AR | 116 | 1 | 4 | 4 | 2 |
| BANCA | 208 | 1 | - | 1 | 12 |
| CAS-PEAL | 66 – 1040 | 21 | 9 – 15 | 6 | 2 |
| FERET | 1199 | 9 – 20 | 2 | 2 | 2 |

a set of measured data and derives values to be used for subsequent learning. The speeded up robust features (SURF) extraction technique extracts the features using the nearest neighbors (Patel & Shah, 2017). The application of SURF features for face recognition in (Du, Su, & Cai, 2009) by utilizing the FERET database achieved the face recognition rate of 96%. Although the recognition rate of SURF is only slightly better than scale invariant feature transform (SIFT) with recognition rate of 95.9%, an improvement on matching speed is observed.

SIFT extraction method has been widely used to extract the features in face recognition (Lenc & Král). SIFT forms descriptors of the region of interest which are invariant to scale and rotation, and provides good performance under illumination changes. Purandare et al. utilized SIFT and contour matching for effective heterogeneous face recognition (Purandare & Talele, 2014). It has been shown in their work that the proposed algorithm gave better results in efficiency and accuracy, where this method is robust for illumination changes, facial expression changes and the changes in pose.

Gabor wavelet provides analysis of images, considering different scales or resolution and orientations (Liu & Wechsler, 2003). Chung et al. applied Gabor filter as part of the face recognition method (Chung, Kee, & Kim, 1999). The Gabor filter method has been combined with the principal component analysis (PCA) to recognize the face. Due to the images are sensitive to illumination and pose variant, Gabor filter responses as an input of PCA are used to overcome the problems. The experimental result of the proposed method showed the enhancement of recognition rate of 19% and 11% in SAIT dataset and Olivetti dataset, respectively.

Eigenfaces decomposes facial images into a small set of characteristic feature images. The lower dimensional space is found by using the eigenfaces (Turk & Pentland, 1991). An automatic face annotation using face features, outfit colors and period has been proposed by Nursuriati et al. (Jamil & Sa'Dan, 2014). The face is first detected by the Viola and Jones Haar-like detector in this approach. The extracted facial features, colors of clothing and date of picture are then stored as feature vectors after the face detection. The facial features are extracted by eigenfaces approach, while the clothing colors are extracted by color histogram and Julian date format is used.

## Face Recognition Classifier

Classification is the problem of identifying to which of a set of categories belongs, on the basis of a training set of data containing observations whose category membership is known. An example will be assigning the features belong to which person. Regression model is one of the methods that has been utilized in face recognition. Huang et al. (Huang, Lai, Gao, Yang, & Yang, 2016) applied linear regression classification (LRC) and its improved form, called linear discriminant regression classification (LDRC) to boost the effectiveness of LRC. The adaptive linear discriminant regression classification (ALDRC) algorithm was also proposed in which consideration of different contributions of the training samples was taken into account. Simulation on some face databases showed the advantage of using ALDRC. Machining learning approaches, too, have been widely used for classification of face images. Machine learning is a field of computer science that uses statistical techniques to provide computer systems the ability to "learn" itself without being clearly programmed. Machine learning involves understanding of the complex patterns until it can learn new pattern adeptly or recognize existing one (Christopher, 2016). One of the most outstanding machine learning techniques is artificial neural networks (ANNs), which use some parallel strategies such as simulating neurons and layering in order to learn concepts from experience. Réda and Aoued (Réda & Aoued, 2004) utilized ANNs based face recognition on face images with and without noise. The experimental result showed that the recognition rates of 100% and 94.68% are attained for images without and with Gaussian noise, respectively. The k-Nearest Neighbor (kNN), a variant of machine learning, has been used by Wrosey (Worsey, 2016) in his work. The features are extracted by the SIFT and each descriptor is matched using a Euclidean distance based kNN. The best result achieved in his work was approximately 86% matching rate. Jingyu (Jingyu, 2018) applied three popular algorithms, specifically, K-means clustering, auto-encoder, and convolutional neural network (CNN), to deal with face recognition problem, in terms of sentiment classification from images. It was shown that the classification using CNN produced the highest accuracy. The advent of the deep learning (DL) methodology has successfully overcome the issues with real time face recognition system of ANNs (Vinay et al., 2015). DL operates by modelling high-level abstractions based on how the human brain recognizes patterns. Deep Neural Networks (DNNs) apply a large number of layers for the purpose of mimicking human learning. It can adjust the strength of connections between the simulated neurons within the multiple layers accordingly (Vinay et al., 2015). It has been shown that DNNs are capable of easily being scaled to substantially large datasets which other methods such as SVM and LDA cannot perform well (Vinay et al., 2015). The DNN has been introduced in (Vinay et al., 2015), where it has been shown that the DNN performed perfectly in face recognition even in images with various illuminations and camera angles. The outstanding accuracy of about 97.3% on the Labelled Faces in the Wild (LFW) database has been obtained.

## Attendance Monitoring Prior Work

Shilwant and Karwankar (Shilwant & Karwankar, 2012) designed a simple web based attendance monitoring system that can be used across campus. The developed system worked in two different ways, first was actual face recognition and second was wider system administrative purposes from post processing of the gathered information. Before passing the captured image with face coordinates to the server for recognition, they used the continuously operating web cam to detect the faces. Alia et al. (Alia et al., 2013) developed a semi-automated system where the camera was used to capture the student's image when they entered the class. The lecturer can instruct the system to process the images and to confirm the recognition. Before submitting a final attendance report to the administrative system, the lecturer can manually add undetected or unrecognized attendees. Worsey (Worsey, 2016) presented an automated system to monitor the attendance. Students' images were recorded using the camera. It is then assigned to the identity of the library image that it best matched for each captured face image. The identity with all related data was excluded from further consideration when the identity of the best matching face image was assigned. Kar et al. (Kar, Debbarma, Saha, & Pal, 2012) presented an automated system to monitor the attendance. The attendance of the students in classroom environment will be recorded automatically by this system. The student's information can be accessed easily because the system provides the facilities to the faculty to maintain a log for clock-in and clock-out time. The system takes attendance of each student at the entry and exit points. Their work showed the improvement of this system as compared to the traditional black and white attendance system. Chintalapati and Raghunadh (Chintalapati & Raghunadh, 2013) developed an automated attendance management system. The system will automatically mark the attendance by recognizing the student when it detects the student enters the classroom, using the camera at the entrance of the classroom. For further processing, face region was extracted and pre-processed. Due to the size of entrance, no more than two persons can enter the classroom at the same time. It has been shown that this system is less time consuming and with high security.

## RESEARCH METHODS

Nowadays, institutions utilize several methods for student attendance system. In Faculty of Mechanical and Manufacturing Engineering (FKMP), Universiti Tun Hussein Onn Malaysia (UTHM), attendance monitoring using the traditional approach, where students are required to sign on the attendance list. This approach is slow if the size of attendee is large, and it may be disruptive, since the attendance list is passed around in class during an important part of the lecture. Also, taking attendance using the sign-in attendance sheet, or maybe a short-in-class quiz, may lead to the issue of fraud attendance, where the student who is present may fraudulently sign on the behalf of an absent friend. At times, lecturers call the name one by one to take the attendance in order to prevent fraud attendance at the expense of the available teaching time. All these manual approaches are not only time-consuming, but also less efficient for keeping the student attendance record validly and correctly.

UTHM has started to implement Student Attendance System (SASAR) by using the QR code since Semester 2, 2017/2018. Students scan the QR code using their registered student account during the class as proof of attendance. SASAR may be more efficient than the traditional sign-in attendance sheet; however, the issues of time-consuming and validity of attendance are remained unsolved. Lecturers have to display the QR code for the students to scan at the expense of the available teaching time. Also, fraudulent behavior still cannot be prevented. By using two or more smartphones, student can help their absent friends to scan the QR code easily. Hence, the feasibility of applying face recognition to monitor student attendance in FKMP, UTHM is used as the case study in this work.

This section discusses the methods used to develop the students' attendance monitoring system using face recognition in this study. A standard face recognition pipeline, consists of face images acquisition, face detection, pre-processing of face images, feature extraction, dimension reduction and face recognition, are introduced in this section. The technique used in each stage of face recognition is also presented in this section.

## Standard Face Recognition Pipeline

Basically, the face recognition system consists of five main stages, specifically, collection of face images, face detection, feature extraction, dimension reduction and face recognition, as illustrated in Figure 9. The details of each main stage are explained in the following section. Various conditions of the face images were recorded in the data collection stage. The different conditions, specifically, pose, facial expression, illumination, time, and accessory are considered in this study. Continuing from the data collection, face detection which is to detect the face in the raw image, is performed. Face detection detects the face region and removes the unwanted background for further process. Prior to face detection, the raw image is transformed into grayscale, and is resized to smaller size for faster computation. For the feature extraction stage, HOG technique is applied to extract the features from the face images. Gradients are calculated to generate the histogram in this stage. Subsequently, PCA is used in dimension reduction stage. The purpose of applying the PCA dimensionality reduction approach is to reduce the feature dimension because

*Figure 9. Standard pipeline for face recognition*

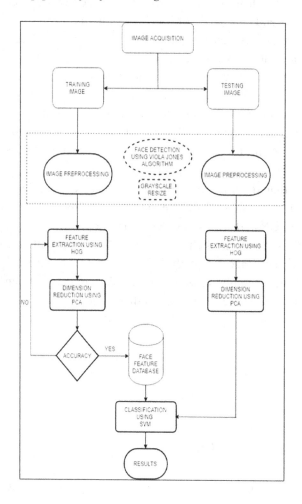

the original data dimension of the extracted features is high. Face recognition is the last stage for the entire system, where SVM classifier has been chosen in this study. The SVM finds the optimal hyperplane to separate different samples into their corresponding categories, such that the owner of the face image can be identified correctly.

## Face Image Acquisition

For the face recognition system, data acquisition plays an important role. The condition of the face image will affect the accuracy of the entire face recognition system indirectly. After scrutinizing some publicly available database, the recording condition of face images used in this study are poses, facial expression, illumination, time and accessory. For pose, the face images are taken from left side of the face until right side of the face, which is 90° to −90°, with the difference of 45° in each time of recording. In addition, the images of frontal face looking upside and downside are taken. For the facial expression, the images are taken in smile, neutral, frown, open mouth, close eye, and speech conditions. For the illumination, lights are put in parallel with face, with the sequence set at 45°, 0°, and −45°. Indoor, outdoor, light on and light off conditions are also considered in the illumination of the image. For the time factor, the image is taken 1 to 5 times over a 6 weeks period. Lastly, for the accessory condition, the images of subject with and without glasses are considered. All of these images are taken by Apple IPhone 6s, in the dimension of 3024×4032. The examples of face images in all different recording conditions are shown in Figure 10. The conditions are (A1) glasses, (E1) neutral, (E2) smile, (E3) frown, (E4) closed eye, (E5) open mouth, (E6) speech, (I) outdoor, (I2) on light, (I3) light -45°, (I4) light 0°, (I5) light 45°, (P1) pose -90°, (P2) pose -45°, (P3) pose 0°, (P4) pose 45°, (P5) pose 90°, (P6) look up, (P7) look down.

*Figure 10. Face image record conditions*

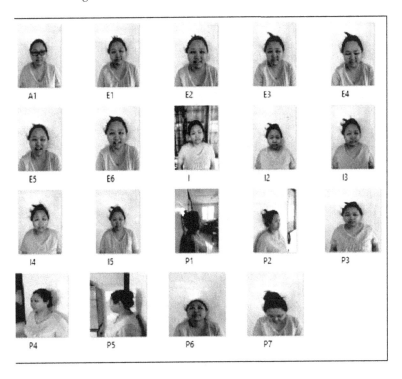

## Face Detection Using Viola Jones Algorithm

Following from the face image acquisition, face detection is generally considered the first step in face recognition. The original image is converted to grayscale prior to face detection as shown in Figure 11. In addition, since the acquired images are in hundreds in this study, longer processing time is required to process the image if large size of image is used. Hence, the original image with dimension 3024×4032 is resized to dimension 1512×2016, which is 50% of the original image. This is to speed up the image processing.

Face detection, basically, is to detect the faces from non-faces from the image. The Viola Jones algorithm (Viola & Jones, 2004) is the face detection technique used in this study. It is selected due to the advantages of its robustness and high computational efficiency (Chaudhari, Shanta, & Vanjare, 2015). There are four stages involved in the Viola Jones algorithm to detect the object, specifically:

1.  Haar-like feature
2.  Integral image for rapid features detection
3.  AdaBoost machine-learning method
4.  Cascade classifier

*Figure 11. Grayscale image after converting*

## Haar-Like Feature

Human faces have similar characteristics, for instance, the eyes are normally darker than the surrounding areas, and the nose bridge region is usually brighter than the eye region. Hence, the variation in the black and light portion of the image can be detected by Haar-like features. The Haar-like features with two-, three- or four-rectangles, are used as a template to scalable geometric structures, as shown in Figure 12.

Haar-like feature computes the differences between distinct rectangular areas within the image space. For example, as shown in Figure 13, a two-rectangles Haar-like features can locate the eye region by searching the areas within the image such that the upper rectangle contrasts the lower rectangle significantly. If a three-rectangles Haar-like features is used, the areas of image with the most distinctive difference between the two outer rectangles and the inner rectangle, are potentially the eye region.

## Integral Images

A main key of the Viola Jones detection algorithm is the use of the integral image. The image space transformed by a single pass can be defined as

$$ii\left(x,y\right) = \sum i\left(x',y'\right) | \left(x' \le x\right) \wedge \left(y' \le y\right) \tag{1}$$

where *ii* is the integral image, the summation of the pixels taken from *i* from the column and row location by *x* and *y*. The integral image is a simple summation. Without using the integral image to compute the sum of pixels in a rectangular area of the image space would require the summation of every pixel. Simple calculation

*Figure 12. Haar-like features are identified by the number of rectangles here contain (2, 3, 4) and the position of the rectangles (Worsey, 2016)*

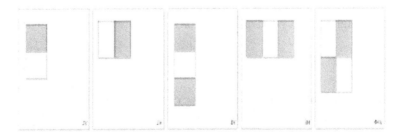

*Figure 13. Illustrating the strength inherent within the domain knowledge in Haar-like features (Worsey, 2016)*

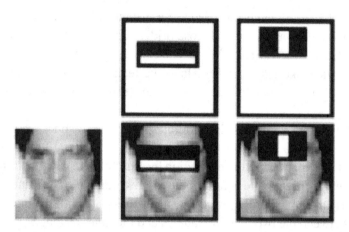

of the four corners of the integral image that sums up the pixel intensity values of the target rectangle area is given as:

$$\sum_{x=a}^{b}\sum_{y=c}^{d} i(x,y) \equiv ii(b,d) + ii(a,c) - ii(a,d) - ii(b,c) \qquad (2)$$

where $ii$ is the integral image and $i$ is the source image. This is illustrated in Figure 14.

## Adaboost Training

Adaboost training can make the Viola Jones algorithm fast and easy computation because the Adaboost algorithm can help to find little features from the face (Viola & Jones, 2001). AdaBoost algorithm provides desired area of the object by discarding pointless background. Neural networks can be used to interpret the working model (Viola & Jones, 2001). The learning process of Adaboost is fast and gives more number of wanted data. This data can be classified by a classifier. A classifier holds minor features of the face. It is frequently utilized for pattern detection. This technique has high accuracy and fast detection but required more time to train (Viola & Jones, 2001).

The explanation of Adaboost machine learning is as follows:

- Given image is in the form $(x_1, y_1)...(x_n, y_n)$
- $y_i = 0,1$ for negative and positive examples

*Figure 14. Integral image to compute the total pixel intensities of an image source rectangle (Worsey, 2016)*

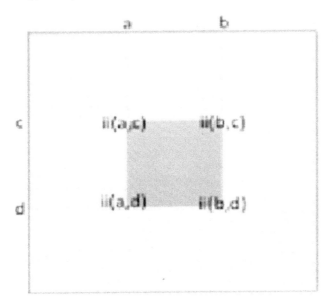

- Initialize the weights $w_{1,i} = \dfrac{1}{2m}, \dfrac{1}{2l}$ for $y_i = 0, 1$ respectively, where m and $l$ are number of positives and negatives respectively.
- For t = 1,...,:
  1. Normalize the weights,

$$w_{t,i} = \frac{w_{t,i}}{\sum_{j=1}^{n} w_{t,i}} \tag{3}$$

   $w_t$ is the probability distribution
  2. For each feature $j$, train a classifier $h_j$ which is restricted to use a single feature. The error is evaluated with respect to

$$w_t, E_t = \sum_i w_i \left| h_j(x_i), y_i \right| \tag{4}$$

  3. Choose the classifier $h_t$ with the lowest error $E_t$
  4. Update the weights

$$w_{t+1,i} = w_{t,i} B_t^{1-e_i} \tag{5}$$

where $e_i = 0$ examples $x_i$ is classified correctly; $e_i = 1$ otherwise

$$B_t = \frac{e_t}{1-e_t} \tag{6}$$

- The final classifier is:

$h(x)=1$

$$\sum_{t=1}^{T} a_t h_t(x) \geq \frac{1}{2} \sum_{t=1}^{T} a_t \tag{7}$$

where $a_t = \log \dfrac{1}{B_t}$

## Cascading Classifier

Using a cascade of stages in the Viola Jones face detection algorithm can quickly eliminates face candidates. The cascade in each stage has stricter requirement to eliminate candidates. After that, it will be more difficult to pass at later stage. A candidate will exit the cascade if they fail in any stage or pass at final stage. If a candidate passes at final stage, then a face will be detected. The process of cascade classifier is shown in Figure 15. A face will be show up when a candidate pass all stages in the cascade. The face will be detected when these four main stages in Viola Jones approach has been done. Figure 16 shows the detected face on the image using the Viola-Jones algorithm.

*Figure 15. The example cascade of stages (Chaudhari et al., 2015)*

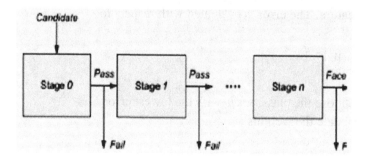

*Figure 16. The example of detected face on image using the Viola-Jones algorithm*

**Face Detection**

**Cropped Face**

## Feature Extraction by Using Histogram of Oriented Gradients

Features can be extracted once the face detection has been done. The technique of histogram of oriented gradients (HOG) (Shu, Ding, & Fang, 2011) is used as the feature extraction method in this study, due to its advantages of low computational complexity. Apart from this, HOG are not sensitive to both light and geometric changes. The steps to extract the HOG features are explained in the following section. The first step is to calculate the difference value for $x$ and $y$ directions, using the following equations:

$$\begin{cases} f_x(x,y) = f(x+1,y) - f(x-1,y) \\ f_y(x,y) = f(x,y+1) - f(x,y-1) \end{cases} \tag{8}$$

where $f(x,y)$ is the brightness value of the image in $(x,y)$. Subsequently, the calculation of magnitude *Arg* and direction $\theta$ in $(x,y)$ is performed, according to Equation (3.8) and Equation (3.9), respectively.

$$Arg(x,y) = \sqrt{f_x(x,y)^2 + f_y(x,y)^2} \tag{9}$$

$$\theta(x,y) = \arctan \frac{f_x(x,y)}{f_y(x,y)} \tag{10}$$

For example, consider an image of 64×128 dimension as in Figure 17, a 8×8 pixel cell is used to divide the image, forming 8×16 = 128 cell.

*Figure 17. Window division process (Xiang-Yu Li et al., 2018)*

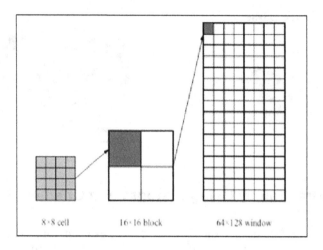

A 2×2 cells compose a block of 16×16 pixels, then 7x15 blocks are composed. The block is with step size of 8 pixels. (64−16)/8 + 1 = 7 is the number of blocks in the horizontal direction, and (128−16)/8 + 1 = 15 is the number of blocks in the vertical direction, as shown in Figure 18.

For example, each cell takes a histogram of 9 gradient directions. Such a block has 4x9 = 36 feature vectors, an image of 36x105 = 3780 HOG features are formed by 105 blocks of feature vectors that are connected in series. The HOG feature extraction display are shown in Figure 19.

*Figure 18. The example of block stepping process (Xiang-Yu Li et al., 2018)*

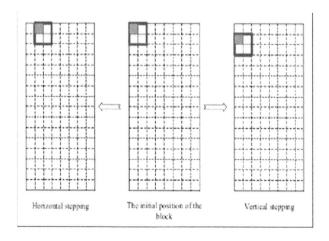

*Figure 19. The example of the HOG feature extraction display*

## Feature Extraction by Using Histogram of Oriented Gradients

The dimension of features is often higher than the number of samples. Although the classification still can be performed well using the raw extracted features, the computational complexity needs to be addressed. Hence, to achieve faster computation, the dimension reduction using the principal component analysis (PCA) is used in this study. PCA is a widely used technique for dimension reduction (Abdi & Williams, 2010; Jolliffe, 2002; Zhu, Zhu, & Li, 2018). PCA is an unmanaged learning algorithm which makes a linear transformation of the dimensions within the original area to an area that excellent describes the significance of every dimension. In theoretical, it determines the coordinates of the information that minimizes the mean square error over all linear changes of coordinate. It is done by locating the eigenvectors and eigenvalues of a related covariance matrix. A set of vectors is ordered by the variance. Since the quantity of the information contained is proportional to the variance within the component, thus, the components of low variance with less impact can be removed, contributing to dimensionality reduction. An outline of how to carry out the PCA on a set of image is described as follows:

1. Define X as a matrix of stacked images where each image is a column. The images are the $x_n$ component of the set of training data.

$$\{(x_n, t_n)\}, n = 1 \dots N \tag{11}$$

2.  Averaging the rows of X to compute the mean vector $\bar{x}$ by using

$$\bar{x}_i = \frac{1}{N} \Sigma X_i \tag{12}$$

where $i$ is the $i^{th}$ row of X.

3.  Subtract the mean and placing the resultant column in a matrix to center the data by using

$$A = X - 1\bar{x}^T \tag{13}$$

where 1 is a vector for 1s

4.  Compute the sample covariance matrix C by

$$C = \frac{1}{N-1} AA^T \tag{14}$$

5.  Compute the eigenvectors and the corresponding eigenvalue for the covariance matrix C by solving

$$Cv = \lambda v \tag{15}$$

where $v$ are the eigenvectors and $\lambda$ are the eigenvalues. The eigenvectors are orthonormal. The eigenvalues show the significance of the eigenvectors.

A two dimensional examples obtained from Figure 20 in which the biggest component is clearly the direction with the best variance. The second component is shown perpendicular to the first component.

## Face Recognition using Support Vector Machine

The classification is the last stage for face recognition, where the support vector machine (SVM) is used as the classifier in this study. SVM is selected due to its superiority of strong classification ability for small samples and high dimension data (Li & Lin, 2018). SVM is supervised learning algorithm that maximizes separation between classes by constructing a hyperplane (Cortes & Vapnik, 1995). Figure 21 shows an optimal hyperplane which separates the data points into positive class and negative class.

*Figure 20. A simple example of the principal components of a set of two dimensional data is shown (Worsey, 2016)*

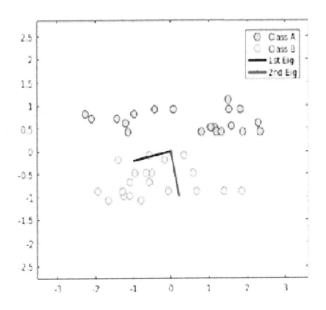

*Figure 21. A two state classification (Cortes et al., 1995)*

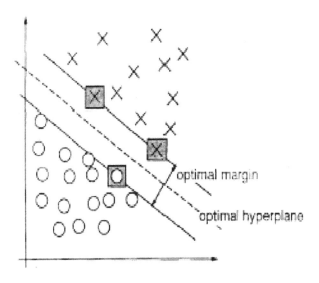

To classify a sample as being either positive or negative class, a decision rule given by

$$w \cdot u + b >= 0 \begin{cases} TRUE\,(positive) \\ FALSE\,(negative) \end{cases}$$

(16)

is applied, where $u$ is an unclassified sample, $w$ is perpendicular to the decision boundary and scalar $b$ defines the boundary. To decide which side of the boundary the unclassified sample resides, $u$ is projected onto a vector that is perpendicular to the boundary.

Initially, the vector $w$ and the corresponding scalar $b$ are in unknown conditions to describe the maximum boundary. To find the extrema, the Lagrange multiplier is applied. Its partial derivatives are solved by defining a set of constraints. The constraints are derived using:

$$y_i(w \bullet x_i + b) - 1 >= 0$$

(17)

and

$$y_i(w \bullet x_i + b) - 1 = 0$$

(18)

where $y_i$ is a positive sample $x_i$ for $+1$ and negative sample for $-1$. Those values of $y$ that equal to zero in the constraint are samples that reside at the edges closest to the boundary.

When the boundary edges reside by both positive $x_+$ and negative $x_-$ sample, the width of the boundary is computed by projecting the difference between $x_+$ and $x_-$ unto a unit normal version of $w$. In fact, this simplifies to $2/\|w\|$ and the minima of the magnitude of $w$ which maximizes the width needs to be identified. This can be done using the Lagrange multiplier. The Lagrangian L is described by

$$L = \frac{1}{2}\|w\|^2 - \sum \alpha_i \left[ y_i (w \cdot x_i + b) - 1 \right]$$

(19)

$$\frac{\partial L}{\partial w} = w - \sum \alpha_i y_i x_i = 0$$

(20)

$$\frac{\partial L}{\partial w} = -\sum \alpha_i y_i = 0$$

(21)

where the partial derivatives for both $w$ and $b$ can be solved.

The vector $w$ is a linear sum of samples of $x$ where the Lagrange multiplier $\alpha$ is not zero. The extremum is dependent on the dot product of pairs from the sample space by substituting the Equation of 3.21 and 3.22 into the Lagrange, as:

$$w = \sum \alpha_i y_i x_i \tag{22}$$

$$\sum \alpha_i y_i = 0 \tag{23}$$

## DATA ANALYSIS AND DISCUSSION

In this section, the results obtained from the developed face recognition monitoring attendance system were discussed. The developed system uses histogram of oriented gradients (HOG) as the feature extraction method and support vector machine (SVM) is selected as classifier. The Viola Jones algorithm is used to detect the face in the image. The principal component analysis (PCA) is used to reduce the dimension of the data.

### Face Detection

Face detection is the first important step to deploy this attendance monitoring system, in which Viola Jones algorithm is utilized in this regard. Prior to face detection, the face images are resized to smaller size (150x150) for fast computation, and are converted from RGB images to grayscale images. Figure 22 presents the original image, and the converted grayscale face images. The original image is in the size of 3024x4032 and is converted into grayscale image in the size of 520x600. The final image that used for feature extraction has been resized to 150x150.

Viola Jones algorithm uses cascade object detector to detect the faces, mouth, noses, eyes or upper body. In this study, frontal face has been selected for the cascade object detector in Viola Jones algorithm. Figure 23 shows the detected frontal face using Viola Jones algorithm.

As been discussed in the previous section, during image acquisition, the face images are taken from different angles, which is 90° to -90°, including frontal face looking upside and downside. In addition, different facial expressions, and different lighting conditions are considered, as illustrated in Figure 10. As illustrated in Figure 24, among 588 acquired face images, the face detection using Viola Jones algorithm could not work for 82 images – mostly associated with images with side

*Figure 22. Original image (left) and the grayscale image (right)*

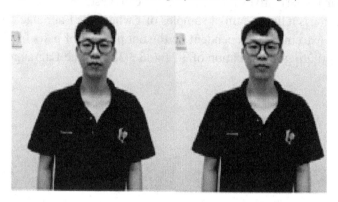

*Figure 23. The face was detected successfully using Viola Jones algorithm*

faces and some of 45° faces. This is due to frontal face detector is used in Viola Jones algorithm for face detection and thus, the effectiveness to detect side face is less promising in this case.

It is pertinent to note that changing the cascade object detector from frontal face to mouth, noses, eyes or upper body detector does not solve the aforesaid limitation. Figure 25 presents some example of face images that the Viola Jones algorithm fails to detect the face.

*Figure 24. The success rate of face detection using Viola Jones algorithm*

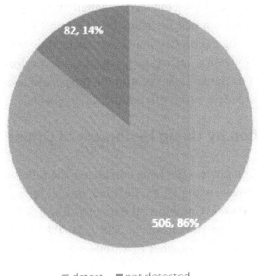

*Figure 25. Example of face images that the Viola Jones algorithm fails to detect the face*

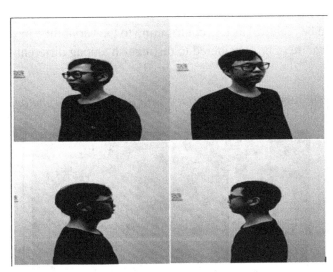

Since development of a fully automated attendance monitoring system is the main focus of this study, cropping the faces manually for those images which could not be handled using Viola Jones algorithm is not feasible in this case. As such, for these images, morphological processing of edge detection, contrast enhancement, noise removal, skeletonization and image segmentation is performed. Subsequently, the face is identified as the largest object in the image and is extracted. Figure 26 shows the detected side face using this additional approach.

## Feature Extraction by Using Histogram of Oriented Gradients

After the face detection process has been completed, the following step is to extract the features of each image using HOG. For each image, the extracted feature is in the dimension of 1x10404. Combing all extracted features from all 588 images, the raw features are in the dimension of 588 x 10404, meaning the number of observations is 588 while the number of variables or features is 10404. It can be observed that the dimension of features is higher than the number of observations. Hence, the dimension reduction using the PCA is required in order to address the computational complexity. From the dimension reduction, the explained variance in PCA shows that only the first 14 principal components (PCs) explain more than 1% of the variance. Explained variance in the PCA means the percentage of the variance explained by each principal component. For the PCs with less than 1% of variance, it can be regarded as less contributing to the variability, meaning that not a significant feature to be considered to distinguish among different observations.

*Figure 26. The successful detected side face using additional morphological operation*

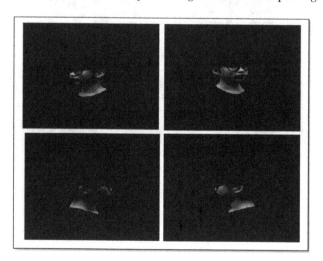

Hence, first 14 PCs are selected in this study for the face recognition using SVM subsequently. The input to SVM has been reduced to the dimension of 588×14, comparing to 588 x 10404 originally.

## Face Recognition Using Support Vector Machine

Following from the dimension reduction using PCA, face recognition using SVM classifier is performed. In this case, the 588 images are separated into training samples and testing samples, in which the training samples are used to build the SVM classification model, while the testing samples are used to evaluate the predictive capability of the developed SVM classifier. The 588 face images of 33 students are acquired in this study. For each individual, two face images are randomly selected as the testing samples, while the remaining are used as the training samples. Hence, the training data in the dimension of 522x14 and testing data in the dimension of 66x14 are obtained. Initially, all 14 PCs are used as the input of SVM. However, it has been found that the recognition accuracy is less satisfying, with 55% of accuracy is attained. Hence, further analysis on the effect of the number of PCs with the classification accuracy is conducted. The number of PCs is varied from 1 to 14, and the obtained recognition accuracy is summarized in Figure 27. As shown in this figure, the highest face recognition accuracy is achieved, when the SVM classifier is trained on 9 PCs. It can be seen that the classification accuracies are increasing from 1 PC to 9 PCs. After the maximum classification accuracy achieved at 9 PCs, the accuracy starts to decline, implying that adding more PCs does not improve the SVM predictive competence. From here, the SVM with 9 PCs as the input is selected as the face recognition model in the following process.

*Figure 27. The effect of using different number of PCs with the recognition accuracy*

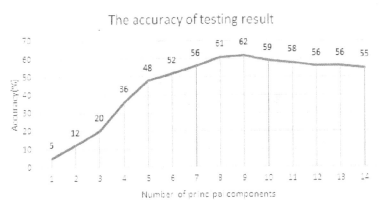

## Design of the Graphical User Interface for Race Recognition Attendance Monitoring System

Following from the training and testing process of SVM using different number of PCs as the input, the best model of SVM with 9 PCs has been selected and constructed as the face recognition model in the attendance monitoring system. Subsequently, the GUI of the attendance monitoring system is developed using MATLAB software. When the user run the system, the first shown window is as illustrated in Figure 28. Figure 29 shows the attendance monitoring system interface developed using MATLAB software, while Figure 28 is the resulted interface during execution.

The attendance monitoring system window shown in Figure 28 is the main part of the developed attendance system, as it will classify the captured face of student, and try to match it with the available database using the developed SVM classifier, and display his/her name if there is a match of face. As shown in Figure 29, there are 2 axes on both sides of the window. The axes 1 on the left hand side is to display the live video taken using the built in webcam of computer, while the axes 2 is to display the image captured from webcam. There are two pushbuttons been designed, which are snap pushbutton with caption 'Take Your Picture' and namelist pushbutton with caption 'Generate Table'. When the snap pushbutton is activated, it will capture the current frame of the video in axes 1, and display the captured image in axes 2. Subsequently, all the image process, feature extraction, dimension reduction and face recognition using the predefined SVM classifier are performed. The identified student's ID is then displayed in the static textbox, located

*Figure 28. Window for monitoring attendance system*

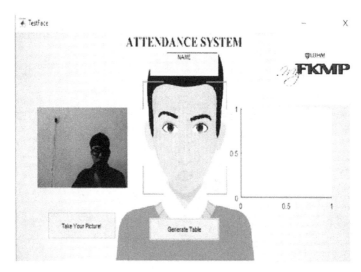

*Figure 29. Interface for monitoring attendance system*

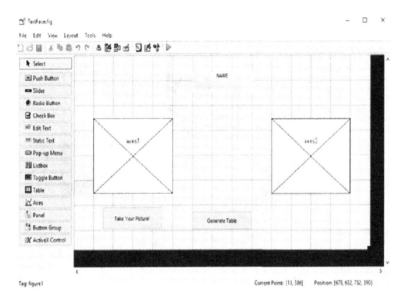

at the top of the window. The namelist pushbutton is to generate the excel file for attendance recording purposes. Figure 30 shows the window of the monitoring attendance system with the displayed name. The red colour rectangular in axes 2 is the detected face using the cascade object detector. All preprocessing methods are run at background. When the face is matched with the database, the name will be displayed, for example, the "id16" shown in Figure 30.

## FUTURE RESEARCH DIRECTIONS

From the results and analysis, the obtained face recognition accuracy of 62% using SVM with 9 PCs is less satisfying. As such, several recommendations are proposed in order to increase the predictive accuracy of SVM.

During the image acquisition, it has been found that the position and the pose of the student are critical problems that need to be dealt with. The face detection using Viola Jones algorithm works effectively for front face, but not for side face. Hence, it is recommended that in future work, only the images with frontal face are considered, with the assumption that student will stand still in front the system during image acquisition. Furthermore, the lighting condition during image acquisition is a critical problem that may affect the results. The images in this study are captured in different places and under different lighting conditions. Some images are taken under

*Figure 30. Window of the monitoring attendance system with matched ID*

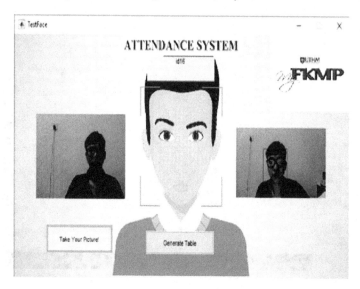

the natural light, and glare been induced in the images. In future, the images of all students should be captured under stable lighting condition and in the same venue.

From the obtained results, it seems that using HOG for feature extraction needs more work since only 43.34% variance been explained by the PCA. In future, it is suggested that feature extraction using HOG can be replaced with Speeded Up Robust Features (SURF). This is due to from literature review, it has been shown that the face recognition rate using the FERET database for SURF is up to 96%.

## CONCLUSION

This study proposes an attendance monitoring system that automatically records student's name when the matched face is detected successfully. The automated student attendance system using face recognition technique has been successfully developed. However, due to the frontal face detector is utilized in the Viola Jones algorithm for face detection, only images with frontal face are detected correctly. The detection of the side face and 45° face are less promising. From the results obtained, the first 14 PCs only explain 43.34% of variance, and the face recognition accuracy of only 62% is attained, by using SVM with 9 PCs, which warrants further improvement.

# REFERENCES

Abdi, H., & Williams, L. J. (2010). Principal component analysis. *Wiley Interdisciplinary Reviews: Computational Statistics, 2*(4), 433–459. doi:10.1002/wics.101

Alia, M. A., Tamimi, A. A., & Al-Allaf, O. N. (2013). Integrated system for monitoring and recognizing students during class session. *The International Journal of Multimedia & Its Applications, 5*(6), 45. doi:10.5121/ijma.2013.5604

Bailly-Bailliére, E., Bengio, S., Bimbot, F., Hamouz, M., Kittler, J., Mariéthoz, J., . . . Porée, F. (2003). *The BANCA database and evaluation protocol.* Paper presented at the International Conference on Audio-and video-based biometric person authentication. doi:10.1007/3-540-44887-X_74

Baumann, J. (1993, Fall). Voice recognition. *Human Interface Technology Laboratory.*

Carlos-Roca, L. R., Torres, I. H., & Tena, C. F. (2018, 8-13 July 2018). *Facial recognition application for border control.* Paper presented at the 2018 International Joint Conference on Neural Networks (IJCNN). doi:10.1109/IJCNN.2018.8489113

Chaudhari, M., Shanta, S., & Vanjare, G. (2015). A review on Face Detection and study of Viola-Jones method. *International Journal of Computer Trends and Technology, 25*(1), 54–61. doi:10.14445/22312803/IJCTT-V25P110

Chintalapati, S., & Raghunadh, M. V. (2013). *Automated attendance management system based on face recognition algorithms.* Paper presented at the 2013 IEEE International Conference on Computational Intelligence and Computing Research. doi:10.1109/ICCIC.2013.6724266

Christopher, M. B. (2016). *Pattern recognition and machine learning.* Springer-Verlag.

Chung, K.-C., Kee, S. C., & Kim, S. R. (1999). Face recognition using principal component analysis of Gabor filter responses. *Proceedings International Workshop on Recognition, Analysis, and Tracking of Faces and Gestures in Real-Time Systems. In Conjunction with ICCV'99 (Cat. No. PR00378).*

Cortes, C., & Vapnik, V. (1995). Support-vector networks. *Machine Learning, 20*(3), 273–297. doi:10.1007/BF00994018

Du, G., Su, F., & Cai, A. (2009). *Face recognition using SURF features.* Paper presented at the MIPPR 2009: Pattern Recognition and Computer Vision.

Gao, W., Cao, B., Shan, S., Zhou, D., Zhang, X., Zhao, D., & Al, S. (2004). *The CAS-PEAL large-scale Chinese face database and evaluation protocols*. Technique Report No. JDL-TR_04_FR_001, Joint Research & Development Laboratory, CAS.

Huang, P., Lai, Z., Gao, G., Yang, G., & Yang, Z. (2016). Adaptive linear discriminant regression classification for face recognition. *Digital Signal Processing*, *55*, 78–84. doi:10.1016/j.dsp.2016.05.001

Jain, A. K., Flynn, P., & Ross, A. A. (2007). *Handbook of biometrics*. Springer Science & Business Media.

Jain, A. K., Ross, A., & Prabhakar, S. (2004). An introduction to biometric recognition. *IEEE Transactions on Circuits and Systems for Video Technology*, *14*(1), 4–20. doi:10.1109/TCSVT.2003.818349

Jamil, N., & Sa'Dan, S. A. (2014). *Automated face annotation for personal photo management*. Paper presented at the 2014 International Conference on Computational Science and Technology (ICCST). doi:10.1109/ICCST.2014.7045176

Jingyu, Q. (2018). A Survey on Sentiment Classification in Face Recognition. *Journal of Physics: Conference Series*, *960*(1), 012030.

Jolliffe, I. T. (2002). Principal component analysis and factor analysis. *Principal Component Analysis*, 150-166.

Joseph, J., & Zacharia, K. (2013). Automatic attendance management system using face recognition. *International Journal of Science and Research*, *2*(11), 328–330.

Kar, N., Debbarma, M. K., Saha, A., & Pal, D. R. (2012). Study of implementing automated attendance system using face recognition technique. *International Journal of Computer and Communication Engineering*, *1*(2), 100.

Klokova, A. (2010). Comparison of various biometric methods. In *Interactive Multimedia Systems*. University of Southampton.

Li, X.-Y., & Lin, Z.-X. (2018). *Face Recognition Based on HOG and Fast PCA Algorithm*. Academic Press; doi:10.1007/978-3-319-68527-4_2

Liu, C., & Wechsler, H. (2003). Independent component analysis of Gabor features for face recognition. [PubMed]. *IEEE Transactions on Neural Networks*, *14*(4), 919–928. doi:10.1109/TNN.2006.875987

Mahbub, U., Sarkar, S., & Chellappa, R. (2019). Partial face detection in the mobile domain. *Image and Vision Computing*, *82*, 1–17. doi:10.1016/j.imavis.2018.12.003

Martinez, A. M. (1998). *The AR face database*. CVC Technical Report24.

Oh, S. J., Benenson, R., Fritz, M., & Schiele, B. (2018). Person Recognition in Personal Photo Collections. [PubMed]. *IEEE Transactions on Pattern Analysis and Machine Intelligence*, 1–1. doi:10.1109/TPAMI.2018.2877588

Patel, T., & Shah, B. (2017). *A survey on facial feature extraction techniques for automatic face annotation.* Paper presented at the 2017 International Conference on Innovative Mechanisms for Industry Applications (ICIMIA). doi:10.1109/ICIMIA.2017.7975607

Phillips, P. J., Moon, H., Rizvi, S. A., & Rauss, P. J. (2000). The FERET evaluation methodology for face-recognition algorithms. *IEEE Transactions on Pattern Analysis and Machine Intelligence*, 22(10), 1090–1104. doi:10.1109/34.879790

Phillips, P. J., Wechsler, H., Huang, J., & Rauss, P. J. (1998). The FERET database and evaluation procedure for face-recognition algorithms. *Image and Vision Computing*, 16(5), 295–306. doi:10.1016/S0262-8856(97)00070-X

Purandare, V., & Talele, K. (2014). *Efficient heterogeneous face recognition using scale-invariant feature transform.* Paper presented at the 2014 International Conference on Circuits, Systems, Communication and Information Technology Applications (CSCITA). doi:10.1109/CSCITA.2014.6839277

Réda, A., & Aoued, B. (2004). *Artificial neural network-based face recognition.* Paper presented at the Control, Communications and Signal Processing, 2004. First International Symposium on. doi:10.1109/ISCCSP.2004.1296323

Saini, R., & Rana, N. (2014). Comparison of various biometric methods. *International Journal of Advances in Science and Technology*, 2(1), 24–30.

Shilwant, D. S., & Karwankar, A. (2012). Student Monitoring By Face Recognition System. *International Journal of Electronics Communication and Soft Computing Science & Engineering*, 2(2), 24.

Shu, C., Ding, X., & Fang, C. (2011). Histogram of the oriented gradient for face recognition. *Tsinghua Science and Technology*, 16(2), 216–224. doi:10.1016/S1007-0214(11)70032-3

Szczuko, P., Czyżewski, A., Hoffmann, P., Bratoszewski, P., & Lech, M. (2019). Validating data acquired with experimental multimodal biometric system installed in bank branches. *Journal of Intelligent Information Systems*, 52(1), 1–31. doi:10.100710844-017-0491-2

Turk, M. A., & Pentland, A. P. (1991). Face recognition using eigenfaces. *1991 IEEE Computer Society Conference on Computer Vision and Pattern Recognition.* doi:10.1109/CVPR.1991.139758

Vinay, A., Shekhar, V. S., Rituparna, J., Aggrawal, T., Murthy, K. B., & Natarajan, S. (2015). Cloud-based big data analytics framework for face recognition in social networks using machine learning. *Procedia Computer Science, 50,* 623–630. doi:10.1016/j.procs.2015.04.095

Viola, P., & Jones, M. (2001). Rapid object detection using a boosted cascade of simple features. *Computer Vision and Pattern Recognition, 2001. CVPR 2001. Proceedings of the 2001 IEEE Computer Society Conference on.* doi:10.1109/ CVPR.2001.990517

Viola, P., & Jones, M. J. (2004). Robust real-time face detection. *International Journal of Computer Vision, 57*(2), 137–154. doi:10.1023/B:VISI.0000013087.49260.fb

Worsey, J. N. (2016). *Face recognition in an unconstrained environment for monitoring student attendance.* Academic Press.

Zafar, U., Ghafoor, M., Zia, T., Ahmed, G., Latif, A., Malik, K. R., & Sharif, A. M. (2019). Face recognition with Bayesian convolutional networks for robust surveillance systems. *Eurasip Journal on Image and Video Processing, 2019*(1). doi:10.118613640-019-0406-y

Zhang. (2013). *Automated biometrics: Technologies and systems* (Vol. 7). Springer Science & Business Media.

Zhu, Y., Zhu, C., & Li, X. (2018). Improved principal component analysis and linear regression classification for face recognition. *Signal Processing, 145,* 175–182. doi:10.1016/j.sigpro.2017.11.018

## ADDITIONAL READING

Damale, R. C., & Pathak, B. V. (2018, June). Face Recognition Based Attendance System Using Machine Learning Algorithms. In *2018 Second International Conference on Intelligent Computing and Control Systems (ICICCS)* (pp. 414-419). IEEE. doi:10.1109/ICCONS.2018.8662938

Devan, P. A. M., Venkateshan, M., Vignesh, A., & Karthikraj, S. R. M. (2017). Smart attendance system using face recognition. *Advances in Natural and Applied Sciences, 11*(7), 139–145.

Elias, S. J., Hatim, S. M., Hassan, N. A., Latif, L. M. A., Ahmad, R. B., Darus, M. Y., & Shahuddin, A. Z. (2019). Face recognition attendance system using Local Binary Pattern (LBP). *Bulletin of Electrical Engineering and Informatics*, *8*(1), 239–245. doi:10.11591/eei.v8i1.1439

Guo, G. (2018). Design and Implementation of Smart Campus Automatic Settlement PLC Control System for Internet of Things. *IEEE Access : Practical Innovations, Open Solutions*, *6*, 62601–62611. doi:10.1109/ACCESS.2018.2877023

Hossain, M. I. A., Hossain, I., Banik, M., & Alam, M. A. (2018, June). IOT based Autonomous Class Attendance System using Non-Biometric Identification. In *2018 Joint 7th International Conference on Informatics, Electronics & Vision (ICIEV) and 2018 2nd International Conference on Imaging, Vision & Pattern Recognition (icIVPR)* (pp. 268-271). IEEE.

Jain, A. K., Nandakumar, K., & Ross, A. (2016). 50 years of biometric research: Accomplishments, challenges, and opportunities. *Pattern Recognition Letters*, *79*, 80–105. doi:10.1016/j.patrec.2015.12.013

Khaleel, A., & Yussof, S. (2016). An investigation on the viability of using iot for student safety and attendance monitoring In Iraqi primary schools. *Journal of Theoretical and Applied Information Technology*, *85*(3), 394.

Kumar, N. A., Swarnalatha, P., Chowdary, P., Naidu, J. K., & Kumar, K. S. (2019). Smart Attendance Marking System using Facial Recognition. *Research Journal of Science and Technology*, *11*(2), 101–108. doi:10.5958/2349-2988.2019.00016.0

Kumar, P. M., Gandhi, U., Varatharajan, R., Manogaran, G., Jidhesh, R., & Vadivel, T. (2017). Intelligent face recognition and navigation system using neural learning for smart security in Internet of Things. *Cluster Computing*, 1–12.

Kutty, N. M., & Mathai, S. (2017). Face Recognition–A Tool for Automated Attendance System. *International Journals of Advanced Research in Computer Science and Software Engineering*, *7*(6), 334–336. doi:10.23956/ijarcsse/V7I6/0268

Labati, R. D., Genovese, A., Muñoz, E., Piuri, V., Scotti, F., & Sforza, G. (2016). Computational intelligence for biometric applications: A survey. *International Journal of Computing*, *15*(1), 40–49.

Li, C., Wei, W., Li, J., & Song, W. (2017). A cloud-based monitoring system via face recognition using Gabor and CS-LBP features. *The Journal of Supercomputing*, *73*(4), 1532–1546. doi:10.100711227-016-1840-6

Limkar, S., Jain, S., Kannurkar, S., Kale, S., Garsund, S., & Deshpande, S. (2019). iBeacon-Based Smart Attendance Monitoring and Management System. In *First International Conference on Artificial Intelligence and Cognitive Computing* (pp. 637-646). Springer, Singapore. doi:10.1007/978-981-13-1580-0_61

Mohammed, K., Tolba, A. S., & Elmogy, M. (2018). Multimodal student attendance management system (MSAMS). *Ain Shams Engineering Journal, 9*(4), 2917–2929. doi:10.1016/j.asej.2018.08.002

Olagunju, M., Adeniyi, E. A., & Oladele, T. O. (2018). Staff Attendance Monitoring System using Fingerprint Biometrics. *International Journal of Computers and Applications, 179*(21), 8–15. doi:10.5120/ijca2018916370

Pathak, P., Paratnale, M. M., Khairnar, D. R., Yadhav, P. V., & Wadgaonkar, P. R. (2016). Student Attendance Monitoring System Via Face Detection and Recognition System. *International Journal of Science Technology & Engineering, 2*(11).

Prakash, C., Kumar, R., & Mittal, N. (2018). Recent developments in human gait research: Parameters, approaches, applications, machine learning techniques, datasets, and challenges. *Artificial Intelligence Review, 49*(1), 1–40. doi:10.100710462-016-9514-6

Priya, S., & Mukesh, R. (2018). Multimodal Biometric Authentication using Back Propagation Artificial Neural Network. International Journal of Simulation--Systems, Science & Technology, 19(6).

Rewari, S., Shaha, A., & Gunasekharan, S. (2016). Facial Recognition Based Attendance System. *Journal of Image Processing & Pattern Recognition Progress, 3*(2), 43–49.

Rjeib, H. D., Ali, N. S., Al Farawn, A., Al-Sadawi, B., & Alsharqi, H. (2018). Attendance and information system using RFID and web-based application for academic sector. *International Journal of Advanced Computer Science and Applications, 9*(1).

Samy, S. S., & Parthiban, L. (2018). A Novel Feature Extraction Approach Using Principal Component Analysis and Quantum behaved Particle Swarm Optimization-Support Vector Networks for Enhancing Face Recognition. *Journal of Computational and Theoretical Nanoscience, 15*(9-10), 3012–3016. doi:10.1166/jctn.2018.7582

Sayeed, S., Hossen, J., Kalaiarasi, S. M. A., Jayakumar, V., Yusof, I., & Samraj, A. (2017). Real-time face recognition for attendance monitoring system. *Journal of Theoretical & Applied Information Technology, 95*(1).

Surekha, B., Nazare, K. J., Raju, S. V., & Dey, N. (2017). *Attendance recording system using partial face recognition algorithm. Intelligent techniques in signal processing for multimedia security* (pp. 293–319). Cham: Springer; doi:10.1007/978-3-319-44790-2_14

Vidya, M. S., & Arul, K. (2016). Automated Attendance System Through Eigen Faces Using Image Processing. International Journal of Informatics and Communication Technology (IJ-ICT), 111-118.

Wagh, P., Thakare, R., Chaudhari, J., & Patil, S. (2015, October). Attendance system based on face recognition using eigenface and PCA algorithms. In *2015 International Conference on Green Computing and Internet of Things (ICGCIoT)* (pp. 303-308). IEEE. doi:10.1109/ICGCIoT.2015.7380478

Zaman, F. H. K., Sulaiman, A. A., Yassin, I. M., Tahir, N. M., & Rizman, Z. I. (2017). Development of mobile face verification based on locally normalized Gabor wavelets. International Journal on Advanced Science. *Engineering and Information Technology*, 7(4), 1198–1205.

## KEY TERMS AND DEFINITIONS

**Biometric Verification:** It's an application which conducts measurement and identification based on physical or behavioral characteristics about a person (such as fingerprint or voice patterns), that can be applied to differentiate personal identities between individuals.

**Face Detection:** Face detection attempts to identify a human face in digital images. Face detection is not the same as face recognition.

**Face Recognition:** Face recognition involves an analysis of facial features, where in general, a computer system is utilized to identify an individual automatically from a digital image or video framework.

**Image Acquisition:** In image processing, image acquisition is an action of retrieving image from an external source for further processing. It's always the foundation step in the workflow since no process is available before obtaining an image.

**Principal Component Analysis:** Principal component analysis is a statistical approach that transforms a set of observations of possibly correlated variables into a set of linearly uncorrelated principal components using orthogonal transformation.

**Support Vector Machine:** Support vector machine is a supervised learning model with an associated learning algorithm that primarily used for classification.

**Viola Jones Algorithm:** Viola-Jones algorithm is an object detection framework, with primary concern to solve the problem of face detection. Four stages are involved in the algorithm, namely, Haar feature selection, creating an integral image, Adaboost training, and cascading classifier.

# Chapter 2
# Deep Learning in Computational Neuroscience

**Sanjay Saxena**
ⓘ https://orcid.org/0000-0002-8288-1010
*Department of Computer Science and Engineering, IIIT Bhubaneswar,*
*Bhubaneswar, India*

**Sudip Paul**
ⓘ https://orcid.org/0000-0001-9856-539X
*North-Eastern Hill University, India*

**Adhesh Garg**
*Department of Computer Science and Engineering, IIIT Bhubaneswar,*
*Bhubaneswar, India*

**Angana Saikia**
*North-Eastern Hill University, India*

**Amitava Datta**
*The University of Western Australia, Australia*

## ABSTRACT

*Computational neuroscience is inspired by the mechanism of the human brain. Neural networks have reformed machine learning and artificial intelligence. Deep learning is a type of machine learning that teaches computers to do what comes naturally to individuals: acquire by example. It is inspired by biological brains and became the essential class of models in the field of machine learning. Deep learning involves several layers of computation. In the current scenario, researchers and scientists around the world are focusing on the implementation of different deep models and architectures. This chapter consists the information about major architectures of*

DOI: 10.4018/978-1-7998-0182-5.ch002

*deep network. That will give the information about convolutional neural network, recurrent neural network, multilayer perceptron, and many more. Further, it discusses CNN (convolutional neural network) and its different pretrained models due to its major requirements in visual imaginary. This chapter also deliberates about the similarity of deep model and architectures with the human brain.*

## INTRODUCTION

Computational neuroscience is the area of investigation in which different mathematical tools and theories are implemented to investigate brain function. It achieves human-level execution in specific undertakings, and new analyses demonstrate that they can do. It is designed to empower the shallow models, enhance their performance. This type of networks addresses the fundamental question of how the brain processes the information, how a nervous system processes the information given to it, audio video or in any other form. These models commonly outline stimuli to neural response or potentially neural to functional responses. Feedforward neural network and recurrent neural networks architecture have gain popularity over the recent years. The biological brain inspires these deep learning neural networks. Their reflections add to their computational productivity, empowering to perform complex accomplishments of insight, running from perceptual errands (for example visual item and sound-related discourse acknowledgment) to intellectual errands (for example machine interpretation), and on to motor control errands (for example controlling a robot arm).

Over the years several models were designed to process the information with the of revolutionizing artificial intelligence. Neural networks inspired by the brain are at the center of this development. Deep neural networks have given better results than any of the other existing models. Neural networks differ from the biological neural network, but they exhibit structural similarity. For example, convolutional neural networks used in computer vision inspired by the natural view and processes segments of the given data, its neurons exhibit spatial restricted receptive fields that increase the invariance, size, and complexity along with the different levels and similar feature detector exists. These models are very less complicated as compared to the actual biological neural network, but they possess a certain degree of similarity, which is providing an edge in the current computation scenario. One of the major problems faced by the researchers concerning neural networks is, what the system is precisely doing. The interface can predict the data, but it is like a black box scenario where exactly it is too complex to understand the functioning of the neural network (Aggarwal, C. C.,2018), (Gulshan, V., Peng, L., Coram, M., Stumpe, M. C., Wu, D., Narayanaswamy, A., Webster, D. R., 2016). Historically simpler models present were easy to understand with a degree of freedom nevertheless since the brain has over billions of parameters and is a very complex structure. We have drawn insights from such complex models by considering a high level of abstraction. It leads us to another argument that states that neural networks are too abstract from the biological reality. A model can be more straightforward and sophisticated at the same time concerning different frames. The main questions researchers are trying to solve to which feature to model and which to omit from the biological brain while deigning network. The merit of these models is not dependent on how exactly they replicate the natural brain but on how accurately they can provide insights into the working of the mind at a given scenario (Waoo, N., Kashyap, R., & Jaiswal, A.,2010). This chapter summarizes the different architecture of deep models inspired by neuroscience. Further, it will draw the attention of the researchers who are working on the field of deep neural network.

## SIMILARITY OF DEEP NEURAL NETWORK AND BRAIN

Deep neural networks are a set of algorithms that are modeled loosely after the human brain. They have an input layer, an output layer, and a minimum of one hidden layer in between. Each layer aims to extract features from the input to recognize patterns. The general structure of the deep neural network given in figure 1.

The hidden layer sums up the inputs, taking their respective weights into account, and makes a non-linear decision to activate a feature by identifying it and sends the activation calculation further to another layer of neurons as input. In terms of the brain, a neuron is the fundamental processing unit of mind as well as a deep neural network. Inside the brain, these are the cells responsible for every action/function in the body with just simple inputs from the external world.

The general structure of the brain neuron shown in figure 2, a brain neuron has three main components at a high level: dendrites, cell body (soma), and axon. Dendrites act as the input mechanism as they receive connections from other neurons. The cell body or soma is the calculation mechanism in which receives inputs from all dendrites and calculates a response such as to whether spike a signal or not. The axon carries out the output mechanism as a delivery agent of the message to the other dendrite of the next neuron layer if the soma decides to fire an output. The point at which the axon joins the dendrite of another neuron is called a synapse, and this connection is called a synaptic connection.

In brain neurons, the signals transfer from one neuron to another with the help of chemical transmitters released by synapse causing the variation of potential in the soma of another neuron. The neuron does not carry any signal in the resting state. In the given an example below shown in figure 3, a minimum of 15 mV (-55

*Figure 1. Deep neural network*

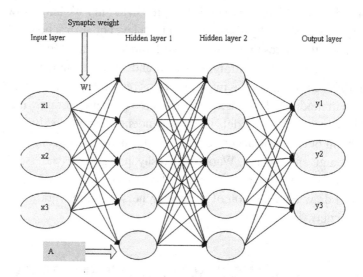

- -70) is required to fire an output. It called the threshold, as shown in figure 3. It means that the total 'sum' of all the input signals received must cross the limit for the message to pass through that neuron. On crossing the threshold, the impulse reaches the other dendrite through a synapse, and this process goes on ("Conduction of Nerve Impulse," 2019), ("CS231n Convolutional Neural Networks for Visual Recognition", 2019).

*Figure 2. Structure of the brain neuron*

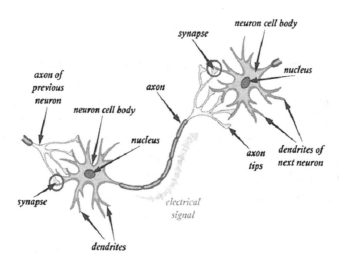

*Figure 3. The response of a single neuron to an incoming signal from its dendrite*

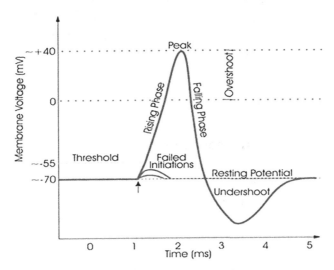

This process is very similar to DNN (Deep Neural Networks) in which the inputs added before being passed to further neurons. Other such similarities include synaptic weight, neural backpropagation, and plasticity in the learning method. Synaptic weight in DNNs refers to the strength of the connection between two nodes belonging to consecutive layers of the neural network. Its magnitude can be determined by the intensity of propagation of the signal through the axon, density of neurotransmitter vesicle and receptors, as well as the no. of synapses (i.e., the connections in between axon and dendrites. In biological neurons, as the signal passes through dendrites, the dendrites have some potential charge or intensity values which move from one cell to another. Deep neural networks these connection strengths known as synaptic weights. In DNN, each neuron in one layer connected to a neuron in the next layer through this synaptic weight. It has some value associated with the connection link that informs about the strength of the connection and the intensity of that feature.

Synaptic plasticity is the term coined to the occurrence of changes in synaptic weight. Another similarity is the neural backpropagation. It is the phenomenon in which after the action potential of a neuron fires a voltage spike through the axon (feedforward propagation) another impulse is produced from the cell body and spreads towards the tip of dendrites from which the original input signal originated. Though the backpropagating action potential can cause alteration in the synaptic weights, yet there is no such process for an error signal to move through multiple neural layers, as seen in the computer backpropagation algorithms. The brain learns and memorizes using local methods like Hebbian learning or STDP (Spike Timing Dependent Plasticity). These methods strengthen the connections between neurons that frequently transfer signals. A fundamental principle in training the deep neural networks is the concept of plasticity. During backpropagation in DNNs, the weights in between two consecutive neural layers in altered in every propagation based on the inputs and their corresponding outputs.

## LITERATURE REVIEW

### Major Architectures of Deep Network

Several architectures implemented in deep learning. This section describes different deep learning architectures in the last few years.

### Convolutional Neural Network (CNN)

A convolutional neural network (CNN) is a combination of multiple convolutional layers, pooling, or fully connected layers. Variations of a multilayer perceptron are used to design the system. Convolutional operations performed at convolution layers to the input data passing the result to the next layer. With much fewer parameters, convolution operation allows the network to be more profound. Image and speech recognition applications show outstanding results in convolutional neural networks. Semantic parsing, paraphrase detection are also the applications of CNN's.

### Multilayer Perceptron (MLP)

Multilayer perceptron network (MLP) has three or more layers. The general structure of the MLP shown in figure 5. It classifies data that is not linearly separable using mainly nonlinear activation function that is hyperbolic tangent or logistic function. It is a fully connected network, i.e., every node in a layer connects to each node in

*Figure 4. Convolutional neural network Ma, Y., Xiang, Z., Du, Q., & Fan, W. (2018), (Peng, M., Wang, C., Chen, T., & Liu, G., 2016)*

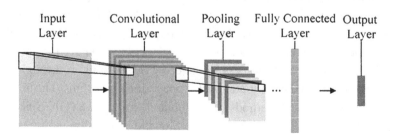

*Table 1. Work done in last 5 years*

| YEAR | AUTHOR | WORK DONE |
|---|---|---|
| 2019 | Santiago A. et.al | They modeled spiking activity in the primary visual cortex of monkeys using deep convolutional neural networks (CNN), which have been successful in computer vision. CNN's were directly trained to fit the data, and have used CNN's trained to solve a high-level task. With these approaches, they were able to outperform previous models and improve the state of the art in predicting the responses of early visual neurons to natural images (Cadena, S.A., Denfield, G.H., Walker, E.Y., Gatys, L.A., Tolias, A.S., Bethge, M. and Ecker, A.S., 2019). |
| 2019 | Ullman. S | He discovered that some additional aspects of brain circuitry could supply clues for guiding network models toward broader aspects of cognition and general AI (Artificial Intelligence). He concluded that combining the empirical and computational approaches to the problem is likely to benefit in the long run of both neuroscience and AGI(Artificial General Intelligence), and could eventually be a component of a theory of intelligent processing that will apply to both (Ullman, S., 2019). |
| 2018 | Pandarinath et al. | They described an artificial neural network model that captures some key aspects of the activity of populations of neurons in the primary motor cortex (Batista, A.P. and DiCarlo, J.J., 2018). |
| 2018 | Gruber et. al | In this study, they created non-dynamic visual competitions for humans by briefly presenting the mixtures of two images. They tested feed-forward DNNs with similar combinations and examined their behavior and found that both humans and DNNs tend to perceive only one picture when presented with a mixture of two. These findings can be used to both improve DNNs as models, as well as potentially improve their performance by imitating biological behaviors (Gruber, L.Z., Haruvi, A., Basri, R. and Irani, M., 2018). |
| 2017 | Dinggang et.al | They found that computational modeling for medical image analysis had a significant impact on both clinical applications and scientific research. Recent progress in deep learning has shed new light on medical image analysis by enabling the discovery of morphological and textural patterns in images solely from data (Shen, D., Wu, G. and Suk, H.I., 2017). |
| 2017 | Jordan et. al | They showed that a deep learning algorithm that utilizes multi-compartment neurons help to understand how the neocortex optimizes cost functions. Like neocortical pyramidal neurons, neurons in their model receive sensory information and higher order feedback in electrotonically segregated compartments. This work demonstrates that deep learning can be achieved using segregated dendritic compartments, which may help to explain the morphology of neocortical pyramidal neurons (Guerguiev, J., Lillicrap, T.P., and Richards, B.A., 2017). |
| 2016 | Irina et. al | They implemented an unsupervised approach for learning disentangled representations of the underlying factors of variation. By enforcing redundancy reduction, encouraging statistical independence, and exposure to data with transform continuities analogous to those to which human infants are exposed, they obtained a Variational autoencoder (VAE) framework capable of learning disentangled factors. This approach makes few assumptions and works well across a wide variety of datasets. Furthermore, their solution has useful emergent properties, such as zero-shot inference (Higgins, I., Matthey, L., Glorot, X., Pal, A., Uria, B., Blundell, C., Mohamed, S. and Lerchner, A., 2016). |

*continues on following page*

*Table 1. Continued*

| YEAR | AUTHOR | WORK DONE |
|------|--------|-----------|
| 2016 | Migel et.al | They present a method for synthesizing deep neural networks using Extreme Learning Machines (ELMs) as a stack of supervised autoencoders. They tested the technique using standard benchmark datasets for multi-class image classification and showed that the classification error rate could progressively improve with the inclusion of additional auto encoding ELM modules in a stack. This approach simultaneously offers a significantly faster training algorithm to achieve its best performance relative to a single ELM hence offers lower error rates and rapid implementation (Tissera, M.D. and McDonnell, M.D., 2016). |
| 2015 | Peter et. al | They analyzed the effects of converting deep ANNs (Analog Neural Network) into SNNs (Spiking Neural Network) concerning the choice of parameters for spiking neurons such as firing rates and thresholds (Tiwari S., Gupta R.K., & Kashyap R. 2019). A set of optimization techniques was presented to minimize performance loss in the conversion process for ConvNets and fully connected deep networks. The presented analysis and optimization techniques boost the value of spiking deep networks as an attractive framework for neuromorphic computing platforms which aimed at fast and efficient pattern recognition (Diehl, P.U., Neil, D., Binas, J., Cook, M., Liu, S.C. and Pfeiffer, M., 2015). |

the next layer making the network. For example, speech recognition and machine translation are applications of multilayer perceptron natural language processing (NLP).

## Recursive Neural Network (RNN)

A recursive neural network (RNN), shown in figure 6, is designed by applying the same set of weights recursively over a structure is one of the simple deep neural networks. It is intended to predict input structures of variable-size, or by traversing given data in topological order, a scalar prediction on it (Kashyap, R., 2019c). In the most straightforward architecture, nodes are combined into parents using nonlinearity like tanh, and a weight matrix that shared across the entire network.

## Recurrent Neural Network (RNN)

A recurrent neural network (RNN), as shown in figure 7, is a class of a recursive artificial neural network in which neurons make directed cyclic connections. Unlike a feedforward neural network output depends on the previous step's neuron state and the present inputs also. It has a memory that lets users solve NLP following data problems like handwriting recognition or speech recognition. It can build a relationship between the data most recently processed to the data processed now. They are mainly used in the case of sequential data and can generate new sentences and document summaries as it has a better understanding of the data fed to the system.

*Figure 5. Multilayer perceptron (Guo, W. W., & Xue, H.,2014)*

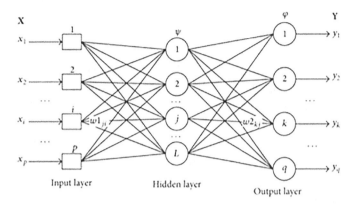

*Figure 6. Recursive neural network (Le, P., & Zuidema, W., 2015)*

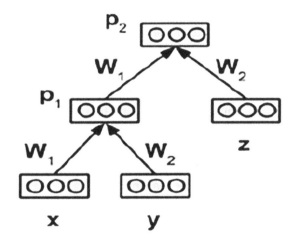

*Figure 7. Recursive neural network*

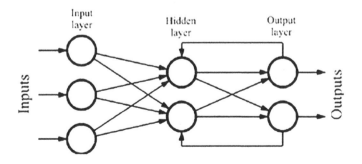

## Long Short-Term Memory (LSTM)

Long Short-Term Memory (LSTM) was designed to increase the accuracy in models with temporal sequences and their long-range dependencies. It is a specific type of recurrent neural network (RNN) architecture. It is a type of memory element. Within its repetitive component's activation functions are not used by LSTM, the values stored are not modified, and during training, the gradient tend does not vanish. LSTM, several units are implemented in "blocks." These blocks generally have three or four "gates" that is the input gate, forget gate, output gate that controls the logistic function drawing the information flow. LSTM as a fundamental element into their products incorporated by companies such as Apple, Amazon, Google, Microsoft, and others.

## Sequence-To-Sequence Models

A sequence-to-sequence model has of two recurrent neural networks: one to process the input an encoder and one to produce the output a decoder as presented in figure 8. Same or different sets of parameters can be used by the encoder and decoder or by the networks (Shukla R., Gupta R.K., & Kashyap R., 2019). Question answering systems, chatbots, and machine translation mainly use the sequence-to-sequence models. Sequence-to-Sequence models have multi-layer cell structure, which used for reading in Neural Networks study with Sequence to Sequence Learning. The encoder takes the input data sequence, and train model on it then it passes the last state of its recurrent layer as an initial state to the first recurrent layer of the decoder, the input of the decoder is the output sequence.

*Figure 8. Sequence to sequence models*

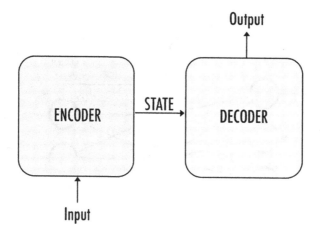

## CONVOLUTIONAL NEURAL NETWORK (CNN) AND ITS DIFFERENT ARCHITECTURES

CNN or Convnet is a distinct type of multi-layer neural networks, intended to identify graphic patterns unswervingly from pixel images with nominal preprocessing. In a convolutional network (ConvNet), there are three types of layers: Convolution layer, Pooling layer, Fully connected layer. As shown in figure 4. Convolution layer: The Convolution layer is the core building block of a Convolutional Network that does most of the computational heavy lifting. The Convolution layer's parameters consist of a set of learnable filters. Every filter is small spatially (along width and height), but extends through the full depth of the input volume. For example, a typical filter on the first layer of a ConvNet might have size 5x5x3 (i.e., 5 pixels width and height, and three because images have depth 3, the color channels). During the forward pass, we slide (more precisely, convolve) each filter across the width and height of the input volume and compute dot products between the entries of the screen and the input at any position Cui, Z., Yang, J., & Qiao, Y. (2016), Duggal, R., Gupta, A., Gupta, R., Wadhwa, M., & Ahuja, C. (2016), Georgakopoulos, S. V., Iakovidis, D. K., Vasilakakis, M., Plagianakos, V. P., & Koulaouzidis, A. (2016), (Raina, R., Madhavan, A., & Ng, A. Y.,2009).

Pooling layer: This layer is used to diminish the size of the inputs and henceforth speed up the calculation. Let suppose a 4 X 4 matrix, as shown below:

*Table 2.*

| 1 | 5 | 6 | 2 |
|---|---|---|---|
| 2 | 9 | 1 | 1 |
| 2 | 3 | 3 | 6 |
| 5 | 6 | 2 | 1 |

Applying max pooling on this matrix will result in a 2 X 2 output:

*Figure 9. Explanation of pooling layer*

53

Fully Connected Layer: The convolution and pooling layers would only be able to extract features and reduce the number of parameters from the original images (Deng, J., Dong, W., Socher, R., Li, L., Li, K., & Fei-Fei, L., 2009), (Grósz, T., & T., I. N.,2014). However, to generate the final output need to apply a fully connected layer to create an output equal to the number of classes we need. Till now, there are several trained popular CNN architectures are there. By following the transfer learning of the different existing buildings, we can implement in our dataset. Now we are going to give a brief introduction of different networks architectures of CNN (Krizhevsky, A., Sutskever, I., & Hinton, G. E.,2017), (Das, S., & Das, S.,2017).

**AlexNet:** Test accuracy of 84.6% Toronto's best deep CNN that won the 2012 ImageNet competition. It is designed using five convolutional layers, max-pooling layers, ReLUs as activation function, three fully-convolutional layers, and dropout.

**VGG-16 (Visual Geometry Group-16):** With 92.7% accuracy this Oxford's model won the 2013 ImageNet competition. It uses a stack of convolution layers with small receptive fields in the first layers instead of few layers with big receptive fields.

**VGG-19 (Visual Geometry Group-19)**: VGG-19 is a convolutional neural network that trained on more than a million images from the ImageNet database. The system is 19 layers deep and can classify images into 1000 object categories, such as a keyboard, mouse, pencil, and many animals. As a result, the network has learned rich feature representations for a wide range of images. The system has an image input size of 224-by-224.

**Google Net:** With the accuracy of 93.3% this Google's network won the 2014 ImageNet competition. It composed of 22 layers and a newly introduced building block called inception module. The module consists of a Network-in-Network layer, a pooling operation, a large-sized convolution layer, and small-sized convolution layer.

**ResNet:** With 96.4% accuracy this Microsoft's model won the 2016 ImageNet competition. It is well-known due to the introduction of residual blocks and to its depth (152 layers). The remaining blocks address the problem of training a profound architecture by introducing identity skip connections so that sheets can copy their inputs to the next layer.

**Shuffle Net:** It is an extremely efficient CNN architecture, designed for mobile devices with the computing power of 10–150 MFLOPs (Mega floating-point operations per second). While maintaining accuracy, the Shuffle Net utilizes pointwise group convolution and channel shuffle to reduce computation cost. It manages to obtain lower top-1 error than the Mobile Net system on Image Net classification (Kashyap, R., 2020).

**Squeeze Net:** For the same accuracy of AlexNet, SqueezeNet can be three times faster and 500 times smaller. The squeeze module only contains 1x1 filters, which means it works like a fully-connected layer working on feature points in the same position. As its name says, one of its benefits is to reduce the depth of the feature map. Reducing thickness means the following 3x3 filters in the expand layer has computation to do. It boosts the speed as a 3x3 filter need as nine times computation as a 1x1 filter.

**Dense Net:** DenseNet connects each layer to every other layer in a feed-forward fashion. It has L layers L(L+1)/ 2 direct connections. For each layer, the feature-maps of all other layers used as inputs, and its feature-maps used as inputs into all subsequent layers. DenseNets have several compelling advantages: they alleviate the vanishing-gradient problem, strengthen feature propagation, encourage feature reuse, and substantially reduce the number of parameters.

**ENet:** Efficient Neural Network gives the ability to perform pixel-wise semantic segmentation in real-time. ENet is up to 18x faster, requires 75x fewer FLOPs (Floating point operations per second), has 79x fewer parameters, and provides similar or better accuracy to existing models. Enet is the fastest model in semantic segmentation.

**Inception:** The Inception network was an essential milestone in the development of CNN classifiers. Before its inception CNN's just stacked convolution layers deeper and deeper, hoping to get better performance. It performs convolution on input, with three different sizes of filters (1x1, 3x3, 5x5). Additionally, max pooling is also shown (Kashyap, R., & Piersson, A. D., 2018). The outputs are concatenated and sent to the next inception module. Following table illustrate different CNN models, year of establishment, and its accuracy.

*Table 3. Summary table of CNN architecture*

| S.N. | Year | CNN | Developed By | Top Accuracy |
|------|------|-----|--------------|--------------|
| 1 | 2012 | AlexNet | Alex Krizhevsky, Ilya Sutskever and Geoffrey Hinton | 55% |
| 2 | 2014 | VGG-16 | Simonyan and Zisserman | 72% |
| 3 | 2014 | VGG-19 | Simonyan and Zisserman | 71% |
| 4 | 2014 | Inception | Szegedy | 80% |
| 5 | 2014 | GoogleNet | Google | 68% |
| 6 | 2015 | ResNet | Kaiming | 74% |
| 7 | 2016 | SqueezNet | DeepScale, University of California | 58% |
| 8 | 2016 | ENet | Adam Paszke, Abhishek Chaurasia, Sangpil Kim, Eugenio Culurciello | 69% |
| 9 | 2017 | ShuffleNet | Xiangyu Zhang, Xinyu Zhou, Mengxiao Lin, Jian Sun | 62% |
| 10 | 2017 | DenseNet | Gao Huang, Zhuang Liu, Laurens van der Maaten and Kilian Weinberger | 75% |

*Figure 10.*

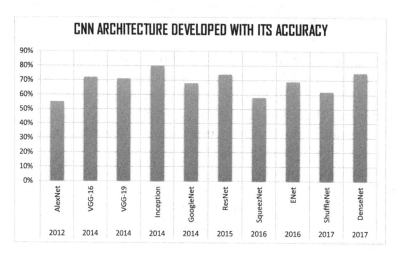

From the above figure, we can see that the accuracy has been gradually increasing in most of the cases with time (Years). Hence, it can deep learn has taken over most of the learning systems in the field of neuroscience due to its high accuracy and efficiency.

## NEUROSCIENCE AND ITS APPLICATIONS THROUGH DEEP LEARNING

The word Neuroscience is on the application of computation, studying neural codes, dynamics, and various circuits replicating the human brain. In deep learning, neural networks tend to design systems, dynamics, or circuits (LeCun, Bengio & Hinton, 2015). Two recent developments have emerged within machine learning that creates an opportunity to connect these perspectives. They are:

1)   Structured architectures: These include systems for attention, recursion, and various forms of short- and long-term memory storage (Kashyap, R., 2019a).
2)   The cost functions and training procedures have become more complex and are varied across layers and over time.

Such a heterogeneously optimized system, enabled by a series of interacting cost functions, serves to make learning data-efficient and precisely targeted to the needs of the organism.

Neuroscience is the study of the nervous system, which includes the brain, spinal cord, and nerves. The brain controls every aspect of the body, from emotion and memory to necessary bodily activities such as movement, breathing, and managing the heartbeat. It is also concerned with the causes and treatment of nervous system disorders (Kashyap, R., 2019b). There are many branches of neuroscience. Since the brain is a complex organ that carries out a variety of functions and the nerves of the rest of the nervous system extend throughout the entire body, a plethora of neuroscience topics exist. The following are some of the main branches of neuroscience (Hassabis, D., Kumaran, D., Summerfield, C. and Botvinick, M., 2017):

1) Affective neuroscience: It is the study of the neural mechanisms involved in emotion, typically through experimentation on animal models.

2) Behavioral neuroscience: It is the application of the principles of biology to the study of genetic, physiological, and developmental mechanisms of behavior in humans and non-human animals.

3) Cellular neuroscience: It is the study of neurons at a cellular level, including morphology and physiological properties.

4) Clinical neuroscience: It is the study of neurons at a cellular level, including morphology and physiological properties.

5) Cognitive neuroscience: It is the study of the biological mechanism underlying cognition.

6) Computational neuroscience: It is the theoretical study of the nervous system.

7) Developmental neuroscience: It studies the processes that generate, shape, and reshapes the nervous system and seeks to describe the cellular basis of neural development to address underlying mechanisms.

8) Neural engineering: It uses engineering techniques to interact with, understand, repair, replace, or enhance neural systems.

9) Systems neuroscience: Systems neuroscience is the study of the function of neural circuits and system.

With increasing advancements in technology, neuroscientists can collect data in higher volumes and with more exceptional resolution. Understanding how the brain works are consequently shifting away from the amount and type of data; one can collect data. There has been a growing interest in acquiring this vast volume of data across levels of analysis, measurement techniques, and experimental paradigms to gain more insight into brain function. At multiple stages and levels of neuroscience investigation, deep learning plays an additional role in the analysis of various tools for discovering how the brain works (Ravì, D., Wong, C., Deligianni, F., Berthelot, M., Andreu-Perez, J., Lo, B. and Yang, G.Z., 2017).

The artificial neural networks are prominent in machine learning was initially inspired by neuroscience. Neuroscience has continued to play a role in many of the significant developments. These guided by insights into the mathematics of efficient optimization, rather than neuroscientific findings. This field has advanced from simple linear systems to nonlinear networks, to deep and recurrent nets. Methods of training have improved to include momentum terms, better weight initializations, conjugate gradients, and so forth, evolving to the current breed of networks. These developments have a connection to neuroscience. Some of the applications of neuroscience in deep learning are as follows (Haines, D.E. and Mihailoff, G.A., 2017):

1)   Detection of various neuronal disorders like Parkinson's disease, Alzheimer's diseases, etc.
2)   DNA (Deoxyribonucleic Acid) microarray analysis.
3)   Immunology.

Some of the primary roles of deep learning in neuroscience are:

1)   Creating a solution to engineering problems.
2)   Identifying predictive variables.
3)   Setting the benchmark for brain models.
4)   Serving itself as a model for the brain.

The Figure 11 below demonstrates the roles:

*Figure 11. Role of learning in neuroscience ("Neuroscience and its applications through deep learning - Google Search," 2019)*

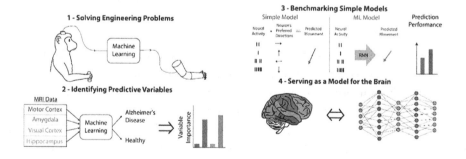

# CONCLUSION

Deep learning has transformed machine learning and artificial intelligence expressively. Recently, it moved back into computational neuroscience. Deep learning offers a fascinating novel framework that permits computational neuroscientists to report essential queries about the computation of the brain. In this chapter, we have gone through in-depth learning, its different models, and different Convolutional neural network architectures.

Moreover, we have discussed the similarities between human biological brains with in-depth learning architecture. After going through the several deep models, we have concluded that each model has its individuality and can use as per the essential requirements. For example, Multilayer perceptron is appropriate for classification forecast complications wherever inputs are allocated a class or label, whereas CNN is designed to plot image data to an output variable. Further, we have also discussed different architectures of CNN such as Alex Net, VGG16, VGG19 and many more and we have concluded classic CNN architectures were encompassed merely of different stacked convolutional layers, modern designs reconnoiter novel and advanced ways for constructing convolutional layers in a mode which permits for more effective learning.

# REFERENCES

Aggarwal, C. C., (2018). Training Deep Neural Networks. *Neural Networks and Deep Learning*, 105-167. doi:10.1007/978-3-319-94463-0_3

Batista, A. P., & DiCarlo, J. J. (2018). Deep learning reaches the motor system. *Nature Methods*, *15*(10), 772–773. doi:10.103841592-018-0152-6 PMID:30275586

CS231n Convolutional Neural Networks for Visual Recognition. (2019). Retrieved from http://cs231n.github.io/convolutional-networks/

Cadena, S. A., Denfield, G. H., Walker, E. Y., Gatys, L. A., Tolias, A. S., Bethge, M., & Ecker, Λ. S. (2019). Deep convolutional models improve predictions of macaque V1 responses to natural images. *PLoS Computational Biology*, *15*(4), e1006897. doi:10.1371/journal.pcbi.1006897 PMID:31013278

Conduction of Nerve Impulse. (2019). Retrieved from http://simplebiologyy.blogspot.com/2014/08/conduction-of-nerve-impulse.html

Cui, Z., Yang, J., & Qiao, Y. (2016). Brain MRI segmentation with patch-based CNN approach. *2016 35th Chinese Control Conference (CCC)*. doi:10.1109/chicc.2016.7554465

Das, S., & Das, S. (2017, November 16). *CNN Architectures: LeNet, AlexNet, VGG, GoogLeNet, ResNet, and more...* Retrieved from https://medium.com/@sidereal/cnns-architectures-lenet-alexnet-vgg-googlenet-resnet-and-more-666091488df5

Deng, J., Dong, W., Socher, R., Li, L., Li, K., & Fei-Fei, L. (2009). ImageNet: A large-scale hierarchical image database. *2009 IEEE Conference on Computer Vision and Pattern Recognition*. 10.1109/CVPR.2009.5206848

Diehl, P. U., Neil, D., Binas, J., Cook, M., Liu, S. C., & Pfeiffer, M. (2015, July). Fast-classifying, high-accuracy spiking deep networks through weight and threshold balancing. In *2015 International Joint Conference on Neural Networks (IJCNN)* (pp. 1-8). IEEE. 10.1109/IJCNN.2015.7280696

Duggal, R., Gupta, A., Gupta, R., Wadhwa, M., & Ahuja, C. (2016). Overlapping cell nuclei segmentation in microscopic images using deep belief networks. *Proceedings of the Tenth Indian Conference on Computer Vision, Graphics and Image Processing - ICVGIP 16*. 10.1145/3009977.3010043

Georgakopoulos, S. V., Iakovidis, D. K., Vasilakakis, M., Plagianakos, V. P., & Koulaouzidis, A. (2016). Weakly-supervised Convolutional learning for detection of inflammatory gastrointestinal lesions. *2016 IEEE International Conference on Imaging Systems and Techniques (IST)*. 10.1109/IST.2016.7738279

Grósz, T. (2014). Document Classification with Deep Rectifier Neural Networks and Probabilistic Sampling. *Text, Speech, and Dialogue Lecture Notes in Computer Science*. doi:10.1007/978-3-319-10816-2_14

Gruber, L. Z., Haruvi, A., Basri, R., & Irani, M. (2018). Perceptual dominance in brief presentations of mixed images: Human perception versus deep neural networks. *Frontiers in Computational Neuroscience*, *12*, 57. doi:10.3389/fncom.2018.00057 PMID:30087604

Guerguiev, J., Lillicrap, T. P., & Richards, B. A. (2017). Towards deep learning with segregated dendrites. *eLife*, *6*, e22901. doi:10.7554/eLife.22901 PMID:29205151

Gulshan, V., Peng, L., Coram, M., Stumpe, M. C., Wu, D., Narayanaswamy, A., & Webster, D. R. (2016). Development and Validation of a Deep Learning Algorithm for the Detection of Diabetic Retinopathy in Retinal Fundus Photographs. *Journal of the American Medical Association*, *316*(22), 2402. doi:10.1001/jama.2016.17216 PMID:27898976

Guo, W. W., & Xue, H. (2014). Crop Yield Forecasting Using Artificial Neural Networks: A Comparison between Spatial and Temporal Models. *Mathematical Problems in Engineering, 2014*, 1–7. doi:10.1155/2014/857865

Haines, D. E., & Mihailoff, G. A. (2017). *Fundamental neuroscience for basic and clinical applications*. Elsevier Health Sciences.

Hassabis, D., Kumaran, D., Summerfield, C., & Botvinick, M. (2017). Neuroscience-inspired artificial intelligence. *Neuron, 95*(2), 245–258. doi:10.1016/j.neuron.2017.06.011 PMID:28728020

Higgins, I., Matthey, L., Glorot, X., Pal, A., Uria, B., Blundell, C., . . . Lerchner, A. (2016). *Early visual concept learning with unsupervised deep learning*. arXiv preprint arXiv:1606.05579

Kashyap, R. (2019a). Security, Reliability, and Performance Assessment for Healthcare Biometrics. In D. Kisku, P. Gupta, & J. Sing (Eds.), Design and Implementation of Healthcare Biometric Systems (pp. 29-54). Hershey, PA: IGI Global. doi:10.4018/978-1-5225-7525-2.ch002

Kashyap, R. (2019b). The sensation of Deep Learning in Image Processing Applications. In A. Hassanien, A. Darwish, & C. Chowdhary (Eds.), *Handbook of Research on Deep Learning Innovations and Trends* (pp. 72–96). Hershey, PA: IGI Global. doi:10.4018/978-1-5225-7862-8.ch005

Kashyap, R. (2019c). *Big Data Analytics Challenges and Solutions*. doi:10.1016/B978-0-12-818146-1.00002-7

Kashyap, R. (2020). Applications of Wireless Sensor Networks in Healthcare. In P. Mukherjee, P. Pattnaik, & S. Panda (Eds.), *IoT and WSN Applications for Modern Agricultural Advancements: Emerging Research and Opportunities* (pp. 8–40). Hershey, PA: IGI Global. doi:10.4018/978-1-5225-9004-0.ch002

Kashyap, R., & Piersson, A. D. (2018). Impact of Big Data on Security. In G. Shrivastava, P. Kumar, B. Gupta, S. Bala, & N. Dey (Eds.), *Handbook of Research on Network Forensics and Analysis Techniques* (pp. 283–299). Hershey, PA: IGI Global. doi:10.4018/978-1-5225-4100-4.ch015

Krizhevsky, A., Sutskever, I., & Hinton, G. E. (2017). ImageNet classification with deep convolutional neural networks. *Communications of the ACM, 60*(6), 84–90. doi:10.1145/3065386

Le, P., & Zuidema, W. (2015). Compositional Distributional Semantics with Long Short Term Memory. *Proceedings of the Fourth Joint Conference on Lexical and Computational Semantics.* 10.18653/v1/S15-1002

LeCun, Y., Bengio, Y., & Hinton, G. (2015). Deep learning. *Nature, 521*(7553), 436–444. doi:10.1038/nature14539 PMID:26017442

Ma, Y., Xiang, Z., Du, Q., & Fan, W. (2018). Effects of user-provided photos on hotel review helpfulness: An analytical approach with deep leaning. *International Journal of Hospitality Management, 71,* 120–131. doi:10.1016/j.ijhm.2017.12.008

Neuroscience and its applications through deep learning - Google Search. (2019). Retrieved from https://www.google.com/search?q=Neuroscience+and+its+applic ations+through+deep+learning&safe

Peng, M., Wang, C., Chen, T., & Liu, G. (2016, October 27). *NIRFaceNet: A Convolutional Neural Network for Near-Infrared Face Identification.* Retrieved from https://www.mdpi.com/2078-2489/7/4/61

Raina, R., Madhavan, A., & Ng, A. Y. (2009). Large-scale deep unsupervised learning using graphics processors. *Proceedings of the 26th Annual International Conference on Machine Learning - ICML 09.* 10.1145/1553374.1553486

Ravì, D., Wong, C., Deligianni, F., Berthelot, M., Andreu-Perez, J., Lo, B., & Yang, G. Z. (2017). Deep learning for health informatics. *IEEE Journal of Biomedical and Health Informatics, 21*(1), 4–21. doi:10.1109/JBHI.2016.2636665 PMID:28055930

Shen, D., Wu, G., & Suk, H. I. (2017). Deep learning in medical image analysis. *Annual Review of Biomedical Engineering, 19*(1), 221–248. doi:10.1146/annurev-bioeng-071516-044442 PMID:28301734

Shukla, R., Gupta, R. K., & Kashyap, R. (2019). A multiphase pre-copy strategy for the virtual machine migration in the cloud. In S. Satapathy, V. Bhateja, & S. Das (Eds.), *Smart Intelligent Computing and Applications. Smart Innovation, Systems and Technologies* (Vol. 104). Singapore: Springer. doi:10.1007/978-981-13-1921-1_43

Tissera, M. D., & McDonnell, M. D. (2016). Deep extreme learning machines: Supervised autoencoding architecture for classification. *Neurocomputing, 174,* 42–49. doi:10.1016/j.neucom.2015.03.110

Tiwari, S., Gupta, R. K., & Kashyap, R. (2019). To enhance web response time using agglomerative clustering technique for web navigation recommendation. In H. Behera, J. Nayak, B. Naik, & A. Abraham (Eds.), *Computational Intelligence in Data Mining. Advances in Intelligent Systems and Computing* (Vol. 711). Singapore: Springer. doi:10.1007/978-981-10-8055-5_59

Ullman, S. (2019). Using neuroscience to develop artificial intelligence. *Science*, *363*(6428), 692–693. doi:10.1126cience.aau6595 PMID:30765552

Waoo, N., Kashyap, R., & Jaiswal, A. (2010). DNA nanoarray analysis using hierarchical quality threshold clustering. In *Proceedings of 2010 2nd IEEE International Conference on Information Management and Engineering* (pp. 81-85). IEEE. 10.1109/ICIME.2010.5477579

# Chapter 3
# Advanced Diagnosis Techniques in Medical Imaging

**Ramgopal Kashyap**

ⓘD https://orcid.org/0000-0002-5352-1286

*Amity School of Engineering and Technology, Amity University, Raipur, India*

## ABSTRACT

*The Boltzmann distribution was derived in this chapter. The Boltzmann equation was explained next to the main difficulty of this equation, the integral of the collision operator, which was solved by the BGK-approximation where a long-term substitute is essential. The discretization of the Boltzmann comparison with the BGK-approximation was introduced along with the lattice and the different lattice configurations to define the lattice framework where the method is applied. Also, in this framework, the algorithm of the process was described. The boundary conditions were summarised, where one can see that they represent macroscopic conditions acting locally in every node.*

## INTRODUCTION

Accurate segmentation of medical images is the biggest challenge in computer vision, other than the application itself; image segmentation plays a significant role as a base technique in other computer vision problems. Despite the development of the various unsupervised image, segmentation methods limit the performance. Hence, for better practicability, semi-supervised image segmentation methods that are known as interactive image segmentation are gaining popularity in segmenting the object with less human effort (A. Ducournau and A. Bretto, 2014). In an interactive segmentation, the user intervention tightly coupled with an automatic segmentation

DOI: 10.4018/978-1-7998-0182-5.ch003

algorithm needs the knowledge and the automated method's computational capability. Real-time visualisation on the screen enables the user to quickly validate and correct the automatic segmentation results in a subdomain where the variational model's statistical assumptions do not agree with the user's expert knowledge. The user intervention mainly includes initialisation of the methods, and horizontal lines, respectively. Checking the accuracy of the results produced by automatic segmentation and corrections to the segmentation results using specialised interactive segmentation tools. Interactions in the segmentation of medical images can broadly classify into three types: pictorial input on an image grid, parameter tuning, and menu option selection (O. Pauplin, P. Caleb-Solly and J. Smith, 2010). The segmentation results obtained with new configurations like mouse clicking or drawing, new parameter values; another menu option visualised on the screen in real-time for further user evaluation. Among all the three types of user interactions, menu option selection is most efficient, but it constrains the degrees of freedom of the user's choice of selections. Pictorial input is simple, but it could be time-consuming in case the interaction requires a user to draw precisely on an image grid. Parameter tuning is easy to operate, but it may require specific training for an insight into the automatic computational part.

## INTERACTIVE IMAGE SEGMENTATION

Interactive segmentation techniques are essential for fast and reliable extraction of the ROI. The level of user interaction in different methods varies in terms of the amount and type of information provided by the users because it requires iterative manual inputs, an acceptable interactive segmentation method has to minimise the human effort and produce a result quickly. That is to say, the seeds needed to obtain the desired outcome must be neither too accurately localised nor too numerous, and the time to compute a segmentation must aim to a few seconds (Y. Chen, A. Cremers and Z. Cao, 2014). The user chooses some pixels named seeds and indicators for each of them the element to which it belongs. Features like location, colour, texture, etc. of desired regions deduced by analysing and adding or removing some seeds can improve the produced result, allowing the user to get any desired segmentation results. It generally accepted that segmentation methods could be classified into an edge-based, region-based and energy-based methods. When an interactive segmentation method searches for the boundaries, then the user gives some points of these boundaries. One of the most representative edge-based interactive segmentation methods is Intelligent Scissors (N. Suetake, E. Uchino and K. Hirata, 2007). However, for highly textured images, a lot of boundary pixels are used for detection of the correct object that makes segmentation task complex.

Regarding most of the region based methods; the user must draw some strokes on the different areas. With this modality of interaction, if picture elements are small when compared to the brush size, sometimes the user selects the wrong initialisation of the seed that gives false processing results. Some methods attempt to deal with this noise needs image preprocessing for getting better results Weiner filter is better for correction of distortion in the images that results can be significantly better.

## PROPOSED METHOD

The problem of interactive image segmentation is the typical use of small foreground or background seeds from users to extract the foreground region. One major issue of the existing algorithms for such interactive segmentation using their preference of the bounding box that covers the object which is to be segmented. The proposed method will make user-defined bounding boxes with external energy that inspect the segmentation results. To compute the fit box to the ground-truth foreground and slightly dilate it by 5% of the total pixels in all directions and to take it as the bounding box along with energy. It is required to expand this bounding box according to the energy needed in the instructions and after performing collision and streaming the bounding box will give accurate result, selection of the object will not dependent on the position user will get same results from selecting anywhere in the image this is the significant achievement of the proposed method (H. Li, D. Zhou and Y. Wu, 2011). It is for interactive capturing of images and better segmentation results and an interactive captured image for fast processing that done through using computational fluid dynamics techniques for medical image segmentation with some modifications. The lattice Boltzmann method has developed from the cradle of statistical mechanics as a whole alternative numerical approach for modelling physical phenomena in fluid flows (S. Balla-Arabe, Xinbo Gao and Bin Wang (2013), M. Tsutahara (2012).

In contrast to the traditional numerical schemes such as the finite difference method (FDM) and spectral element method (SEM) uses macroscopic equations for processing. The first room starts full of particles while the second room starts empty. From the physical point of view, the Boltzmann method can be interpolated as a microscope for fluid mechanics while a telescope for molecular dynamics and it has successfully applied for the coupling of molecular dynamics in the microscopic world and fluid dynamics in the macroscopic (Q. Lou, Z. Guo and B. Shi, 2012). The fundamental idea behind lattice gas automata is that microscopic interactions of artificial particles living on the microscopic lattice can lead to the corresponding macroscopic equations to describe the same fluid flows. During the interaction, which is consisting of collision and propagation or streaming with lattice velocities, lattice symmetry plays a crucial role in conserving mass and momentum as well as ensuring the angular momentum conservation. Hardy developed the first lattice gas automata with 4-fold rotational symmetry in a square lattice, de Pazzis and Pomeau achieving only mass and momentum conservation. The hexagonal symmetry was sufficient to conserve the angular energy to retrieve not only diffusion equation, reaction-diffusion equation, but also the Navier-Stokes equations and the proposed two-phase nine velocity model it is much faster than the traditional models with linearization and simplification of the collision operator in Boltzmann equation.

The major challenge with the Boltzmann method is it is tough to achieve higher than the second order of accuracy for both temporal and spatial discretisation. Moreover, because there are more distribution functions than the hydrodynamic variables to keep track of, it cannot avoid the relatively intensive computation as a trade-off for simplicity. In the proposed method a fuzzy external force (FEF) (B. Amarapur and P. Kulkarni, 2011) is making the segmentation fast, robust against noise and efficient whatever the position or the shape of the initial contour it can capture objects accurately. It has, first the advantage of the FCM which controls the evolving curve through the membership degree of the current pixels. Second, the benefits of the energy-based method are that it is independent of the topological change of shape, size and orientation of the object and, third, the advantages are it very suitable for parallel programming due to its local and explicit nature. The novelty of the proposed approach lies first in the handling of segmentation. Here made two enhancements to the traditional method: "iterative estimation" and "perfect boundary condition" that decreases the user interaction for a given quality of the result and fast segmentation.

The traditional model in which the grid is two-dimensional and square so that each node in the grid has four neighbours. The particles can have four possible velocities, $c1 = (1, 0)$, $c2 = (0, 1)$, $c3 = (-1, 0)$, and $c4 = (0, -1)$ as shown in Figure 1.

For each time step, each particle is moved forward one step in the direction of its velocity, and when two or more particles meet at the same node after a time step, a collision occurs. To conserve mass and momentum, the number of particles and the total velocity of all the particles in the node must be the same before and after the collision. When two particles collide head-on, they are thrown out at right angles to their original velocities (M. Benedict, J. Kovács and A. Czirják, 2012), as shown in Figure 2.

It conserves momentum, as the sum of the velocities of the two particles is zero in both configurations. When three or four particles meet at the same node, the only setting that satisfies conservation of mass and momentum is the same configuration as before the collision. Therefore, a clash between three or four particles cannot and does not result in a change of setting and the particle stream on as if no collision occurred. The crashes are entirely deterministic, meaning that each crash has one and only one possible result. Because of this, the proposed model has a property

*Figure 1. The velocity vectors of the model*

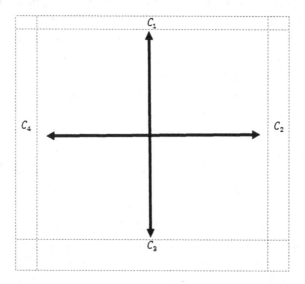

*Figure 2. The head of collision rules of the model*

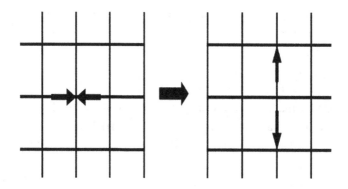

called time-reversal invariance, which means that the model can be run in reverse to recover an earlier state. Two rooms separated by a wall with a small opening (O. Utyuzh, G. Wilk and Z. Wodarczyk, 2007). The first room starts full of particles while the second room starts empty. When the simulation begins, particles escape from the first room to the second until the system reaches an equilibrium of roughly equal particle densities. The model is then run in reverse until all particles in the second room have retraced their steps and gone back to their initial positions in the first room. The proposed method has some advantages compared to other numerical methods. The state of each node in the grid can be described entirely by four bits: Bit $I$ represent the presence or absence of one particle moving in the direction $c_i$. It

*Figure 3. Four particles with different directions moving in the model from one time step to the next*

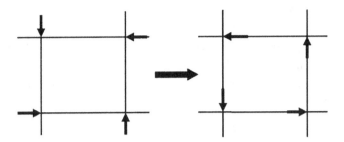

means that very little storage space and memory are required. Another advantage is that due to the Boolean nature of the system, no floating-point numbers used in the model, which means that all names are entirely exact, and no round-off errors occur.

The precise and deterministic nature of the model also means that it has a property called time-reversal invariance, which means that the system can be run in reverse to reproduce an earlier state perfectly. A third advantage is the inherently parallel nature of the system. The events in each node are not related to the simultaneous developments in another node since the only communication between nodes is through streaming of particles. Also, the nature of particle streaming is such that each particle can only have one origin. It means that several processors can process the collisions or particle streaming in different sections of the grid simultaneously without a need for communication, apart from distributing the work among each other and sending back results (C. Sun, F. Pérot, R. Zhang, D. Freed and H. Chen, 2013). There are also many inherent weaknesses in the traditional model. Due to the little scope of the model, it can never be said to be incomplete equilibrium. The system will never by itself reach a state where the system is identical from one step to the next. It is evident from the model's property of time-reversal invariance: For the system to be in a state where the future state is identical to the current state, all previous states must have been equal to the current state. Therefore, it is only possible to reach a permanent status by setting them as the initial condition.

A trivial example is a system with all possible particles presents everywhere, but this can hardly be said to be a natural equilibrium. For this reason, the microscopic state of the system is always changing. As mentioned earlier, the macroscopic quantities of the system can found by averaging the tiny amounts over space or time. The constant change in the small state, there will always be statistical noise in the macroscopic quantities; this problem can be reduced by broadening the average, but never avoided. Possibly the greatest weakness of the active contour model is that it fails to achieve rotational invariance, which means that its behaviour becomes anisotropic (O. Utyuzh, G. Wilk and Z. Wodarczyk, 2007). For instance, in a system with particles evenly spread out, apart from a high concentration in the centre, this high concentration will spread out from the centre in a diamond pattern. As a result of this, active contour systems fail to behave in accordance to the Navier-Stokes equations. This weakness alone is crippling to the point that the HPP model is not useful for fluid simulations. The quantities used in the simulation relate to real numbers through the lattice spacing $\Delta x$ and the time step $\Delta t$. For instance, the physical particle speeds $\overline{c}_i, p$ in the lattice is given by

$$\overline{c}_i, p = \frac{\Delta x}{\Delta t} \cdot \overline{c}_i, l \tag{1}$$

Here say that the vector is in lattice units, which are units normalised by $\Delta x$ and $\Delta t$. In lattice units, that $= 1$ for all i in the active contour model, and that $\Delta t = 1$. For the vector, which is in physical units, that $= \Delta x / \Delta t$. The particle density in each node can be calculated simply from the number of particles present in the node, or

$$p(\overline{x}, t) = \sum_i n_i(\overline{x}, t) \tag{2}$$

where $p(\overline{x}, t)$ is the particle density at the node with a position at time $t$, and is the Boolean occupation number, meaning the number of particles present (0 or 1) at this node with velocity . The quantities And $t$ is in lattice units. Similarly, the total momentum in each node calculated from where u is the mean velocity of the particles at this node. Hard walls can create an active contour model as nodes, which cause incoming particles to reflect. The boundaries of the simulated system can be hard walls, or they can be periodic. Periodic boundaries imply that a particle which exits the system at one edge will re-enter the system at the opposite edge. With hard boundaries, the behaviour of a fluid trapped in a box is simulated, while with periodic boundaries, it is the behaviour of a fluid in a periodic system which simulated. It is naturally possible to combine the two boundaries, for instance, by having hard vertical boundaries on two sides and periodic boundaries on the other two. Force can be simulated in the proposed method randomly changing some particle velocity in the direction of the force with a given probability. With all these rules known, it is possible to perform a simulation. First, certain geometry is created using hard walls, and initial distribution of particles with certain positions and velocities is created (J. Kundu and R. Rajesh, 2015). The system is then left to run for a while until it reaches a sort of equilibrium. Then, the macroscopic particle density can be found by averaging over space (several nodes) and time (several time steps) to find the average number of particles in each area. The macroscopic momentum can found by a similar average of the nodes' momentum. The lattice vectors in the proposed model are $c1 = (1, 0)$, $c2 = (1/2, \sqrt{3}/2)$, $c3 = (-1/2, \sqrt{3}/2)$, $c4 = (-1, 0)$, $c5 = (-1/2, -\sqrt{3}/2)$ and $c6 = (1/2, -\sqrt{3}/2)$ given in Figure 4.

A hexagonal lattice allows two possible resolutions for a head-on collision which conserve both mass and momentum, illustrated in Figure 6.5. It is different from the HPP model, where there is only one possible resolution, which is to occur, is chosen randomly for every collision, with equal probability. Due to this stochastic element in the model, it is no longer fully deterministic and does not have the time-reversal property of the four-velocity model.

*Figure 4. The velocity vector of the model*

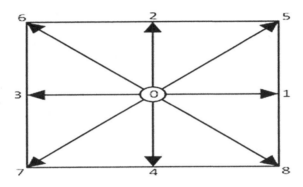

*Figure 5. Common set of two-dimensional vectors*

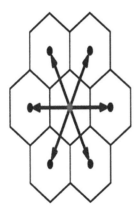 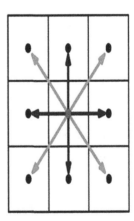

*Figure 6. Evolution of all the vectors of the model*

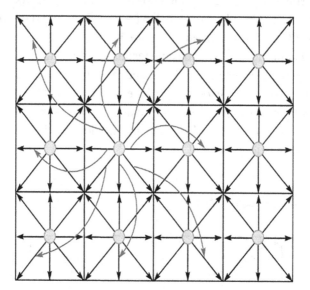

As mentioned, it can derive that the proposed model gives behaviour by the incompressible Navier-Stokes equations [269]. From the derivation, one can show that the kinematic viscosity of the system must be

$$V = \frac{\Delta x^2}{\Delta t} \left( \frac{1}{2\rho \left(1 - \rho \frac{\rho}{6}\right)^3} - \frac{1}{8} \right) \tag{3}$$

where $\rho$ is the equilibrium density of the gas, this can found at the average particle density of the entire system. To see from this equation that the viscosity can become arbitrarily large in the limits $\rho \to 0$ and $\rho \to 6$, indicating no particles in the system and a maximum number of particles in the system, respectively. The minimal viscosity for the model found when $\rho = 3/2$.

Varieties exist in the proposed model the additional collisions introduced. The proposed model is essentially the Lattice Boltzmann model (M. Beneš and P. Kučera, 2015) and active contour model (A. Mohamad and A. Kuzmin, 2012). with a change of the lattice and the collision rules. Thus, it retains all the advantages of the traditional model such as small storage space demands, exact dynamics and parallelism. It removes the most critical disadvantage, that of the inherent anisotropy of the conventional model, giving a behaviour consistent with the incompressible

*Figure 7. The head-on collision rule for the proposed model*

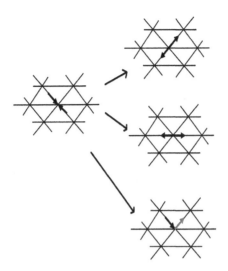

Navier-Stokes equations. The problem of statistical noise remains. It is a general problem when trying to recover macroscopic quantities from microscopic-scope simulations, as the microscopic system is subject to random fluctuations that disappear in the continuum limit. On the other hand, if the subject of interest is studying such changes in real systems, this statistical noise is a desired property.

A valuable property the proposed method retains from its lattice gas ancestors is locality in each step given above, each node is updated separately from the others because of this parallelism can achieve, and the method can use as many processors as there are nodes in the grid. Nothing has been said yet about the problem of initial conditions. Finite volume method subdivided domain into small control volumes that are known as cells through the grid, and the network describes the boundaries of the control volumes while the computational node at the centre of the control volume and the integral conservation is satisfied exactly over the control volume.

The net flux through the control volume boundary is the total of the integrals over the four control volume faces (six in 3D). The control volumes do not overlap, and the value of the integrand is not available at the control volume faces and determined by interpolation.

The conservation equations play essential roles in CFD for digitisation the species transport equation for constant density, and incompressible flow is given by:

$$\frac{\delta c}{\delta t} + \frac{\delta(u_i, c)}{\delta x_i} = \frac{\delta y}{\delta x}\left(D\frac{\delta c}{\delta t}\right) + s \tag{4}$$

*Figure 8. The proposed method collision handling*

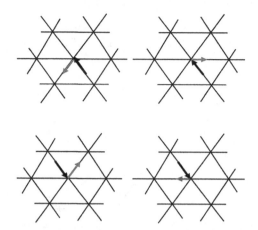

*Figure 9. The boundary and node representation*

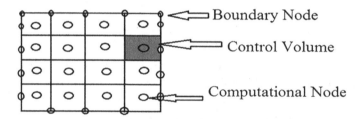

*Figure 10. The computational node and boundary calculation*

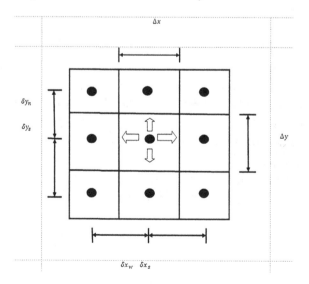

Here c is the concentration of the chemical species and D is the diffusion coefficient. S is a source term. It will discretise this equation (convert it to a solvable algebraic form) for the single flow field shown on the right, assuming steady-state conditions.

The balance over the control volume is given by:

$$A_e u_e C_e - A_w u_w C_w + A_n u_n C_n - A_s u_s C_s$$
$$= \left( DA_e \frac{\delta c}{\delta x_e} \right) - \left( DA_w \frac{\delta c}{\delta x_w} \right) + \left( DA_n \frac{\delta c}{\delta y_n} \right) - \left( DA_s \frac{\delta c}{\delta y_s} \right) + s_p \tag{5}$$

It contains values at the faces, which need to determine from interpolated from the values at the cell centres.

*Figure 11. Discretization of node according to velocity*

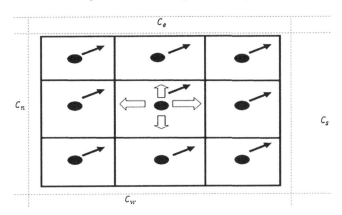

*Figure 12. Control volume of the nodes*

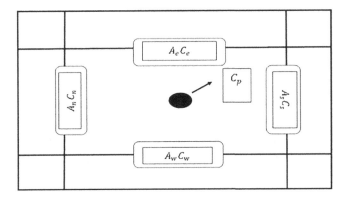

Where,

$A_e A_s A_w A_n$ are the area of the faces
$C_E C_S C_W C_N$ are the concentrations at the cell centres
$c_s c_s c_w c_n$ are the concentrations at the faces
$u_e u_s u_w u_n$ is the Velocity at the faces
$u_E u_S u_W u_N$ is the Velocity at the cell centres
D is the Diffusion Coefficient
$S_p$ is a source in the cell

The simplest way to decide the values at the faces done through first-order upwind differencing. Here, let's assume that the amount on the face is equal to the centre and using that method results in:

$$A_e u_p C_p - A_w u_w C_w + A_n u_p C_p - A_s u_s C_s$$
$$= DA_e \left( C_E - C_P \right) - DA_w - \left( C_P - C_W \right) + DA_n \left( C_N - C_P \right) - DA_s \left( C_P - C_S \right) + s_p$$

(6)

This equation rearranged at the centre of cell P as a function of the concentrations in the adjacent cells, the path, and the grid. This equation can now be simplified:

$$a_e c_p = a_e c_e + a_s c_s + a_w c_w + a_n c_n + b$$

(7)

$$a_e c_p = \sum_{nb} a_n c_n + b$$

(8)

Here n refers to the neighbouring cells. The coefficients $a_n$ And b will change according to the domain of the cells. The species concentration field can calculate recalculating $c_p$ for all the cells.

The Periodic edges act as if they connected to the opposite side of the system. If the left and right sides of a system are periodic, a particle distribution which streams left at the left corner of the order will reappear at the right edge, heading left. In a 2D system, the left, right boundaries and the top-bottom boundaries can be periodic. Figure 12 shows neighbouring nodes across natural barriers. A periodic limit naturally implies that the system is regular, where a cyclic behaviour is studied, such as the propagation of a plane sound wave in a duct, where the length of the system equals the wavelength (J. Wu and H. Guo, 2014).

*Figure 13. Particle streaming paths from a corner node in 3 x 3 nodes*

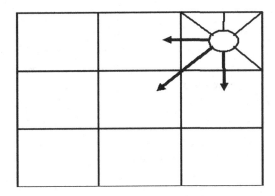

The other simple lattice Boltzmann boundary is the hard wall, which reflects particles and guarantees a non-slip condition with zero velocity at the wall. There are two variations on this method, the on-grid or full-way bounce-back method and the mid-grid or half-way bounce back method (S. Krithivasan, S. Wahal and S. Ansumali, 2014).

In these two methods, individual nodes in the grid are marked as walls and are thus not a part of the fluid. The particle distributions in-wall nodes are not relaxed towards equilibrium and do not act by the lattice Boltzmann evolution equation.

*Figure 14. Particle streaming on the possible paths*

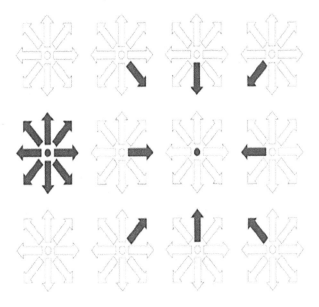

The on-grid method is the simpler of the two methods. In the collision step of the iteration, where the fluid nodes are relaxed, all particles' directions reversed so that the particles are sent back in the direction they came from, as shown in Figure 14. The collision step modified for the wall nodes, but the streaming level is unchanged. In the mid-grid method, particles which are set to flow into a wall node are reflected instead of streamed, as shown in Figure 15.

Here, the streaming step is modified while the collision step remains the same. In both bounce-back methods, the current position of the wall is actually between the wall nodes and the fluid nodes adjacent to it. It can be seen, for instance, by comparing the mid-grid method is somewhat more challenging to implement than the on-grid way, but the mid-grid method gives better accuracy. It is the reason to use mid-grid walls in the process of a system. They are periodic, a particle distribution which streams left at the left edge of the order will reappear at the right edge, heading left [274]. In a 2D mode, the left-right boundaries and the top-bottom boundaries can be periodic and hard wall the proposed method which reflects particles and guarantees a non-slip condition with zero velocity at the wall. There are two variations on this method, the on-grid or full-way bounce-back method and the mid-grid or half-way bounce back method. In these two methods, individual nodes in the grid are marked as walls and are thus not a part of the fluid. The particle distributions in-wall nodes are not relaxed towards equilibrium and do not act by the lattice Boltzmann evolution equation. The on-grid method is the simpler of the two methods. In the collision step of the iteration, where the fluid nodes are relaxed, all particles' directions reversed so that the particles are sent back in the direction they came from, as shown in Figure 16. The collision step modified for the wall nodes,

*Figure 15. The on-grid bounce-back method*

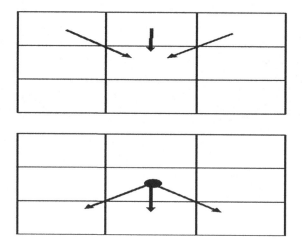

*Figure 16. The mid-grid bounce-back method*

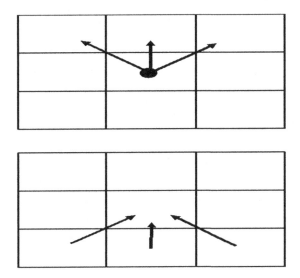

but the streaming level is unchanged. In the mid-grid method, particles which are set to flow into a wall node are reflected instead of streamed, as shown in Figure 16. Here, the streaming step is modified while the collision step remains the same. In both bounce-back methods, the current position of the wall is actually between the wall nodes and the fluid nodes adjacent to it.

The distribution $f(,,t)$ $rv$ gives the probability of finding a single a molecule inside a small volume $r$, around the position with a certain velocity At time $t$. So in principle, the probability of finding a molecule with a velocity between and $+d$ and at a specific position between and $+d$ at time $t$ is given by the following relation.

$$f(\bar{r} + d\bar{r}, \bar{v} + d\bar{v}, t) = f(\bar{r}, \bar{v}, t)d\bar{r}\ d\bar{v} \tag{9}$$

In the supposed situation where collisions do not exist, every molecule is able to move freely as they do not interact with other molecules. Then, a given the external force is introduced, which acts on a molecule of unit mass. Therefore the velocity of the molecule will change to $+dt$, which can be expressed as

$$\bar{v} + \bar{F}dt = \bar{v} + \left(\frac{d\bar{v}}{dt}\right)dt = \bar{v} + d\bar{v} \tag{10}$$

and the position will change as well from $\bar{r}$ to $\bar{r} + \bar{v}\ dt$, which also can be simplified

$$\overline{r} + \overline{v}dt = \overline{r} + \left(\frac{d\overline{r}}{dt}\right)dt = \overline{r} + d\overline{r} \tag{11}$$

Hence, since there are no collisions allowed, the distribution density before applying the external force $\overline{F}$ and the distribution after a differential time step $dt$ follows this relation.

$$f(+d,+d,t+dt)dd=f(,,t)dd \tag{12}$$

It is because molecules can move freely, that every particle with a given initial state is free to arrive at a final state after is applied. If collisions are considered, the relation changes because molecules are not able to move with complete freedom around the domain. Hence, a collision term must be added about restrain the liberty of the molecules. This term is the rate of change between the number of particles that are between $+ d$ and $+ d$ after a time differential $dt$.

The rate of change can express as:

$$\frac{df}{dt} = \Omega \tag{13}$$

This equation shows that the total rate of change in the distribution function is equal to the rate of collisions, plus the fluxes of particles entering and leaving the volume of study. Eq.(6.7) implies that the total rate of change of the distribution function is equal to the speed of collisions. It is not easy to solve the Boltzmann equation due to the collision term. The Chapman-Enskog expansion, collision term can be related to the viscosity when deriving the NS equation. An approximation without introducing significant error in the result. This approximation by Bhatnagar, Gross and Krook (BGK) as a simplification of the collision operator.

$$\Omega = \omega(-f) = (-f) \tag{14}$$

Where $\omega$ is the collision frequency, and its inverse $\tau$ is the relaxation time. The term Denotes the distribution function value at the local equilibrium. The relaxation time is related to the viscosity in this framework, $\nu lb$, by the following formula

$$v_{lb} = \frac{1}{3}\left(\tau - \frac{1}{2}\right) \tag{15}$$

This factor takes a significant role in the numerical stability of the method. The modified Boltzmann equation with the BGK approximation results

$$\frac{\partial f}{\partial t} + \overline{v}\nabla f = \frac{1}{\tau}\left(f^{eq} - f\right) \qquad (16)$$

Moreover, this equation works on a more fundamental level than NS equations, so it is possible to derive NS equations from the Boltzmann equation. In this discrete form of the *Boltzmann equation,* basic steps in the LBM.

$$fi(\overline{r} + \overline{ei}\Delta t, t + \Delta t) = fi(\overline{r}, t) + \frac{\Delta t}{\tau}[fi^{eq}(\overline{r}, t) - fi(\overline{r}, t)] + \qquad (17)$$

$fi(\overline{r} + \overline{ei}\Delta t, t + \Delta t) = fi(\overline{r}, t)$ is streaming step and $\frac{\Delta t}{\tau}[fi^{eq}(\overline{r}, t) - fi(\overline{r}, t)]$ is the collision step. The beauty of this equation is its simplicity. Thus, it can be easily modified to introduce different simulation properties. The algorithm is

Initialise;
**for** *number of iterations* **do**
Apply boundary conditions;
Streaming Step;
Compute macroscopic quantities;
Compute *f eq*;
Collision Step;
**if** *there are obstacles* **then**
Obstacle treatment;
end
end
Store data;

## BOUNDARY CONDITIONS

Considering the problem simulates, only solid boundaries are implemented to delimit the domain. The stable boundary conditions used in the proposed method based on the so-called bounce-back boundary condition. That is, each particle that collides with a solid border has its velocities $v_i$ reversed $(v_i = -v_i)$ and therefore bounces back from the edge. It is physically appropriate because solid walls have a sufficient roughness to prevent any fluid motion parallel to the wall. Also, the peripheral cells that delimit the domain marked as boundary cells with the bounce-back condition. During their update, these cells still require access to cells that are outside of the area, which is the so-called ghost cells. Special treatment for those cells, another layer of boundary cells put around the area (X. Zhuang, X. Ji and Z. Wei, 2013). However, the additional layer of boundary cells not processed in a lattice Boltzmann step; they only exist to avoid a special treatment for the actual boundary cells. Therefore, all the LBM computations can efficiently accelerate on the GPU; body forces can be added to the LBM as an external input to control the flow behaviour.

## EXPERIMENTS AND RESULT ANALYSIS

The experimental section described in two parts; the first part shows the accuracy and the usefulness of the proposed method by comparing it with the traditional energy-based methods (K. Zhang, H. Song and L. Zhang, 2010), (Y. Wang, C. Shu and L. Yang, 2016), (H. Kang, B. Kim, J. Lee, J. Shin and Y. Shin, 2014), (K. Zhang, H. Song and L. Zhang, 2010). The second part exemplifies the ability of the proposed method concerning speed and efficiency. In the implementation of the proposed approach, the value of the fuzzy parameter set to three, and Convection coefficient kept 0.08. All the techniques have been implemented using Matlab R2014b installed on a PC Pentium(R) Dual-Core CPU E5500 processor with a clock speed of 2.80 GHz and 2 GB of RAM.

## Comparison in Terms of Effectiveness and Accuracy

In this part, the contrast of the proposed method with four segmentation methods given, the first one is active contours without edges introduced by T. Chan and L. Vese *et al* for image segmentation submitted by Kaihua Zhang *et al.*((K. Zhang, H. Song and L. Zhang, 2010) provided by Huihui Song et *al.* (H. Kang, B. Kim, J. Lee, J. Shin and Y. Shin, 2014), and the last one submitted by Chunming Li *et al.* (Chunming Li, Rui Huang, Zhaohua Ding, J. Gatenby, D. Metaxas and J. Gore, 2011). Figure 6.17 is showing other methods and the proposed method result.

To examine that the proposed method provides the best segmentation results, it gives discontinue and efficient object boundary. The method by Chen *et al.* and the method by Li *et al.* both are not succeeding because due to the identification of the weak edges. The method by Huihui Song et *al.* spend more time in the iterations. Furthermore, the resulting contours present many discontinuities. The process by Li *et al.* gives over segmented results and takes more time; it is, therefore, less robust than the proposed method, and furthermore, the quality of the segmentation using the proposed method is robust to noise and gives the best results.

*Figure 17. (a) Shows the segmentation results using the active contour method without edges, fig. (b) shows the segmentation results using the improved chan vese method, fig. (c) shows the segmentation results using the local image fitting energy method, fig. (d) shows the segmentation results using a level set method for image segmentation in the presence of intensity inhomogeneities, fig. (e) shows the segmentation results using the proposed method*

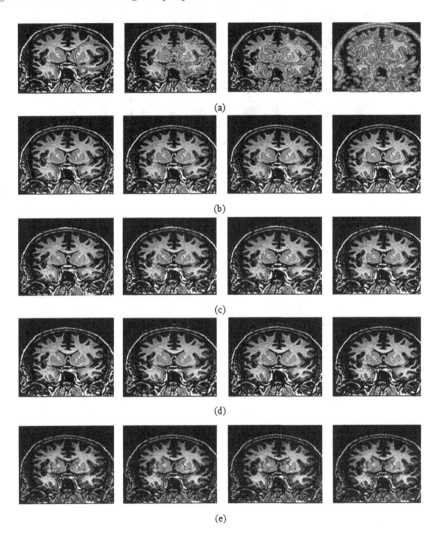

*Figure 18. Shows the segmentation result of mri image of the brain corrupted by salt and pepper noise (noise density value d=0.02)*

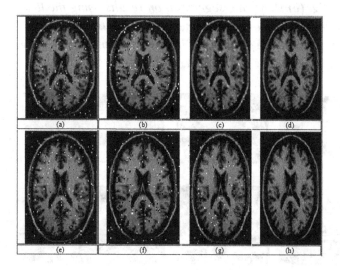

*Table 1. Pearson correlation coefficient comparison of proposed method with geodesic active contour, globally optimal geodesic active contour, local binary fitting model, local region model and local intensity fitting model*

| S.N. | Method | Pearson Correlation Coefficient |
| --- | --- | --- |
| | | Original Image vs Noisy Image |
| 1 | Local Intensity Fitting | 30059.00372 |
| 2 | Geodesic Active Contour | 29641.67067 |
| 3 | Local Binary Fitting | 29743.21324 |
| 4 | GOGAC | 29777.78693 |
| 5 | Local Region Model | 29852.18299 |
| 6 | Proposed Method | 30200.33511 |

## Comparison in Terms of Speed and Efficiency

In this part, comparison of the proposed method with the well-known CV method, improved CV, local image fitting method, improved level set method with bias correction and the proposed method, all the CPU times displayed in Table 1. It can be seen that the proposed method gives better result than the Chan Vese, improved Chan Vese, local image fitting energy method and level set method, whatever the shape and the position of the initial contour the result changes with the initial outline and one should run the algorithm several times in order to choose the best result.

*Table 2. CPU times shown in the experiment*

| Methods | CPU Time(s) Types of Images | | | |
|---|---|---|---|---|
| | Type 1 | Type 2 | Type 3 | Type 4 |
| Proposed Method | 6.073 | 5.220 | 5.668 | 11.747 |
| Chan Vese | 9.179 | 15.453 | 18.038 | 16.496 |
| Improved Chan Vese | 8.270 | 4.525 | 14.556 | 12.723 |
| Local image fitting | 9.851 | 17.364 | 36.987 | 32.966 |
| Level Set Method | 10.531 | 10.796 | 49.453 | 49.750 |

*Figure 19. Shows the segmentation results of medical MRI and CT images of the human body. the results of the proposed method are accurate and clear; the resulting contours are closed and present no discontinuities. figures are showing segmentation results fig (a) using the active contour method without edges, fig. (b) using the improved Chan Vese method, fig. (c) using the active contour method by local image fitting, fig. (d) shows the segmentation result using the level set method for image segmentation in the presence of intensity inhomogeneities with application to MRI and fig. (e) shows the segmentation result using the proposed method*

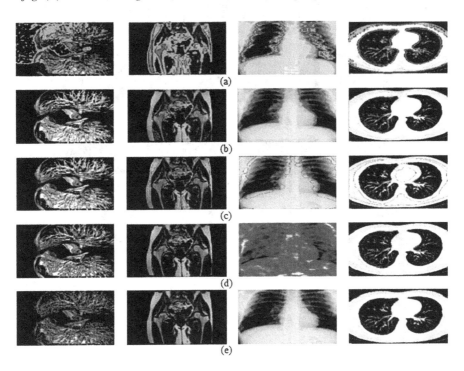

Thus, these methods cannot be suitable for accurate and proper segmentation, C-V model uses region information and considered as one of the most widely used models for segmentation. One of the prominent advantages of the C-V model is that it performs well on the images with fuzzy or even without edges. However, as a limitation, the C-V model always supposes the image with intensity homogeneity, the local image fitting method gives correct results, but the proposed method is much faster.

Here the observation of the proposed method provides the most excellent segmentation results; whatever the form and the location of the initial contour and the resultant contours are smooth and continuous. Figure 21 shows the local image fitting method where the initial contour position affects the final result of segmentation incorrect result downs the accuracy of the process.

*Figure 20. (a, c, e, g) Shows the initial contour and (b, d, f, h) shows the segmentation results by local image fitting*

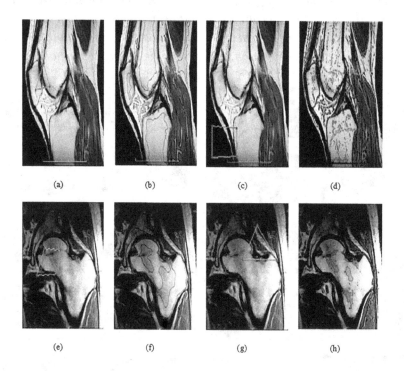

*Figure 21. Shows the initial contours (a-i) and the (j-k) shows the segmentation results of the proposed method*

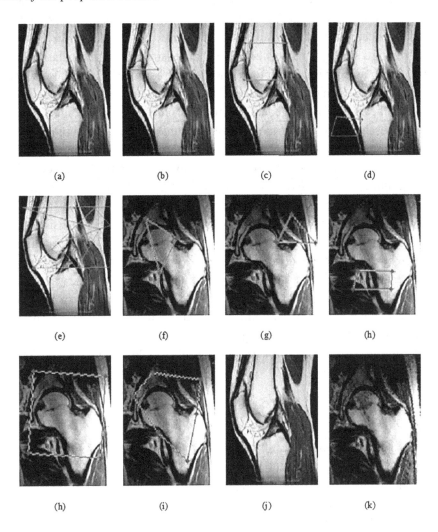

(a)  (b)  (c)  (d)

(e)  (f)  (g)  (h)

(h)  (i)  (j)  (k)

## CONCLUSION

The proposed approach to interactively segment the foreground object of interest from an image is to annotate a bounding box that covers the foreground object. Then, double labelling is performed to achieve a refined segmentation. The lattice Boltzmann method, therefore, is a new and promising alternative to the traditional Navier–Stokes solvers in the domain of Computational Fluid Dynamics (CFD). Because of the great need for memory and computing time, most CFD problems on a single computer insufficient time. Therefore the solvers have to be parallelised. Because of the implicit parallelism of the proposed method, this promises a good speedup. Numerical simulation of the PDEs usually requires high-intensity computation and large consumption of computational resources. To discretise the PDEs that lead to solving a sparse linear system. The parallelisms of computer algorithms are becoming increasingly important today, as the last years' trend in processors was to put more CPUs on each processor instead of drastically improving the speed of each CPU. Also, the emergence of general-purpose graphics processing units, which can look at as massively parallel processors, offers exciting new opportunities for rapid calculation of parallelizable problems. It is a term for issues which are particularly simple to parallelise, and where the speed up in the computation is nearly linear with the number of processor cores used. The reason for the lattice Boltzmann's straightforward parallelisation is that operations on the grid are local so that each node can be updated independently of others. It should not be surprising that the lattice Boltzmann method gives behaviour, according to the wave equation, and that it can be used to simulate acoustics. After all, the compressible Navier-Stokes equation can be simulated using the lattice Boltzmann method and the wave equation can be derived from compressible Navier-Stokes. Of course, for pure wave equation simulations, there will probably be more effective numerical methods. The lattice Boltzmann method's strength is being a full Navier Stokes solver, which means that it can be used to simulate non-linear acoustics in complex flows.

## SUMMARY

In this chapter, the Boltzmann distribution was derived, which is the distribution that holds the statistical treatment of the method. The Boltzmann equation explained next to the main difficulty of this equation, the integral of the collision operator solved by the BGK-Approximation where a long term substitutes this essential. The discretisation of the Boltzmann comparison with the BGK-Approximation introduced, all along with the lattice and the different lattice configurations, to define the lattice framework where the method is applied. Also, in this framework, the algorithm of the process was described. The boundary conditions summarised in this chapter, where one can see that they represent macroscopic conditions acting locally in every node.

# REFERENCES

Ducournau, A., & Bretto, A. (2014). Random walks in directed hypergraphs and application to semi-supervised image segmentation. *Computer Vision and Image Understanding, 120,* 91–102. doi:10.1016/j.cviu.2013.10.012

Pauplin, O., Caleb-Solly, P., & Smith, J. (2010). User-centric image segmentation using an interactive parameter adaptation tool. *Pattern Recognition, 43*(2), 519–529. doi:10.1016/j.patcog.2009.03.007

Chen, Y., Cremers, A., & Cao, Z. (2014). Interactive color image segmentation via iterative evidential labeling. *Information Fusion, 20,* 292–304. doi:10.1016/j.inffus.2014.03.007

Suetake, Uchino, & Hirata. (2007). Separability-Based Intelligent Scissors for Interactive Image Segmentation. *IEICE Transactions on Information and Systems, 90*(1), 137-144.

Li, H., Zhou, D., & Wu, Y. (2011). Collision detection algorithm based on mixed bounding box. *Jisuanji Yingyong, 30*(12), 3304–3306. doi:10.3724/SP.J.1087.2010.03304

Balla-Arabe, S., Gao, X., & Wang, B. (2013). A Fast and Robust Level Set Method for Image Segmentation Using Fuzzy Clustering and Lattice Boltzmann Method. *IEEE Transactions on Cybernetics, 43*(3), 910–920. doi:10.1109/TSMCB.2012.2218233 PMID:23076068

Tsutahara, M. (2012). The finite-difference lattice Boltzmann method and its application in computational aero-acoustics. *Fluid Dynamics Research, 44*(4), 045507. doi:10.1088/0169-5983/44/4/045507

Lou, Q., Guo, Z., & Shi, B. (2012). Effects of force discretization on mass conservation in lattice Boltzmann equation for two-phase flows. *EPL, 99*(6), 64005. doi:10.1209/0295-5075/99/64005

Amarapur, B., & Kulkarni, P. (2011). External Force for Deformable Models in Medical Image Segmentation: A Survey. *Signal and Image Processing: an International Journal, 2*(2), 82–101. doi:10.5121ipij.2011.2208

Benedict, M., Kovács, J., & Czirják, A. (2012). Time dependence of quantum entanglement in the collision of two particles. *Journal of Physics. A, Mathematical and Theoretical, 45*(8), 085304. doi:10.1088/1751-8113/45/8/085304

Utyuzh, O., Wilk, G., & Wodarczyk, Z. (2007). Numerical symmetrization of state of identical particles. *Brazilian Journal of Physics, 37*(2).

Sun, C., Pérot, F., Zhang, R., Freed, D., & Chen, H. (2013). Impedance Boundary Condition for Lattice Boltzmann Model. *Communications in Computational Physics, 13*(03), 757–768. doi:10.4208/cicp.421011.260112s

Utyuzh, O., Wilk, G., & Wodarczyk, Z. (2007). Numerical symmetrization of state of identical particles. *Brazilian Journal of Physics, 37*(2).

Kundu, J., & Rajesh, R. (2015). Asymptotic behavior of the isotropic-nematic and nematic-columnar phase boundaries for the system of hard rectangles on a square lattice. *Physical Review. E, 91*(1), 012105. doi:10.1103/PhysRevE.91.012105 PMID:25679568

Beneš, M., & Kučera, P. (2015). Solutions to the Navier-Stokes equations with mixed boundary conditions in two-dimensional bounded domains. *Mathematische Nachrichten, 289*(2-3), 194–212.

Mohamad & Kuzmin. (2012). The Soret Effect with the D1Q2 and D2Q4 Lattice Boltzmann Model. *International Journal of Nonlinear Sciences and Numerical Simulation, 13*(3-4).

Wu, J., & Guo, H. (2014). Sonar Image Segmentation Based on an Improved Selection of Initial Contour of Active Contour Model. *AMM, 709*, 447–450. doi:10.4028/www.scientific.net/AMM.709.447

Krithivasan, S., Wahal, S., & Ansumali, S. (2014). Diffused bounce-back condition and refill algorithm for the lattice Boltzmann method. *Physical Review. E, 89*(3), 033313. doi:10.1103/PhysRevE.89.033313 PMID:24730973

Zhuang, X., Ji, X., & Wei, Z. (2013). A Novel Deformable Grid Method for Image Segmentation. *AMM, 310*, 624–628. doi:10.4028/www.scientific.net/AMM.310.624

Wang, Y., Shu, C., & Yang, L. (2016). Boundary condition-enforced immersed boundary-lattice Boltzmann flux solver for thermal flows with Neumann boundary conditions. *Journal of Computational Physics, 306*, 237–252. doi:10.1016/j.jcp.2015.11.046

Kang, H., Kim, B., Lee, J., Shin, J., & Shin, Y. (2014). Automatic left and right heart segmentation using power watershed and active contour model without edge. *Biomedical Engineering Letters, 4*(4), 355–361. doi:10.100713534-014-0164-9

Zhang, K., Song, H., & Zhang, L. (2010). Active contours driven by local image fitting energy. *Pattern Recognition, 43*(4), 1199–1206. doi:10.1016/j.patcog.2009.10.010

Li, C., Huang, R., Ding, Z., Gatenby, J., Metaxas, D., & Gore, J. (2011). A Level Set Method for Image Segmentation in the Presence of Intensity Inhomogeneities With Application to MRI. *IEEE Transactions on Image Processing*, *20*(7), 2007–2016. doi:10.1109/TIP.2011.2146190 PMID:21518662

Wang, L., He, L., Mishra, A., & Li, C. (2009). Active contours driven by local Gaussian distribution fitting energy. *Signal Processing*, *89*(12), 2435–2447. doi:10.1016/j.sigpro.2009.03.014

Chapter 4

# Challenges of Applying Deep Learning in Real–World Applications

**Amit Kumar Tyagi**

https://orcid.org/0000-0003-2657-8700

*School of Computing Science and Engineering, Vellore Institute of Technology, Chennai, India*

**G. Rekha**

*Department of Computer Science and Engineering, Koneru Lakshmaiah Educational Foundation, Hyderabad, India*

## ABSTRACT

*Due to development in technology, millions of devices (internet of things: IoTs) are generating a large amount of data (which is called as big data). This data is required for analysis processes or analytics tools or techniques. In the past several decades, a lot of research has been using data mining, machine learning, and deep learning techniques. Here, machine learning is a subset of artificial intelligence and deep learning is a subset of machine leaning. Deep learning is more efficient than machine learning technique (in terms of providing result accurate) because in this, it uses perceptron and neuron or back propagation method (i.e., in these techniques, solve a problem by learning by itself [with being programmed by a human being]). In several applications like healthcare, retails, etc. (or any real-world problems), deep learning is used. But, using deep learning techniques in such applications creates several problems and raises several critical issues and challenges, which are need to be overcome to determine accurate results.*

DOI: 10.4018/978-1-7998-0182-5.ch004

# INTRODUCTION ABOUT DEEP LEARNING

## Defining Multi-Platform

The definition of Artificial Intelligence (AI) is quite long and easy to understand, i.e., it refers to the simulation of intelligent behavior by computer systems. Deep Learning is a subset of Machine Learning, i.e., used to produces prediction from a large collection of data (using analysis techniques or methods, and learning from its own), whereas Machine learning is a subset of Artificial Intelligence, to produces predictions (using human being help in analysis). Machine Learning is defined as "ML is a field of study that gives computers the capability to learn without being explicitly programmed" (Tyagi, A. K. (2019), Samuel, A. L. (2000)), and Awad, M., & Khanna, R. (2015). Machine learning uses algorithms like supervised (regression, decision tree, random forest, classification) and unsupervised (clustering, association analysis, Hidden Markov Model, etc.). Here, supervised, unsupervised and re-enforcement learning are three types of machine learning. Such behavior could encompass any range of tasks for which human intelligence is normally necessary, such as visual pattern recognition, language translations, and decision-making (datafloq.com, (2018)). On the other hand, Deep Learning uses Artificial Neural Networks (ANN) inspired by knowledge of human brain biology, from which emerge algorithms which are highly efficient in solving classification problems. In general terms, deep learning is an aspect of AI that uses complex hierarchical neural networks and lots of precise data to make machines capable of learning things automatically by its own (like a human being learns). Today's the market value of deep learning software is growing at a higher rate, i.e., from $20 million (in 2018) to $930 million (by 2025). Deep Learning is the spearhead of Artificial Intelligence (see figure 1), and it is one of the most exciting technologies of the recent/ past decade. Now days, this kind of learning techniques are being used in several applications/ areas like such as recognizing speech or detecting cancer, etc.

Deep Learning is often compared to the mechanisms that underlie the human mind, and some experts believe that it will continue to advance at an unexpected growth and conquer many more fields/ areas (bdtechtalks.com, (2018)). In some cases, there is fear that deep learning might threaten the very social and economic fabrics that hold our societies together, by either driving humans into unemployment or slavery. There is no doubt that machine learning and deep learning are super-efficient for many tasks (while are interrelated to each other (refer figure 1)). However, there are not universal techniques (even Deep Learning) which can solve all problems and override all previous technologies. This technologies/ learning technique (in many cases) have several/ its distinct limits and challenges which prevent it from competing with the mind of a human being. Human beings can learn abstract, broad relationships (Seymour, V. (2016)) between different concepts and make decisions with little information. In brief, deep learning algorithms are narrow in their capabilities and need precise information to do their job/ analysis information. Note that as discussed above, Deep Learning is a subset of Machine Learning (Tyagi, A. K. (2019)). that achieves great power and flexibility by learning, to represent the world as nested hierarchy of concepts, with each concept defined in relation to simpler concepts, and more abstract representations computed in terms of less abstract ones, cost, mistakes. A deep learning technique learn categories incrementally through its hidden layer architecture, defining low-level to high level categories like letters to words then to sentences, for example, in image recognition it means identifying light/dark areas before categorizing lines and then shapes to allow face recognition.

In deep learning, each neuron or node in the network represents one aspect of the whole and together they provide a full representation of the image. Each node or hidden layer is given a weight that represents the strength of its relationship with the output and as the model develops the weights are adjusted. Today's popular example of Deep Learning (in case of learning itself) is 'Ex-Machina' (a Hollywood movie, released in 2014). In this movie, a machine (a robot: machine with intelligence) tries to attack on human being (with thinking), also fall attached with a human. In near future, this kind of future will be interesting when both machine and people are working together, with understanding each other (without doing any malicious activity). Apart that, Deep learning exciting process are: Face recognition, image classification, speech recognition, text-to-speech generation,

*Figure 1. Relation of deep learning with machine leaning with artificial intelligence*

handwriting transcription, machine translation, medical diagnosis (Cao, C., Liu, F., et.al (2018), & Litjens, G., Kooi, T., et.al (2017), cars (drivable area, lane keeping), digital assistants, Ads, search, social recommendations, game playing with deep RL. Hence now history of Deep Learning is investigated (year-wise) as:

- 1943: Neural Networks
- 1957: Perceptron
- 1974-86: Back-propagation, RBM, RNN
- 1989-98: CNN, MNIST, LSTM, Bi-directional RNN
- 2006: "Deep Learning", DBN
- 2009: ImageNet
- 2012: AlexNet, Dropout
- 2014: GANs
- 2014: DeepFace
- 2016: AlphaGo
- 2017: AlphaZero, Capsule Networks
- 2018: BERT

Further, the history of Deep Learning Tools (year-wise) is included as:

- Mark 1 perceptron – 1960
- Torch – 2002
- CUDA - 2007
- Theano – 2008
- Caffe – 2014
- DistBelief – 2011
- TensorFlow 0.1- 2015
- PyTorch 0.1 – 2017
- TensorFlow 1.0 – 2017
- PyTorch 1.0 – 2017
- TensorFlow 2.0 - 2019

Hence, now each section will discusses essential topics related to deep learning (in detail).

## Deep Learning vs. Machine Learning

Now-a-days, the software industry moving towards/ implementation of machine intelligence in their business, i.e., to boost their product. Generally, Machine Learning is being used in industry to make machine automotive and intelligent. In a simpler way, Machine Learning is set of algorithms that parse data, learn from them, and then apply what they have learned to make intelligent decisions. For example, it is how Netflix knows which shows we need/ want to watch next or how Facebook recognises your friend's face in a digital photo. These videos on Netflix are analysed deeply with collection of data of various users, i.e., at which instance user forwards and at which moment users repeated the scenes. In the past decade, traditional Machine Learning algorithms and data mining techniques were unable to solve such complex problems (due to a lot of data, in different- different format). They require a lot of skilled people and efficient people (in domain expertise), i.e., human being only capable of what they are designed/ skilled for doing a task/work. In an Artificial Intelligence world (or we use it by users/ its manufacturers), deep learning role is much important in several domains like image classification, speech recognition, handwriting transcription, machine translation, etc. Deep learning is far different from machine learning in case of working and producing promises or outputs. Some difference between DL and ML can be included as:

1.  Data Dependencies: Performance is the main key difference between both algorithms. Although, when the data is small, Deep Learning algorithms do not perform well. This is the only reason Deep Learning (DL) algorithms need a large amount of data to understand it perfectly.

2.  Hardware Dependencies: Generally, Deep Learning depends on high-end machines while traditional learning depends on low-end machines. Thus, Deep Learning requirement includes Graphics Processing Units (GPUs). That is an integral part of it is working. They also do a large amount of matrix multiplication operations.

3.  Feature Engineering: In this general process, domain knowledge is kept into the creation of feature extractors to reduce the complexity of the data and make patterns more visible to learn the algorithm working. Although, it is very difficult to process. Hence, it is time consuming and expertise.

4.  Problem Solving Approach: Generally, we use the traditional algorithm to solve problems. However, it needs to break a problem into different parts to solve them individually. To get a result, combine them all. For Example, we have a task of multiple object detection. In this task, we have to identify what the object is and where is it present in the image. In a Machine Learning approach, we have to divide the problem into two steps: object detection and object recognition. First, we use the Grabcut algorithm to skim through the image and find all the possible objects. Then, of all the recognized objects, we would use an object recognition algorithm like Support Vector Machine (SVM) with Histogram of Oriented Gradients (HOG) to recognize relevant objects.

5.  Execution Time: Usually, Deep Learning takes more time to train as compared to Machine Learning. There are so many parameters in a Deep Learning algorithm, whereas Machine Learning takes much less time to train, ranging from a few seconds to a few hours.

6.  Interpretability: We have interpretability as a factor for comparison of both learning techniques. Although, Deep Learning is still thought 10 times before its use in industry/ organisations.

Figure 2 shows the difference of working structure of Machine Learning and Deep Learning Techniques.

In summary in machine learning, supervised learning is used to predict value based on labelled data (e.g., weather-predicting AI), whereas unsupervised learning predicts value based on unlabelled data (e.g., behavior-predicting AI for an e-commerce website), while re-enforcement learning learns from its own or work on feedback process. Re-enforcement learning is also called reward-based learning. ML algorithm typically consists of two phases: training and testing. Training data is used to develop a model whereas testing phase is used to validate model. Basically, Machine Learning used to solve business problems like detecting spam, image recognition, product recommendation and predictive maintenance, etc. While, in Deep Learning solves problems using input layer, output layers and hidden layers. As much hidden layers are there in deep learning, the more complex problems can be solved. Also, as much small data set will be used in deep learning for processing, the result will be similarly inaccurate. In summary, deep learning make prediction using neural network.

*Figure 2. Process of machine learning vs deep learning (Sambit Mahapatra, towardsdatascience.com, (2018))*

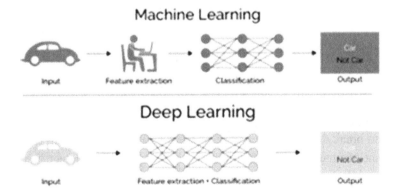

## Distinctive Features of Deep Learning

Generally, Deep Learning is used to extract meaningful data from data (collected from smart things/ internet of things internet connected things) a machine learning method. In general, deep learning is a subset of machine –learning techniques. Initially, concept of deep learning was taken from machine learning. As biggest advantage of deep learning and its popularity is: it works with large amounts of data, while machine learning techniques does not. The "Big Data Era" of technology will provide huge amounts of opportunities for new innovations in deep learning. According to a member of Google-Brain Project, "The analogy to deep learning is that the rocket engine is the deep learning models and the fuel is the huge amounts of data we need to feed to these (existing) algorithms" (Sambit Mahapatra, towardsdatascience.com, (2018)). Deep Learning requires high-end machines contrary to traditional Machine Learning algorithms. Graphical Processing Unit (GPU) has become an essential part in execution of a Deep Learning algorithm. GPU is used to handle large amount of data, in which processor works in parallel. In traditional Machine learning techniques, most of the applied features need to be identified by a domain expert in order to reduce the complexity of the data and make patterns more visible to learning algorithms to work. On another side, the biggest advantage Deep Learning algorithm also is that they try to learn high-level features from data in an incremental manner. This eliminates the need of domain expertise (skilled people) and hard-core feature extraction, i.e., in this extraction of meaningful information is done automatically by reward based learning (without human-intervention).

## Why do we Require Deep Learning?

We used deep learning to process a large amount of data (big data), especially images, prediction of prices, stock prices, etc. This algorithm is used to solve complex problems using neurons or a concept of hidden layers in its working. Apart from above importance, it is far better than machine learning techniques in producing results, i.e., produce results in minimum times. But, a problem with deep learning is that, it does not tell the way of output, i.e., "How it produced", whereas in machine learning, we know "How an output is produced" with having every step of inputs or processing. Another major difference between Deep Learning and Machine Learning technique is the problem-solving approach. Deep Learning techniques tend to solve the problem end to end, whereas Machine learning techniques need the problem statements to break down to different parts to be solved first and then their results to be combine at final stage. For example, for a multiple object detection problem, Deep Learning techniques like Yolo net take the image as input and provide the location and name of objects at output. But, in usual Machine Learning algorithms like SVM, a bounding box object detection algorithm is required first to identify all possible objects to have the Histogram of Oriented Gradients (HOG) as input to the learning algorithm in order to recognize relevant objects. Usually, a Deep Learning algorithm takes a long time to train due to large number of parameters. Popular Residential Network (ResNet) algorithm takes about two weeks to train completely from scratch, whereas traditional Machine Learning algorithms take few seconds to few hours to train. The scenario is completely reverse in testing phase. And at testing time, Deep Learning algorithm takes much less time to run. Whereas, if we compare it with k-nearest neighbors (a type of machine learning algorithm), test time increases on increasing the size of data. Although this is not applicable on all machine learning algorithms, as some of them have small testing times too.

## Strengths of Deep Learning

As discussed above, Deep learning techniques are used with neural network to predict prices of a stock- market, price variation of an airline. In such applications, where prices are dynamic and keep changing everyday (also every hour) based on availability of trade shares/ available seats. Hence in such similar scenario, deep learning has following several strengths over other learning techniques, which are included here as:

1.  No Need for Feature Engineering: Feature Engineering is the process of extracting features from raw data to explain better the selected problem. It is a work of machine learning technique, which improves model accuracy till a certain level. This process requires domain knowledge about a given/ identified problem, for example, in the real- estate business, the location of a land/ house has a significant impact on the selling price. Prices of houses/ land varied according to locations by locations (according to the population density). For a house/ land's location, two parameters like latitude and longitude are essential. With these parameters (in putting together), we can reach to respective location. Note that single parameter has no use at all. Hence, combining the latitude and the longitude to identify a location is an example (feature) of feature engineering. In deep learning, feature engineering is done on its own (by machine) while other learning technique do not support this. A deep learning algorithm will scan the data to search for features that correlate and combine them to enable faster learning without being explicitly told to do so. With this ability, researchers/ data scientists can save a lot of times (months/ weeks of work). Moreover this, neural networks (a deep learning algorithm) is made of can uncover new, more complex features that human miss usually.

2. No Need for Labeling of data: Getting good-quality training data is one of the biggest problems in machine learning because data labeling can be a tedious and expensive job. Sometimes, the data labeling process is simple, but time-consuming. For example, labeling photos "dog" or "muffin" is an easy task, but an algorithm needs thousands of pictures to tell the difference. Other times, data labeling may require the judgments of highly skilled industry experts. So, for some examples, getting high-quality training data can be very expensive. For example, Microsoft's project InnerEye is a tool that uses computer vision to analyze radiological images. To make correct, autonomous decisions, the algorithm requires thousands of well-annotated images where different physical anomalies of the human body are clearly labeled. Such work needs to be done by a radiologist with experience, and a trained eye. Given that around 4-5 images can be analyzed per hours, proper labeling of all images will be expensive (according to Glassdoor, an average base salary for a radiologist is $290.000 a year, i.e., $200 per hour). With deep learning, the need for well-labeled data is made obsolete as deep learning algorithms excel at learning without guidelines. Other forms of machine learning are not successful with this type of learning. In the respective example, a deep learning algorithm would be able to detect physical anomalies of the human body, even at earlier stages than human doctors.

3. Best results with Unstructured Data: According to research from Gartner, up to 80% of a company's data is unstructured because most of it exists in different formats such as texts, pictures, pdf files and more. Unstructured data is hard to analyze for most machine learning algorithms, which means it is also going unutilized. In this area, deep learning can help a lot. Some examples of structured and unstructured data can be discussed in table 1. Deep learning algorithms can be trained using different data formats, and still derive insights, that are relevant to the purpose of its training. For example, a deep learning algorithm can uncover any existing relations between pictures, social media chatter, industry analysis, weather forecast, and predicting future stock prices of a company, etc.

4. Efficient at delivering high-quality results: Humans need as much as rest (because of having laziness) and fuel free of cost/ at lower price. They get tired or hungry and make silly mistakes (time to time, again and again). This case of tiredness, laziness, or feeling hungry is not for neural networks. Once trained correctly, a deep learning brain can perform thousands of repetitive, routine tasks within a shorter period of time than it would take a human being. The quality of its work never diminishes, unless the training data includes raw data that does not represent the problem we are trying to solve.

*Table 1. Comparison of used structured data and unstructured data in deep learning*

|  | Structured data | Unstructured data |
|---|---|---|
| **Characteristics** | Pre-defined data models, usually text only, easy to search | No Pre-Defined Data Model, May Be Text, Images, Sound, Video or Other Formats, Difficult to Search |
| **Resides in** | Relational Databases, Data Warehouses | Application, NoSQL Databases, Data Warehouses, Data Lakes |
| **Generated by** | Human or Machines | Human or Machines |
| **Typical applications** | Airline Reservation Systems, Inventory Control, CRM systems, ERP systems | Word Processing, Presentation Software, Email Clients, Tools for Viewing or Editing Media |
| **Examples** | Dates, Phone Numbers, Social Security Numbers, Credit Card Numbers, Customer Names, Addresses, Product Names and Numbers, Transaction Information. | Test files, Reports, Email Messages, Audio Files, Video Files, Images, Surveillance Imagery. |

In summary, there are some advantages of deep leaning like it (deep learning) gives good performance with problems which require several solutions in multiple domains. This includes speech, language, vision, playing games like Go, etc. It is useful in reducing the need for feature engineering, one of the most time-consuming parts of machine learning practice. In last, it is used an architecture that can be adapted to new problems relatively easily, for example, Vision, Time series, Language etc., are using techniques like Convolutional Neural Networks (CNN), Recurrent Neural Networks (RNN), Long Short-Term Memory (LSTM), etc.

## Weaknesses of Deep Learning

Deep learning (also known as deep structured learning or hierarchical learning) is a family of artificial intelligence to produce intelligent decisions using supervised, semi-supervised or unsupervised learning techniques. It works far better than machine learning techniques. But as discussed above and in (Grm, K., et.al (2017), & Najafabadi, M. M., et.al (2015)], some weaknesses of deep learning are, i.e., it does not work efficiently with bad quality of pictures/ images (having less colours in images), with partial information/ data, small amount of data. Apart that, there are some other/ several disadvantages of deep leaning techniques like

- Deep Learning requires a large amount of data, if we only have thousands of samples, deep learning is unlikely to outperform other approaches.

- Deep Learning is extremely computationally expensive to train. The most complex models take weeks to train using hundreds of machines equipped with expensive GPUs (Graphics Processing Unit).
- Deep Learning does not require strong theoretical foundation.
- Deep Learning determines the topology/ training method/hyper-parameters (Lorenzo, P. R., et.al (2017, July)) for training/ learning purpose, i.e., it is a black art without a theory.
- In Deep Learning, what is learned is not easy to understand/ implement. In this, other classifiers (e.g. decision trees, logistic regression, etc.) make it much easier to understand (in terms of explanation of a process).

Deep Learning means "how much a machine can think deeply (like a human) and can produce efficient results". Using this technique, machine learns by example, i.e., reward or feedback based learning, but still we find several weaknesses of this learning technique, which are discussed in this section in brief. Now, next section of this chapter will discuss several limitations of deep learning techniques.

## The Limitations of Deep Learning

The use of deep learning in several applications is nearly infinite. Many applications are unreachable for current deep learning techniques which had large amounts of human-or machine generated data, for example, we collect a dataset of billions of English language descriptions of the features of a software product (written by a product manager/corresponding source code developed by a team of engineers to meet these requirements). But, with this collected data, we cannot train a deep learning model efficiently, i.e., which can easily read a product description and generate the appropriate codebase. Basically, reasoning method like programming, or applying the scientific method, i.e., long-term planning, and algorithmic-like data manipulation also do not work properly for deep learning models, i.e., it does not matter that how much data we collected or generated (or produced) for those models. Even getting explanation of a sorting algorithm with the help of deep neural network is really a complex process. Now the question is "why a deep learning model is just a chain of simple, continuous geometric transformations mapping one vector space into another"? Generally, deep learning works on Deep Neural Network and on its training and testing of data-set (re-sampling of data again and again). A Deep Neural Network (DNN) can solve a task, even if it training less but accuracy of the algorithm may differ than more trained data. Hence, now some limitations of deep learning are included as:

- **Scaling Deep Learning Techniques:** Scaling Deep Learning techniques by stacking more layers and using more training data create several issues. It will not solve the more fundamental problem that deep learning models are very limited in what they can represent, and all programs which have been learnt, cannot be denoted for simpler (continuous) representation. Scaling of deep learning techniques (for determining expected output) always is a complex task.

- **Risk of Anthropomorphizing Machine Learning Models:** One very real risk with contemporary Artificial Intelligence is that of misinterpreting what deep learning models do, and overestimating their abilities. A fundamental feature of the human mind is our "theory of mind", our tendency to project intentions, beliefs and knowledge on the things around us. Drawing a smiley face on a rock suddenly makes it "happy" in our minds. Applied to deep learning, this means that when we are able to somewhat successfully train a model to generate captions to describe pictures, for example, we are led to believe that the model "understands" the contents of the pictures, as well as the captions it generates. We then proceed to be very surprised when any slight departure from the sort of images present in the training data causes the model to start generating completely absurd captions. In particular, this is highlighted by "adversarial examples", which are input samples to a deep learning network that are designed to trick the model into misclassifying them. Through gradient ascent, one can slightly modify an image in order to maximize the class prediction for a given class. By taking a picture of a panda and adding to it a "gibbon" gradient, we can get a neural network to classify this panda as a gibbon. This evidence both the brittleness of these models, and the deep difference between the input-to-output mapping that they operate and our own human perception.

- **Interpretability:** Interpretability is the main issue why many sectors using other Machine Learning techniques over Deep Learning. For example, suppose we use deep learning to calculate the relevance score of a document. The performance it gives is quite excellent and is near human performance. But there is an issue, i.e., it does not reveal why and how it has given that score (called black box problem). Indeed, mathematically we can find out which nodes of a deep neural network were activated, but we do not know what their neurons were supposed to model and what these layers of neurons were doing collectively. So, we fail to interpret the results. Which is not in case of Machine Learning algorithms like decision trees, logistic regression etc.?

- **Standards:** No unique standards are available to use deep learning technique on different types of data (collected from many devices, enabled in various applications). As we know, deep learning is also applied on images, and audio based content. So "What types of standards of images or audio should be available for applying this concept/ deep learning on collected images/ audio data-sets"? For such issues, we need to find efficient solutions from several research communities in near future.

In simple words, deep learning models do not have any understanding of their input, at least not in any human sense. Our own understanding of images, sounds, and language, is grounded in our sensorimotor experience as humans as embodied earthly creatures. Machine learning models have no access to such experiences and thus cannot "understand" their inputs in any human-relatable way. By annotating large numbers of training examples to (as)input/ feed into our models, we get them to learn a geometric transform that maps data to human concepts on this specific set of examples, but this mapping is just a simplistic sketch of the original model in our minds, the one developed from our experience as embodied agents, it is like an image with low pixel in a mirror. A machine learning practitioner (and keeping this in our mind) should never fall into the trap of believing that neural networks understand the task they perform. They (deep learning models) were trained on a different, far narrower task than the one we wanted to teach them, that of merely mapping training inputs to training targets (point by point). If we show them anything that deviates from their training data, and they will break in the most absurd ways, which is a major limitation of Deep Learning. Hence, this section discusses about limitation of deep learning in detail. Now next section will deal with working-phenomena of deep learning.

## Working of Deep Learning

Deep Learning is a technique for classifying information through layered Neural Networks (NN). The working structure of this learning technique is quite similar to human, i.e., it works like how a human brain works. In this process, Neural Networks (NN) has a set of input units, where raw data is given/ fed as input (like pictures, or sound samples, or written text). Then inputs are mapped with the output nodes, which determine the category to which the input information belongs. For example, it can determine that the input picture contains a cat, or that the small sound sample was the word "Hello". Deep Neural Networks (DNN) consist power of deep learning algorithms. It also has several hidden layers between the input and an output node, which makes them capable of making much more complicated classifications of data (see figure 3). Deep learning algorithms need to be trained with large sets of labelled data (for getting higher accuracy of results). For example, we put in/ give it thousands of pictures of cats or dogs before it can start classifying new cat pictures with relative accuracy. The larger the training data set, the better the performance of the used algorithm/ method will be. Also, with using more hidden layers in a Deep Neural Network (DNN), more difficult/ complex problems can be solved. Today's big firms/ companies or Multinational Companies are using more and more data (large amount of data), and are willing to offer their (maximum) services for free of cost (i.e., in exchange for accessing user data). The more classified information about their users they have, the better they will be able to train or implement their deep learning algorithms. With that, firms/ organisations can produce some efficient decision for themselves, i.e., to fight against their market competitors. It is game-changing process, i.e., changing the competition scenario of a market (i.e., related to one product). This will in turn make their services more efficient than those of their competitors and bring them more customers (some of whom will pay for their premium services). Hence, now when and where we can use Deep Learning, with respect to that, some basic facts are discussed as:

- Deep Learning outperforms other techniques if the data size is large. But with small data size, traditional Machine Learning algorithms are preferable.
- Deep Learning techniques need to have high end infrastructure to train in reasonable time.
- When there is lack of domain understanding for feature introspection, Deep Learning techniques outshines others as you have to worry less about feature engineering.
- Deep Learning really shines when it comes to complex problems such as image classification, natural language processing, and speech recognition.
- Deep Learning outperforms other techniques if quality of images in high definition.

## Deep Learning With Neural Network

The neurons are grouped into three different types of layers: Input Layer, Hidden Layer(s) and Output Layer. With these three layers, we can understand the process of figure 3 with one example. We need to identify first an image from a collection of images. Using deep learning models/ techniques, an image can be pre-processed using three phases, i.e., in identifying pattern of local contrasts, face features and in last respective faces (for example: face recognition).

Hence here, the input layer receives input data. In our case, we have four neurons in the input layer: Pictures, local Contrast in a picture, face features and faces. The input layer passes the inputs to the first hidden layer. The hidden layers perform mathematical computations on our inputs. One of the challenges in creating neural networks is deciding the number of hidden layers, as well as the number of neurons

*Figure 3. Deep learning with neural network*
*(Credit: Edureka Videos and Introduction on Deep Learning)*

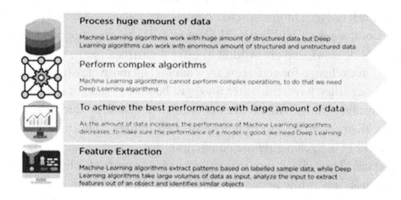

for each layer. Note that the word "Deep" in Deep Learning refers to having more than one hidden layer. And in last, the output layer returns the output data. In our case, it gives us the face recognition with respect to some given features. Hence in summary, we can say that the more hidden layer in a deep learning are being used, the accurate results will be received. Hence, this section discusses the main working of deep learning, in which we found that hidden layers play an important role in processing of deep learning. Now, several problems or issues raised in deep learning will be discussed in next section.

## Problems/Issues With Deep Learning

We have discussed that deep learning technique is too useful (beneficial) in producing some predictions/ decisions based on some data-sets than its other family's fields like machine learning, and artificial intelligence. But it has also raised several issues in it time to time. Apart that, if some algorithms are unable to understand a data then even collected meaningful/ cleaned data also can give inaccurate results. Several problems have been investigated like this problem in deep learning, which will be discussed here. We need to look over such issues in near future.

1.  **Deep Learning is data hungry:** In a world with infinite (i.e., huge) data, and infinite computational resources, we always require some efficient techniques to handle it (Tyagi, A. K., & Reddy, V. K. (2019)). But, were always fail to deliver appropriate tool or methods, because this data is growing everyday (by billions of internet of things or internet connected things). The tools proposed by several researchers do not provide every possible labelled sample of a problem space

to a deep learning algorithm. Therefore, it will have to generalize or interpolate between its previous samples in order to classify data it has never seen before (i.e., a new image or sound that is not contained in its dataset). Currently, Deep Learning lacks a mechanism for learning abstractions through explicit, verbal definition, and works best when there are thousands, millions or even billions of training examples Marcus, G. (2018). Soon essential questions raised here, "what happens when deep learning algorithm does not have enough quality training data"? It can fail instantly, such as mistaking a rifle for a helicopter, or humans for gorillas. The heavy reliance on precise and abundance of data also makes deep learning algorithms vulnerable to spoofing. Testament to the fact are many crazy stories such as deep learning algorithms mistaking stop signs for speed limit signs with a little defacing, or British police software not being able to distinguish sand dunes from nudes (Ben Dickson, bdtechtalks. com, (2018)).

2.  **Deep Learning is Shallow:** Deep Learning algorithms are very good at mapping inputs to outputs but not so much at understanding the context of the data they are handling. In fact, the word "deep" in deep learning is much more a reference to the architecture of the technology and the number of hidden layers it contains rather than an allusion to its deep understanding of what it does. For example, naturally apply to abstract concepts like 'justice,' 'democracy' or 'meddling'" (Ben Dickson, bdtechtalks.com, 2018). In an example like gaming, deep learning algorithms can become very good at playing games, and they can eventually beat the best human players in both video and board games. However, this does not mean that Artificial Intelligence (AI) algorithm has the same understanding as humans in the different elements of the game. It has learned through trial and error that making those specific moves will prevent it from losing. For example, Google DeepMind's mastering of the Atari game. According to the designers of this algorithm (used in respective game), the game realized after 240 minutes that the best way to beat the game is to dig a tunnel in the wall. But it neither knows what a tunnel or a wall is. It has made itself expert through millions of trials and errors combinations, to beat another player (playing, and winning a game with high points in the possible shortest time).

3.  **Deep Learning is Opaque:** While decisions made by rule-based software can be traced back to the last, but in case of machine learning and deep learning algorithms, this facility is not available. This missing feature (of transparency) in deep learning is called as "black box" problem. Deep learning algorithms shift through millions of data points to find patterns and correlations that often go unnoticed to human experts. The decisions they make based on these findings often confound even the engineers who created them. This might not

be a problem when deep learning is performing a trivial task where a wrong decision will cause little or no damage. But, when it is deciding the fate of a defendant in court or the medical treatment of a patient, mistakes can have more serious repercussions. Today's the transparency issue is yet to be solved. It is a potential liability when using deep learning for problem domains like financial trades or medical diagnosis (Cao, C., et.al (2018)), in which human users might like to understand how a given system made a given decision (Ben Dickson, bdtechtalks.com (2018), Hagendorff, T. (2019)). Algorithmic bias as one of the problems stemming from the opacity of deep learning algorithms. Machine learning algorithms often inherit the biases of the training data the ingest, such as preferring to show higher paying job ads to men rather than women, or preferring white skin over dark in adjudicating beauty contests. These problems are hard to debug in development phase and often result in controversial news headlines when the powered software (included deep learning) goes into production.

4.  **Is Deep Learning doomed to fail?** No, but it is bound for a reality check. In general, deep learning is "a perfectly fine way of optimizing a complex system for representing a mapping between inputs and outputs, given a sufficiently large data set" (Ben Dickson, bdtechtalks.com (2018), Marcus, G. (2018)). Deep learning must be acknowledged for what it is, a highly efficient technique for solving classification problems, which will perform well when it has enough training data and a test set that closely resembles the training data set. Note that if we do not have enough training data, or when our test data differs greatly from our training data, or when we are not solving a classification problem, then deep learning becomes a square peg slammed into a round hole, a crude approximation when there must be a solution elsewhere (Marcus, G. (2018)). Deep learning technique need to be combined with other technologies (i.e., with plain-old rule-based programming/ other AI techniques such as reinforcement learning). In (www.wired.com, (2018)), author proposes neuroscience as the key to creating real AI that will be able to achieve human-like problem solving.

5.  **Deep Learning Needs Enough Quality Data:** Deep learning works when it is performed on large amount of data and it improves as the collected data increases. However, when enough quality data simply is not fed into a deep learning system, it can fail badly. In 2017, researchers fooled Google deep learning systems into making errors after altering the available data by adding "noise". While the errors unearthed by the researchers related to trivial matters (i.e., mistaking rifles for turtles in image recognition algorithms). This discusses the dependency of deep learning on the right quantity and quality of data for it (to work accurately). With small input variations in data quality having such profound results on outcomes and predictions, there is a real need to ensure

greater stability and accuracy in deep learning. Furthermore, in some firms/ industries like industrial applications, sufficient data might not be available, it limits deep learning's adoption.

6.  **Artificial Intelligence and its Expectations:** There is a difference between the layman's expectations of Artificial Intelligence (AI) technologies and the actual uses of AI in several applications/ domains. The perception which print-media/ media want to report is one of the super-smart computers with cognitive capabilities which will replace many jobs (done by human beings). But the computer and data science industries have a challenge to address that AI is a tool to enhance productivity with maximum human roles (with providing high accuracy with high productivity). AI requires minimum cases of errors in its process/ execution. In general, AI can do work efficiently with automation of mundane tasks, data-driven predictions, and optimizations, etc. In summary, AI cannot replace a human being, i.e., what a human brain thinks time to time and how he thinks (to do/ solve critical tasks).

7.  **Becoming Production-Ready:** Today's people/ firms are investing in area of Artificial Intelligence (AI), to build more efficient artificial intelligence/ machine, which can work faster, smarter and in a secure way. Providing security to all internets of things, and machines is really a critical task (also biggest challenges). An AI is expected to solve real-life problems/ any worthwhile problem. For that, AI capabilities should be upgraded with new technology infrastructure (to address security concerns). With this, security of the AI platforms, and delivering of solutions to respective (notified) problems will be available instantly (e.g., deliver results, predictions, etc., when needed). A critical goal of AI in the enterprise for machines to assist executives and key stakeholders in making important decisions; both strategic and tactical.

8.  **Deep Learning does not Understand Context Very Well:** The word "deep" in deep learning denotes to its architecture than the level of understanding that these algorithms are currently capable of producing. For example, a deep learning algorithm might become highly proficient at mastering a video game to the point it can easily defeat human players. However, based on a different game, we require to change the setting of neural network to train it again, because to new game or its context it will not understand in first time. For any application, we need to train a neural network once. Similarly, in Internet of Things (IoTs), everyday new data is being generated, for that setting or training neural network is not an easy task.

9.  **Deep Learning Security:** Deep Learning networks require security component in several applications (Najafabadi, M. M., et.al (2015)), i.e., cyber security is needed to be implement in several application (on network). However, giving inputs to these deep learning models and expected outputs from these models

(also networks themselves) have a possibility of altering in input, which may affect output (produced one) completely. Note that deep learning networks may be vulnerable to malicious attacks. For example, self-driving vehicles are partly powered by deep learning. Here, if one was to access the deep learning model and make input alterations, vehicle behaviour could potentially be controlled in a malicious manner. In past, a black-box attack on several deep learning networks has been attacks, i.e., which misclassify the results (making results irrelevant for any future use).

Hence, there are several problems have been investigated with respect to deep learning in the past decade. And many more are still to be count/ focus. Here, we should not forget that deep learning era is an infancy stage too, so much solutions are not available in current. Note that training a Neural Network is hardest part of Deep Learning, because for that we need a large data set. Also, we need a large amount of computational power. In next section, this chapter will discuss about several challenges in deep learning.

## Challenges in Deep Learning

Deep Learning is largely responsible for today's growth (also using Artificial Intelligence (AI)). The technology has given computers a lot of powers in most of the areas, for example, ability to recognize natural language/ speech of a human being, medicine, finance, marketing, etc. Deep Learning has transformed computer vision and improved machine translation. Several areas for Deep learning are still uncovered, but in the existing one, several challenges have been mitigated which are being addressed here as:

1.  **Lots and Lots of data:** Deep Learning algorithms are trained to learn so fast (in minimum time) using data (learning for producing predication/ decision from collected data). Large data sets are required to make sure that the machine delivers desired and accurate results (to respective user/ firms/ organisations). As human brain needs a lot of time, experiences to learn and extract information (or facts), similarly analogous Artificial Neural Network (ANN) requires large amount of data. The more powerful machine/ system we want to build, the more parameters (also features) need to be considered and more parameters require more data. For example, for speech recognition, machine would require data from multiple dialects, demographics and time scales. For that, researchers feed terabytes of data for the algorithm (in a machine) to learn a single (natural) language, which is a time-consuming (also requires tremendous data processing capabilities). Hence using deep learning, we can

solve a problem with providing large amount of data with enough training and testing of respective data-sets. Note that the complexity of a neural network algorithm can be represented with using number of parameters. In deep neural networks, used parameters can be in millions, tens of millions or hundreds of millions (depend on cases/ problems). Remember that if a user's requirements change, then data will change, and then outcomes of an algorithm will change surely. Now here, a question is arising that "How much data is required to train an algorithm efficiently"? For neural networks, the amount of data needed for training will be much higher compared to other machine learning algorithms, because task of a deep learning algorithm is two-folded. First, it needs to learn about the domain, and only then solve the problem. When the training begins, the algorithm starts from scratch. To learn about a given domain, the algorithm needs a huge number of parameters (also require a lot of experiences to learn and collect information about the world around us) to tune and "play around with". With that, a deep learning algorithm can think much like as a human brain (not completely). On reaching such level, deep learning can produce some useful decisions. For example, we know that gas is hot by putting out finger on it, or snow melts at warm temperature when we try to bring it home or in presence of air. Similarly, a neural network learns (with learning patterns, experiences, etc.) about a stock price of a given company, i.e., which one stock will be increased or decreased by end of the day. Note that for getting higher accuracy with respect to stock price, we require large amount of data-sets (i.e., training and testing on it again and again).

2.  **Overfitting in Neural Networks/ the model:** As discussed above, a model is typically trained by maximizing its performance on a particular training data set. The model memorizes the training examples but does not learn to generalize to new situations and data set. In general, Overfitting refers to an algorithm that models the "training data" too well (i.e., one that overtrains the model). Overfitting occurs in complex models when having too many parameters relative to the number of observations. Overfitting occurs when an algorithm learns the detail and noise in the training data to the extent that negatively impacts the performance of the model in real-life scenarios. It is a major problem in neural networks, also in deep learning (because modern network share very large numbers of parameters and thereby a lot of "noise"). Now here, some questions are arising, i.e., "How do we know if our model is overtrained" and "When the accuracy stops improving after a certain number of epochs"? We need to provide answer to such questions, if we are working with neural networks/deep learning.

3.   **Hyperparameter Optimization:** Hyperparameters are the parameters which are defined prior to the starting of a learning process (Lorenzo, P. R., et.al (2017, July)). Changing the value of such parameters by a small amount can create a major change in the performance of our implemented model. Depending on the default parameters and not performing Hyperparameter Optimization can have useful impact on the model performance. Also, having too few hyperparameters and hand tuning them rather than optimizing through proven methods is also a performance driving aspect.

4.   **Requires High-Performance Hardware:** Training a data set for a Deep Learning solution needs lots of data. To solve real world problems using deep learning, the machine needs to be equipped with adequate processing power (e.g., GPU). To ensure better efficiency and less time consumption, researchers move to multi-core high performing GPUs and similar processing units. These processing units are costly and consume a lot of power. Industry level Deep Learning systems require high-end data centers while smart devices such as drones, robots, mobile devices, etc., require small, and efficient processing units. Using deep learning algorithms to solve real world problems is a costlier and power consuming affair.

5.   **Neural Networks are essentially a Blackbox:** Neural networks are essentially Black-boxes and researchers do not know that how they receive results/ conclusions with using neural networks. Basically, we know which data we have feed to machine or deep learning algorithm, but we cannot say anything about outcomes, i.e., how we have received that (operations are largely invisible to humans). Note that we should remember that deep learning uses neural network concept to run itself and do not require human intervention to predict decision. It is one of popular limitations of deep learning, i.e., we do not know that how a neural network reaches at a particular solution (refer section 1.2). It is impossible to look inside of it to see how it works (called black box problem). The lack of ability of neural networks makes it difficult to implement for high-level cognitive functions. Similar to a human brain, the reasoning of a neural network is done with the behavior of thousands of simulated neurons, then it arranged into dozens/ hundreds of intricately interconnected layers. With several hidden layers processing (where inputs are sent from one level to the next level until an overall output is produced), we produce an output. Also, deep learning uses a process known as back-propagation to tweaks individual neurons in such a way that network learn to produce the desired output faster. Hence, lack of transparency, interpretability fails deep learning algorithms (makes it hard to predict), even some time neural networks produce great results. For example, Deep Patient, a deep learning program that was applied to patient records of more than 7,00,000 individuals at Mount Sinai Hospital in New York. After

a long training period, Deep Patient was able to detect certain illnesses better than human doctors. On one hand, this was great news. On the other, if a tool like Deep Patient is actually going to be helpful to medical personnel, it needs to provide the reasoning for its prediction, to reassure their accuracy and to justify a change in someone's treatment. Without the justification, it is difficult to gain the trust of patients or learn why any mistakes in diagnosis were made. This issue is very critical and require a spark/ light to find justification for a received output (by neural network).

6. **Lack of Flexibility and Multitasking:** Deep Learning models, once trained, can deliver efficient and accurate solution to a real-world problem. However, the neural network architectures are highly specialized to specific domains of application. To solve a problem, we require retraining and reassessment, i.e., deep learning models which can multitask without the need of reworking on the whole architecture. In (Manor, R., Mishali, L., & Geva, A. B. (2016)), researchers presented a paper on Multi Model, i.e., a neural network architecture that extract from the success of vision, language and audio networks to simultaneously solve a number of problems spanning multiple domains, including image recognition, translation and speech recognition. Hence, Deep Learning is one of the primary research areas for Artificial Intelligence (AI)/ of using AI. But, while exploring new, or less explored territories of cognitive technology, it is very difficult to solve raised hurdles and difficulties. Today's the future requires the answer for a question "Is Deep Learning our best solution towards real AI"?

In summary, researchers must come with some efficient solutions to overcome above raised challenges (with respecting to adopting/ using deep learning). In summary, deep learning challenges are five-folded, i.e., First, we require to process large amount of data-sets for training using modern tools/ hardware like GPUs (Graphics Processing Units). Emerging techniques like transfer learning and generative adversarial networks show some promise with regard to overcoming this challenge. Second, deep learning works very well, because it uses large number of interconnected neurons, or many parameters (for better accuracy), which allow for capturing subtle nuances and variations in data. However, this also means that it is harder to identify hyper-parameters, parameters whose values need to be fixed before training. As discussed above, there is also a danger of over-fitting data (i.e., when many parameters being used/ when the number of parameters greatly exceeds the number of independent observations).Third, deep learning networks require a lot of time for training, thereby making it very hard to quickly retrain models on the edge using newly available information, i.e., issues like latency and privacy will be lost in era of edge computing. Fourth, due to the large number of layers, nodes, and connections, it is very difficult to understand that "how deep learning networks arrive at particular results"? This issue may not be essential in applications like tagging photos on online social networking, but it is very important in mission-critical applications like predictive maintenance or clinical decision-making. Finally, deep-learning networks are highly susceptible to the butterfly effect small variations in the input data can lead to drastically different results, making them inherently unstable.

Hence, for developing an efficient deep learning algorithm (for tuning and assessing the performance of these algorithm based on empirical data), we require:

1. To measure the complexity of the models, as a function of the number and type of computational units, model topology/structure, model generalization, and learning efficiency;
2. To allow the definition of theoretically grounded strategies for tuning and assessing the performance of models learned from empirical data;
3. To develop regularization schemes. A specific framework for assessment of unsupervised learning is also needed.

Note that computational efficiency is an essential issue in deep learning. In current, deep learning models require a large amount of data to give efficient performances. But this data is growing at a rapid pace every day, so sufficient and efficient model require for handling (analysing) this data (with properly training, with parallel and in distributed computational infrastructures).

## SUMMARY AND DISCUSSION

Generally, Deep learning is used to extract useful patterns from data. It is a sub-field of machine learning (also Artificial Intelligence). It is work with the powers like a human-being (using learning structures based on artificial neural network). Deep learning algorithms with a properly training and testing of large amount of data-sets (available in different data formats) are much useful for various use cases. For example, Deep learning algorithm uncover existing relations between pictures, social media chatter, industry analysis, weather forecast, predict future stock prices of a given company, ticket prices of a journey (in airlines/ airplane ticket price estimator, etc. Hence, Deep learning is summarized with seven essential points:

• Deep Learning uses a Neural Network to imitate animal intelligence.
• There are three types of layers of neurons in a neural network: The Input Layer, the Hidden Layer(s), and the Output Layer.

- Connections between neurons are associated with a weight, dictating the importance of the input value.
- Neurons apply an Activation Function on the data to "standardize" the output coming out of the neuron.
- To train a Neural Network (to get accurate results), we require a large data-set.
- Iterating through the data set and comparing the outputs will produce a Cost Function, indicating how much the AI is off from the real outputs.
- After every iteration through the data set, the weights between neurons are adjusted using Gradient Descent to reduce the cost function.

As discussed above, there three major drivers which caused the breakthrough of (deep) neural networks are: the availability of huge amounts of training data, powerful computational infrastructure, and advances in academia. Today's deep learning systems have started to outperform not only classical methods, but also with other areas like identification of human-benchmarks (i.e., image classification or face recognition). Deep learning has opened a clear road for research community to do their research work or to solve real-world problems. Hence, to make deep learning powerful and more useful in coming era, we need to overcome above discussed challenges like computational efficiency, transparency, interpretability, latency, privacy. In deep learning, most of big questions of intelligence have not been answered nor properly formulated, which is a major issue in this learning technique.

Deep learning is an evolving technology. In spite of promising results stated so far, there is a need for much to be developed. We have seen success of deep learning in the fields of speech, image and language recognition. But in the tasks with non-trivial representations like information retrieval and natural language processing much research need to be carried off. Recent research work showed a vast improvement need in optimization techniques for the architecture of deep learning (Martens, J., & Sutskever, I. (2011), Bengio, Y., et.al (2013, May), Sutskever, I. (2013), Dean, J., (2012), Le, Q. V., et.al (2011, June)). In (Coates, A., (2013, February) experimental results show the need for extending the training of deep features when very large amounts of training data are available. The scope is to find whether full set of parameters are needed in deep learning or not.

One important issue to address is to develop scalable and effective parallel algorithms for training deep architecture with massive datasets at the Web scale. Recent advances in developing asynchronous stochastic gradient learning using large-scale CPU clusters (e.g., (Dean, J., (2012), Le, Q. V., et.al (2011, June)) and GPU clusters (Coates, A., (2013, February) shows promising results. To make deep learning techniques scalable to very large training data, theoretically sound parallel learning algorithms or more effective architectures than the existing ones need to be further developed (e.g., Bengio, Y., et.al (2013, May), Sutskever, I. (2013), Dean, J.,

(2012)). One major barrier to the application of DNNs and related deep models is that it currently requires considerable skills and experience to choose sensible values for hyper-parameters such as the learning rate schedule, the strength of the regularized, the number of layers and the number of units per layer, etc. A solid theoretical foundation of deep learning needs to be established to learn in unsupervised mode.

Moreover this, the interest and enthusiasm of deep learning is growing and already too popular now days in several real-world applications, for example, consumer-related applications like helping voices of Siri and Cortana, Google Photos' tagging feature, Grammarly's proof reader, and Spotify's music recommendations are some example of deep learning algorithm. Also, a bigger impact/ usage of deep learning is also found in the business world, for example, customer data in CRM systems, social media and other online data to better segment clients, predict churn and detect fraud. The financial industry is depending a lot on deep learning algorithms to deliver stock price predictions and execute trades at the right time. In the healthcare industry deep learning networks are exploring the possibility of repurposing known and tested drugs for use against new diseases to shorten the time before the drugs are made available to the general public. Governmental institutions are also turning to deep learning for help to get real-time insights into metric like food production and energy infrastructure by analyzing satellite imagery. There is a long list (of use-cases of deep learning algorithm) to continue. Hence in near future, we can expect large investments to be made to further perfect this technology (deep learning), and more and more of the current challenges to be solved in the future. In last, for solving real world problems and making human life easier, we should say thanks to Deep Learning and Artificial Intelligence for a Bright Future.

## REFERENCES

Awad, M., & Khanna, R. (2015). *Efficient learning machines: theories, concepts, and applications for engineers and system designers.* Apress; doi:10.1007/978-1-4302-5990-9

Bengio, Y., Boulanger-Lewandowski, N., & Pascanu, R. (2013, May). Advances in optimizing recurrent networks. In *2013 IEEE International Conference on Acoustics, Speech and Signal Processing* (pp. 8624-8628). IEEE. doi:10.1109/ICASSP.2013.6639349

Cao, C., Liu, F., Tan, H., Song, D., Shu, W., Li, W., ... Xie, Z. (2018). Deep learning and its applications in biomedicine. [PubMed]. *Genomics, Proteomics & Bioinformatics, 16*(1), 17–32. doi:10.1016/j.gpb.2017.07.003

Coates, A., Huval, B., Wang, T., Wu, D., Catanzaro, B., & Andrew, N. (2013, February). Deep learning with COTS HPC systems. In *International conference on machine learning* (pp. 1337-1345). Academic Press.

Dean, J., Corrado, G., Monga, R., Chen, K., Devin, M., Mao, M., & Ng, A. Y. (2012). Large scale distributed deep networks. In *Advances in neural information processing systems* (pp. 1223–1231). Academic Press.

Dean, J., Corrado, G., Monga, R., Chen, K., Devin, M., Mao, M., . . . Ng, A. Y. (2012). Large scale distributed deep networks. In Advances in neural information processing systems (pp. 1223-1231). Academic Press. Coates

Deng, L., & Yu, D. (2014). Deep learning: methods and applications. *Foundations and Trends® in Signal Processing, 7*(3–4), 197-387.

Grm, K., Štruc, V., Artiges, A., Caron, M., & Ekenel, H. K. (2017). Strengths and weaknesses of deep learning models for face recognition against image degradations. *IET Biometrics*, *7*(1), 81–89. doi:10.1049/iet-bmt.2017.0083

Hagendorff, T. (2019). The Ethics of AI Ethics--An Evaluation of Guidelines. arXiv preprint arXiv:1903.03425

Hinton, G., Deng, L., Yu, D., Dahl, G., Mohamed, A. R., Jaitly, N., ... Sainath, T. (2012). Deep neural networks for acoustic modeling in speech recognition. *IEEE Signal Processing Magazine*, 29.

Huval, B., Wang, T., Wu, D., Catanzaro, B., & Andrew, N. (2013, February). Deep learning with COTS HPC systems. In *International conference on machine learning* (pp. 1337-1345). Academic Press.

Le, Q. V., Ngiam, J., Coates, A., Lahiri, A., Prochnow, B., & Ng, A. Y. (2011, June). On optimization methods for deep learning. In Proceedings of the 28th International Conference on International Conference on Machine Learning (pp. 265-272). Omnipress.

Litjens, G., Kooi, T., Bejnordi, B. E., Setio, A. A. A., Ciompi, F., Ghafoorian, M., ... Sánchez, C. I. (2017). A survey on deep learning in medical image analysis. [PubMed]. *Medical Image Analysis*, *42*, 60–88. doi:10.1016/j.media.2017.07.005

Lorenzo, P. R., Nalepa, J., Ramos, L. S., & Pastor, J. R. (2017, July). Hyper-parameter selection in deep neural networks using parallel particle swarm optimization. In *Proceedings of the Genetic and Evolutionary Computation Conference Companion* (pp. 1864-1871). ACM. doi:10.1145/3067695.3084211

Manor, R., Mishali, L., & Geva, A. B. (2016). Multimodal neural network for rapid serial visual presentation brain computer interface. [PubMed]. *Frontiers in Computational Neuroscience, 10*, 130. doi:10.3389/fncom.2016.00130

Marcus, G. (2018). Deep learning: A critical appraisal. arXiv preprint arXiv:1801.00631

Martens, J. (2010, June). Deep learning via hessian-free optimization. *ICML, 27*, 735–742.

Martens, J., & Sutskever, I. (2011). Learning recurrent neural networks with hessian-free optimization. In *Proceedings of the 28th International Conference on Machine Learning (ICML-11)* (pp. 1033-1040). Academic Press.

Najafabadi, M. M., Villanustre, F., Khoshgoftaar, T. M., Seliya, N., Wald, R., & Muharemagic, E. (2015). Deep learning applications and challenges in big data analytics. *Journal of Big Data, 2*(1), 1. doi:10.118640537-014-0007-7

Samuel, A. L. (2000). Some studies in machine learning using the game of checkers. *IBM Journal of Research and Development, 44*(1.2), 206-226.

Seymour, V. (2016). The human–nature relationship and its impact on health: A critical review. [PubMed]. *Frontiers in Public Health, 4*, 260. doi:10.3389/fpubh.2016.00260

Sutskever, I. (2013). *Training recurrent neural networks*. Toronto, Canada: University of Toronto.

Tyagi, A. K. (2019). *Machine Learning with Big Data*. Retrieved from https://towardsdatascience.com/why-deep-learning-is-needed-over-traditional-machine-learning-1b6a99177063

Tyagi, A. K., & Reddy, V. K. (2019). *Performance Analysis of Under-Sampling and Over-Sampling Techniques for Solving Class Imbalance Problem*. Retrieved from https://www.edureka.co/blog/what-is-deep-learning

Chapter 5

# Challenges and Applications for Implementing Machine Learning in Computer Vision:
## Machine Learning Applications and Approaches

**Hiral R. Patel**
*Ganpat University, India*

**Ajay M Patel**
*AMPICS, India*

**Satyen M. Parikh**
*FCA, India*

## ABSTRACT

*The chapter introduces machine learning and why it is important. Machine learning is generally used to find knowledge from unknown data. There are many approaches and algorithms available for performing machine learning. Different kinds of algorithms are available to find different patterns from the data. This chapter focuses on different approaches with different usage.*

## INTRODUCTION

The world is seeing the ongoing stream of a wide range of organized and unstructured information from internet based life, correspondence, transportation, sensors, and gadgets. World wide Data Corporation (IDC) is gauges that 180 zettabytes of information will be produced by 2025. This blast of information has offered ascend to

DOI: 10.4018/978-1-7998-0182-5.ch005

another economy known as the Data Economy or Importance. Information is the new oil that is valuable yet helpful just when cleaned and prepared. There is a consistent fight for responsibility for between endeavors to get profits by it. The information economy with its tremendous supply is empowering extraordinary development in information sciences, the field which manages extricating helpful data and bits of knowledge from the accessible information. Information science is going toward another worldview where one can instruct machines to gain from information and infer an assortment of helpful experiences. This is known as Artificial Intelligence. Man-made reasoning alludes to knowledge shown by machines that reenact human and creature insight. Computer based intelligence is utilized generally.

The following related task is performed by Artificial Intelligence.

- Self-driving vehicles
- Applications like Siri that comprehend and react to human discourse
- Google's AlphaGo AI has vanquished many Go champions, for example, Ke Jie
- Actualizing AI in chess
- Amazon ECHO item (home control chatbot gadget)
- Hilton utilizing Connie – attendant robot from IBM Watson

The general example of AI that is Amazon pulls in information from its client database to prescribe items to clients. This usefulness gets more clients. More clients produce significantly more information that assistance improves the proposals considerably further.

Alpavdin characterizes Machine Learning as- "Upgrading an execution standard utilizing precedent information and past experience".

The term Machine Learning was begat by Arthur Samuel in 1959, an American pioneer in the field of PC gaming and man-made brainpower and expressed that "it enables PCs to learn without being unambiguously modified".

Also, in 1997, Tom Mitchell gave an "all around presented" scientific and social definition that "A PC program is said to gain as a matter of fact E as for some undertaking T and some execution measure P, if its execution on T, as estimated by P, enhances with experience E.

Machine Learning is a most recent trendy expression coasting around. It has the right to, as it is a standout amongst the most intriguing subfield of Computer Science.

Data is the key idea of machine learning. Analyst can apply its calculations on information to distinguish concealed examples and addition bits of knowledge. These examples and picked up information help frameworks to learn and improve their execution.

Machine learning innovation includes the two insights and software engineering. Measurements enable one to draw deductions from the given information. To actualize proficient calculations we can likewise utilize software engineering. It speaks to the required model, and assesses the execution of the model.

Machine learning includes some progressed factual ideas, for example, demonstrating and enhancement. Displaying alludes to the conditions or likelihood dissemination for the given example information. Improvement additionally incorporates procedures used to locate the most fitting parameters for the given arrangement of information.

The information causes frameworks to learn and improve their execution. We can utilize Modern Learning innovation in a few zones, for example, counterfeit neural systems, information mining, web positioning and so forth.

In Big Data Analytics, Data mining and machine learning are the two most regularly utilized strategies. So people can get befuddled between the two however they are two distinct methodologies utilized for two unique purposes.

Here just the sight view of difference between *Data Mining and Machine Learning*. Data mining is the way toward distinguishing designs in a lot of information to investigate valuable data from those examples. It might incorporate methods of computerized reasoning, machine learning, neural systems, and measurements. The premise of information mining is genuine information. It might have taken motivation and methods from machine learning and measurements yet is put to various finishes. An individual completes information mining in a particular circumstance on a specific informational collection. The objective is to use the intensity of the different example acknowledgment procedures of machine learning.

In any case, machine learning process is a way to deal with creating man-made reasoning. We use Machine Learning calculation to build up the new calculations and strategies. These enable the machine to gain from the examined information or with experience. Most errands that need insight must have a capacity to initiate new information from encounters. Accordingly, a huge region inside AI is machine learning. This includes the investigation of calculations that can separate data without on-line human direction.

Machine Learning identifies with the investigation, structure, and improvement of the calculations. These give PCs the ability to learn without being expressly modified. Information Mining begins with unstructured information and attempts to separate learning or intriguing examples. Amid this procedure, we use machine Learning calculations.

The ability of Artificial Intelligence frameworks to take in by removing designs from information is known as Machine Learning. Machine Learning is a plan to gain from precedents and experience, without being unequivocally modified. Rather than composing code, you feed information to the nonexclusive calculation, and it fabricates rationale dependent on the information given.

## Machine Learning Benefits

Give us a chance to take a gander at a portion of the advantages in this Machine Learning instructional exercise.

- Amazing Processing
- Better Decision Making and Prediction
- Faster Processing
- Precise
- Reasonable Data Management
- Reasonable
- Dissecting Complex Big Data

## Highlights of Machine Learning

Give us a chance to take a gander at a portion of the highlights given beneath in this Machine Learning instructional exercise. Machine Learning is registering escalated and for the most part requires a lot of preparing information. It includes tedious preparing to enhance the learning and basic leadership of calculations.

As more information gets included, Machine Learning preparing can be mechanized for adapting new information designs and adjusting its calculation.

Machine Learning is a field which is raised out of Artificial Intelligence (AI). Applying AI, we needed to assemble better and wise machines. In any case, with the exception of couple of simple errands, for example, finding the most brief way between point A and B, we were not able program increasingly mind boggling and always advancing challenges. There was an acknowledgment that the best way to almost certainly accomplish this assignment was to give machine a chance to gain from itself. This sounds like a youngster gaining from its self. So machine learning was produced as another capacity for PCs. What's more, presently machine realizing is available in such huge numbers of sections of innovation, that we don't understand it while utilizing it.

Discovering designs in information on planet earth is conceivable just for human cerebrums. The information being extremely enormous, the time taken to register is expanded, and this is the place Machine Learning comes without hesitation, to help individuals with huge information in least time.

In the event that huge information and distributed computing are picking up significance for their commitments, machine learning as innovation breaks down those enormous lumps of information, facilitating the undertaking of information researchers in a robotized procedure and increasing equivalent significance and acknowledgment.

The procedures we use for information digging have been around for a long time, however they were not compelling as they didn't have the focused capacity to run the calculations. On the off chance that you run profound learning with access to better information, the yield we get will prompt sensational leaps forward which is machine learning.

This infers the assignments in which machine learning is concerned offers an essentially operational definition instead of characterizing the field in subjective terms. This pursues Alan Turing's proposition in his paper "Registering Machinery and Intelligence", in which the inquiry "Can machines believe?" is supplanted with the inquiry "Can machines do what we (as speculation elements) can do?"

Inside the field of information investigation, machine learning is utilized to devise complex models and calculations that loan themselves to forecast; in business use, this is known as prescient examination. These investigative models permit specialists, information researchers, designers, and examiners to "produce solid, repeatable choices and results" and reveal "concealed experiences" through gaining from authentic connections and patterns in the information set(input).

So on the off chance that you need your program to anticipate, for instance, traffic designs at a bustling convergence (errand T), you can run it through a machine learning calculation with information about past traffic designs (experience E) and, on the off chance that it has effectively "educated", it will at that point improve the situation at foreseeing future traffic designs (execution measure P).

The very unpredictable nature of some genuine issues, however, regularly implies that creating particular calculations that will tackle them superbly every time is unreasonable, if certainly feasible. Instances of machine learning issues incorporate, "Is this malignant growth?", "Which of these individuals are great companions with one another?", "Will this individual like this motion picture?" such issues are astounding focuses for Machine Learning, and in actuality machine learning has been connected such issues with extraordinary achievement.

## Kinds of Machine Learning

There are three common taxonomies of Machine Learning Algorithm based on the result conclusion of the algorithm (Figure 1). The Figure 2 is also the categories of Ml Algorithms using learning Style.

The different methodologies under each category are mentioned in figure 2.

*Figure 1. Kinds of ML & Categorization of ML Algorithms*

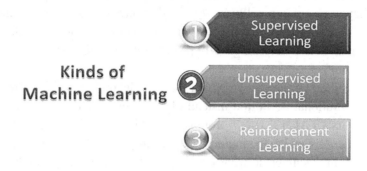

*Figure 2. Categorization of ML Algorithms*

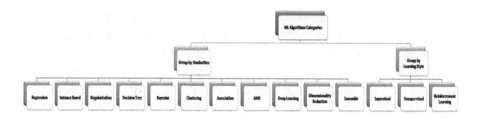

## 1. Supervised Learning

In regulated learning, we are given an informational index and as of now comprehend what our right yield should resemble, having the possibility that there is a connection between the information and the yield. Directed learning issues are additionally sorted into relapse and arrangement issues.

To portray the directed learning issue somewhat more formally, our objective is, given a preparation set, to get familiar with a capacity h: X → Y so that h(x) is a "decent" indicator for the comparing estimation of y. For authentic reasons, this capacity h is known as a theory. Seen pictorially, the procedure is thusly similar to what is shown in Figure 3.

At the point when the objective variable that we're endeavoring to foresee is consistent, for example, in our lodging model, we consider the learning issue a relapse issue. At the point when y can take on just few discrete qualities, (for example, if, given the living territory, we needed to anticipate if a home is a house or a condo, state), we consider it an arrangement issue.

The figure 4 shows the algorithms which are under the Supervised Learning Category of Machine Learning.

*Figure 3. Supervised Learning Style*

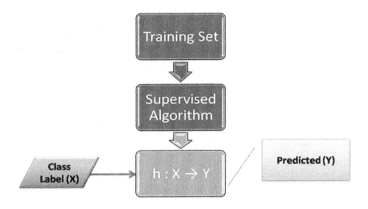

## 2. Unsupervised Learning

Unsupervised learning works by breaking down the information without its marks for the shrouded structures inside it, and through deciding the relationships, and for highlights that really correspond two information things. It is being utilized for bunching, dimensionality decrease, include learning, thickness estimation, and so forth.

*Figure 4. Supervised Learning Algorithms*

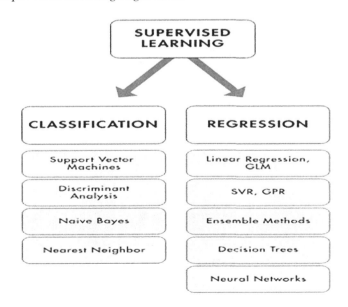

The shrouded structure once in a while called include vector, speaks to the info information such a way, that on the off chance that a similar component vector is being use to recreate the info, at that point one can do that with some satisfactory misfortune. The change in two component vectors of two data sources specifically relative to the difference in the information sources itself. Along these lines this shrouded structure or highlight vector just speaks to highlights in the information that really offer refinement to it.

In this Unsupervised Machine Learning, input information isn't marked and does not have a known outcome.

*Figure 5. Unsupervised Learning Algorithms*

We need to get ready model by deriving structures present in the info information. This might be to extricate general guidelines. It might be through a scientific procedure to lessen excess.

Model issues are bunching, dimensionality decrease, and affiliation rule learning.

Precedent calculations incorporate the Apriori calculation and k-Means.

## 3. Reinforcement Learning

Reinforcement learning is a region of Machine Learning. Reinforcement: It is tied in with making reasonable move to expand compensate in a specific circumstance. It is utilized by different programming and machines to locate the most ideal conduct or way it should take in a particular circumstance. Fortification taking in contrasts from the directed learning in a route that in regulated learning the preparation information has the appropriate response key with it so the model is prepared with the right answer itself while in Reinforcement learning, there is no answer yet the fortification specialist chooses what to do to play out the given errand. Without preparing dataset, it will undoubtedly gain from its experience.

Precedent: The issue is as per the following: We have a specialist and a reward, with numerous obstacles in the middle. The specialist should locate the most ideal way to achieve the reward. The accompanying issue clarifies the issue all the more effectively.

The figure 6 indicates robot, precious stone and flame. The objective of the robot is to get the reward that is the jewel and dodge the obstacles that is fire. The robot learns by attempting all the conceivable ways and after that picking the way which gives him the reward with the least obstacles. Each correct advance will give the robot a reward and each wrong advance will subtract the reward of the robot. The absolute reward will be determined when it achieves the last reward that is the precious stone.

*Figure 6. Reinforcement Learning Example*

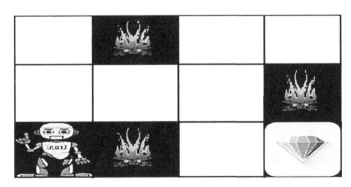

## Main Points for Reinforcement Learning

**Input:** The information ought to be an underlying state from which the model will begin

**Outcome:** There are numerous conceivable output as there are assortment of answer for a specific issue

**Training/Preparing:** The preparation depends on the information, The model will restore a state and the client will choose to remunerate or rebuff the model dependent on its yield.

The model keeps on learning.

The best arrangement of solution is chosen dependent on the most extreme reward.

## Reinforcement Learning vs. Supervised Learning

- Reinforcement Learning is tied in with settling on choices successively. In basic words we can say that the out relies upon the condition of the present information and the following information relies upon the yield of the past input where as In Supervised learning the choice is made on the underlying information or the information given toward the begin.

- In Reinforcement learning choice is reliant, So we offer names to groupings of ward decisions where as Supervised learning the choices are free of one another so names are given to every choice.

- Playing Chess is the example of Reinforcement Learning and Object Recognition is the example of Supervised Learning.

## Applications of Machine Learning

One of the cutting edge developments we've seen is the making of Machine Learning. This fantastic type of man-made consciousness is as of now being utilized in different ventures and callings. For Example, Image and Speech Recognition, Medical Diagnosis, Prediction, Classification, Learning Associations, Statistical Arbitrage, Extraction, Regression.

These are this present reality Machine Learning Applications; we should see them one by one-

## 1. Picture Recognition

It is a standout amongst the most widely recognized AI applications. There are numerous circumstances where you can arrange the item as an advanced picture. For advanced pictures, the estimations depict the yields of every pixel in the picture. On account of a highly contrasting picture, the power of every pixel fills in as one estimation. So if a high contrast picture has N*N pixels, the all out number of pixels and thus estimation is N2.

How about we examine ANN in Machine Learning:

In the hued picture, every pixel considered as giving 3 estimations of the forces of 3 principle shading segments ie RGB. So N*N shaded picture there are 3 N2 estimations.

For face location – The classes may be face versus no face present. There may be a different classification for every individual in a database of a few people.

For character acknowledgment – We can fragment a bit of composing into littler pictures, each containing a solitary character. The classifications may comprise of the 26 letters of the English letter set, the 10 digits, and some unique characters.

## 2. Discourse Recognition

Discourse acknowledgment (SR) is the interpretation of verbally expressed words into content. It is otherwise called "programmed discourse acknowledgment" (ASR), "PC discourse acknowledgment", or "discourse to content" (STT).

In discourse acknowledgment, a product application perceives verbally expressed words. The estimations in this Machine Learning application may be a lot of numbers that speak to the discourse flag. We can fragment the flag into parts that contain particular words or phonemes. In each portion, we can speak to the discourse motion by the forces or vitality in various time-recurrence groups.

Despite the fact that the subtleties of flag portrayal are outside the extent of this program, we can speak to thc flag by a lot of genuine qualities.

Do you think about Artificial Neural Network Model

Discourse acknowledgment, Machine Learning applications incorporate voice UIs. Voice UIs are, for example, voice dialing, call steering, domotic apparatus control. It can likewise use as straightforward information passage, arrangement of organized records, discourse to-content preparing, and plane.

## 3. Medicinal Diagnosis

ML gives strategies, procedures, and devices that can help in tackling symptomatic and prognostic issues in an assortment of therapeutic areas. It is being utilized for the examination of the significance of clinical parameters and of their mixes for visualization, for example expectation of ailment movement, for the extraction of medicinal information for results inquire about, for treatment arranging and support, and for in general patient administration. ML is likewise being utilized for information examination, for example, discovery of regularities in the information by properly managing blemished information, translation of consistent information utilized in the Intensive Care Unit, and for savvy disturbing bringing about successful and proficient checking.

It is contended that the effective execution of ML techniques can help the mix of PC based frameworks in the social insurance condition giving chances to encourage and upgrade crafted by therapeutic specialists and eventually to improve the effectiveness and nature of restorative consideration.

We should take a voyage through Neural Network Algorithms

In restorative conclusion, the principle intrigue is in setting up the presence of an illness pursued by its exact distinguishing proof. There is a different classification for every malady under thought and one class for situations where no illness is available. Here, AI improves the precision of restorative analysis by breaking down information of patients.

The estimations in this Machine Learning applications are ordinarily the aftereffects of certain restorative tests (precedent circulatory strain, temperature and different blood tests) or therapeutic diagnostics, (for example, medicinal pictures), nearness/nonappearance/force of different manifestations and essential physical data about the patient(age, sex, weight and so on). Based on the consequences of these estimations, the specialists slender down on the ailment exacting the patient.

## 4. Measurable Arbitrage

In money, measurable exchange alludes to mechanized exchanging procedures that are regular of a present moment and include countless. In such procedures, the client endeavors to execute an exchanging calculation for a lot of securities based on amounts, for example, verifiable connections and general monetary factors. These estimations can be given a role as an arrangement or estimation issue. The fundamental presumption is that costs will move towards an authentic normal.

Do you think about Kernel Functions

We apply AI strategies to acquire a file exchange methodology. Specifically, we utilize direct relapse and bolster vector relapse (SVR) onto the costs of a trade exchanged store and a surge of stocks. By utilizing foremost part examination (PCA) in lessening the component of highlight space, we watch the advantage and note the issues in the use of SVR. To create exchanging signals, we show the residuals from the past relapse as a mean returning procedure.

On account of arrangement, the classes may be sold, purchase or do nothing for every security. I the instance of estimation one may endeavor to foresee the normal return of every security over a future time skyline. For this situation, one normally needs to utilize the assessments of the normal come back to make an exchanging decision(buy, sell, and so forth.)

## 5. Learning Associations

Learning affiliation is the way toward forming bits of knowledge into different relationship between items. A genuine model is the way apparently inconsequential items may uncover a relationship to each other. At the point when examined in connection to purchasing practices of clients.

How about we talk about Deep learning and Neural Networks in Machine Learning

One utilization of AI Often concentrating the relationship between the items individuals purchase, which is otherwise called bin examination. On the off chance that a purchaser purchases 'X', would the person in question power to purchase 'Y' in view of a relationship that can recognize between them? This prompts the relationship that exists among fish sticks and french fries and so on when new items dispatch in the market a Knowing these connections it builds up another relationship. Realizing these connections could help in proposing the related item to the client. For a higher probability of the client getting it, It can likewise help in packaging items for a superior bundle.

This learning of relationship between items by a machine is learning affiliations. When we found a relationship by inspecting a lot of offers information, Big Data experts. It can build up a standard to infer a likelihood test in learning a contingent likelihood.

## 6. Arrangement

Arrangement is a procedure of putting every person from the populace under examination in numerous classes. This is recognized as autonomous factors.

View Convolutional Neural Networks Architecture

Grouping causes examiners to utilize estimations of an article to recognize the classification to which that object has a place. To set up a productive standard, investigators use information. Information comprises of numerous instances of articles with their right characterization.

For instance, before a bank chooses to dispense an advance, it evaluates clients on their capacity to reimburse the advance. By considering variables, for example, client's acquiring, age, reserve funds and monetary history we can do it. This data is taken from the past information of the credit. Henceforth, Seeker uses to make a connection between client qualities and related dangers.

## 7. Expectation

Consider the case of a bank registering the likelihood of any of credit candidates blaming the advance reimbursement. To figure the likelihood of the blame, the framework will initially need to order the accessible information in specific gatherings. It is portrayed by a lot of tenets recommended by the investigators.

How about we reconsider Recurrent Neural Networks

When we do the characterization, according to require we can figure the likelihood. These likelihood calculations can figure over all parts for fluctuated purposes

The present forecast is one of the most smoking AI calculations. How about we take a case of retail, prior we had the capacity to get bits of knowledge like deals report a month ago/year/5-years/Diwali/Christmas. These sort of announcing is called as verifiable detailing. In any case, as of now business is progressively keen on discovering what will be my deals one month from now/year/Diwali, and so on.

With the goal that business can take a required choice (identified with obtainment, stocks, and so on.) on time.

## 8. Extraction

Data Extraction (IE) is another use of AI. It is the way toward removing organized data from unstructured information. For instance pages, articles, web journals, business reports, and messages. The social database keeps up the yield delivered by the data extraction.

The procedure of extraction accepts contribution as a lot of records and delivers an organized information. This yield is in a condensed structure, for example, an exceed expectations sheet and table in a social database.

These days extraction is turning into a key in the huge information industry.

As we realize that the immense volume of information is getting created out of which the majority of the information is unstructured. The primary key test is taking care of unstructured information. Presently change of unstructured information to organized structure dependent on some example with the goal that the equivalent can put away in RDBMS.

Aside from this in current days information gathering instrument is likewise getting change. Prior we gathered information in clumps like End-of-Day (EOD)

## CONCLUSION

Machine Learning is assuming control over the world-and with that, there is a developing need among organizations for experts to know the intricate details of ML. ML is figuring escalated and by and large requires a lot of preparing information. It includes dull preparing to improve the learning and basic leadership of calculations. As more information gets included, Machine Learning preparing can be computerized for adapting new information designs and adjusting its calculation.

## REFERENCES

Awad, W., & Elseuofi, S. (2011). Machine Learning methods for E-mail Classification. *International Journal of Computers and Applications*, *16*(1), 39–45. doi:10.5120/1974-2646

Cao, C., Liu, F., Tan, H., Song, D., Shu, W., Li, W., ... Xie, Z. (2018). Deep Learning and Its Applications in Biomedicine. [PubMed]. *Genomics, Proteomics & Bioinformatics*, *16*(1), 17–32. doi:10.1016/j.gpb.2017.07.003

Deng & Yu. (2013). Deep Learning: Methods and Applications, Foundations and Trends R. *Signal Processing*, *7*(3-4), 197–387. doi:10.1561/2000000039

Grm, K., Štruc, V., Artiges, A., Caron, M., & Ekenel, H. (2018). Strengths and weaknesses of deep learning models for face recognition against image degradations. *IET Biometrics*, *7*(1), 81–89. doi:10.1049/iet-bmt.2017.0083

Kashyap, R. (2019a). Big Data and Global Software Engineering. In M. Rehman, A. Amin, A. Gilal, & M. Hashmani (Eds.), *Human Factors in Global Software Engineering* (pp. 131–163). Hershey, PA: IGI Global; doi:10.4018/978-1-5225-9448-2.ch006

Kashyap, R. (2019b). Sensation of Deep Learning in Image Processing Applications. In A. Hassanien, A. Darwish, & C. Chowdhary (Eds.), *Handbook of Research on Deep Learning Innovations and Trends* (pp. 72–96). Hershey, PA: IGI Global; doi:10.4018/978-1-5225-7862-8.ch005

Kashyap, R. (2019c). *Big Data Analytics Challenges and Solutions*. doi:10.1016/B978-0-12-818146-1.00002-7

Kashyap, R. (2019d). Computational Healthcare System With Image Analysis. In C. Chen & S. Cheung (Eds.), *Computational Models for Biomedical Reasoning and Problem Solving* (pp. 89–127). Hershey, PA: IGI Global; doi:10.4018/978-1-5225-7467-5.ch004

Kashyap, R. (2019e). Systematic Model for Decision Support System. In A. Mukherjee & A. Krishna (Eds.), *Interdisciplinary Approaches to Information Systems and Software Engineering* (pp. 62–98). Hershey, PA: IGI Global; doi:10.4018/978-1-5225-7784-3.ch004

Kashyap, R. (2019f). Miracles of Healthcare With Internet of Things. In J. Rodrigues, A. Gawanmeh, K. Saleem, & S. Parvin (Eds.), *Smart Devices, Applications, and Protocols for the IoT* (pp. 120–164). Hershey, PA: IGI Global; doi:10.4018/978-1-5225-7811-6.ch007

Kashyap, R. (2019g). Deep Learning: An Application in Internet of Things. In H. Purnomo (Ed.), *Computational Intelligence in the Internet of Things* (pp. 130–158). Hershey, PA: IGI Global; doi:10.4018/978-1-5225-7955-7.ch006

Kashyap, R. (2019h). Machine Learning, Data Mining for IoT-Based Systems. In G. Kaur & P. Tomar (Eds.), *Handbook of Research on Big Data and the IoT* (pp. 314–338). Hershey, PA: IGI Global; doi:10.4018/978-1-5225-7432-3.ch018

Kashyap, R. (2019i). Decision Support Systems in Aeronautics and Aerospace Industries. In T. Shmelova, Y. Sikirda, N. Rizun, D. Kucherov, & K. Dergachov (Eds.), *Automated Systems in the Aviation and Aerospace Industries* (pp. 138–165). Hershey, PA: IGI Global; doi:10.4018/978-1-5225-7709-6.ch005

Kashyap, R. (2019j). Medical Image Segmentation and Analysis. In C. Chakraborty (Ed.), *Advanced Classification Techniques for Healthcare Analysis* (pp. 132–160). Hershey, PA: IGI Global; doi:10.4018/978-1-5225-7796-6.ch007

Kashyap, R. (2019k). Big Data and High-Performance Analyses and Processes. In A. Voghera & L. La Riccia (Eds.), *Spatial Planning in the Big Data Revolution* (pp. 45–83). Hershey, PA: IGI Global; doi:10.4018/978-1-5225-7927-4.ch003

Kashyap, R. (2019l). Artificial Intelligence Systems in Aviation. In T. Shmelova, Y. Sikirda, N. Rizun, & D. Kucherov (Eds.), *Cases on Modern Computer Systems in Aviation* (pp. 1–26). Hershey, PA: IGI Global; doi:10.4018/978-1-5225-7588-7.ch001

Kashyap, R. (2020). Applications of Wireless Sensor Networks in Healthcare. In P. Mukherjee, P. Pattnaik, & S. Panda (Eds.), *IoT and WSN Applications for Modern Agricultural Advancements: Emerging Research and Opportunities* (pp. 8–40). Hershey, PA: IGI Global; doi:10.4018/978-1-5225-9004-0.ch002

Kashyap, R., & Rahamatkar, S. (2019b). Healthcare Informatics Using Modern Image Processing Approaches. In B. Singh, B. Saini, D. Singh, & A. Pandey (Eds.), *Medical Data Security for Bioengineers* (pp. 254–277). Hershey, PA: IGI Global; doi:10.4018/978-1-5225-7952-6.ch013

Litjens, G., Kooi, T., Bejnordi, B., Setio, A., Ciompi, F., Ghafoorian, M., ... Sánchez, C. I. (2017). A survey on deep learning in medical image analysis. [PubMed]. *Medical Image Analysis*, *42*, 60–88. doi:10.1016/j.media.2017.07.005

Manor, R., Mishali, L., & Geva, A. (2016). Multimodal Neural Network for Rapid Serial Visual Presentation Brain Computer Interface. [PubMed]. *Frontiers in Computational Neuroscience*, *10*. doi:10.3389/fncom.2016.00130

Najafabadi, M., Villanustre, F., Khoshgoftaar, T., Seliya, N., Wald, R., & Muharemagic, E. (2015). Deep learning applications and challenges in big data analytics. *Journal Of Big Data*, *2*(1), 1. doi:10.118640537-014-0007-7

# Chapter 6
# Medical Imaging Importance in the Real World

**Ramgopal Kashyap**

ⓘD https://orcid.org/0000-0002-5352-1286

*Amity School of Engineering and Technology, Amity University, Raipur, India*

## ABSTRACT

*In the medical image resolution, automatic segmentation is a challenging task, and it's still an unsolved problem for most medical applications due to the wide variety connected with image modalities, encoding parameters, and organic variability. In this chapter, a review and critique of medical image segmentation using clustering, compression, histogram, edge detection, parametric, variational model. and level set-based methods is presented. Modes of segmentation like manual, semi-automatic, interactive, and automatic are also discussed. To present current challenges, aim and motivation for doing fast, interactive and correct segmentation, the medical image modalities X-ray, CT, MRI, and PET are discussed in this chapter.*

## INTRODUCTION

In the medical image resolution, automatic segmentation is a challenging task, and it's still an unsolved problem for most medical applications due to the wide variety connected with image modalities, encoding parameters and organic variability. Manual segmentation is time-consuming and frequently not applicable in clinical routine. Semi-automatic segmentation methods which required-user interaction can use in instances where automatic algorithms fail. A wide variety of semi-automatic segmentation methods exist that will roughly classify into voxel-based approaches, where the end-user draws seed things to define fore and background voxels and

DOI: 10.4018/978-1-7998-0182-5.ch006

surface-based means, where the shape of a functional object is reconstructed depending on contours or subject models. Image segmentation can smoothly proceed on three other ways, manually, interactive, semi-automatic and automatic.

Segmentation is the process of partitioning an image into semantically interpretable regions. The purpose of segmentation is to decompose the image into parts that are meaningful concerning a particular application. Image segmentation is typically used to locate objects and boundaries like lines, curves in images. The result of image segmentation is a set of regions that collectively cover the entire image or a set of contours extracted from the image. Each of the pixels in a region is similar concerning any characteristic or computed property, such as colour, intensity, or texture. Adjacent areas are significantly different concerning the same characteristic.

Segmentation subdivides an image into its constituent regions or objects. That is, it partitions an image into distinct areas that are meant to correlate strongly with objects or features of interest in the image. Segmentation can also be regarded as a process of grouping together pixels that have similar attributes. The level to which the subdivision carried depends on the problem solved (Anderson, C. W., 1987). That is, segmentation should stop when the objects of interest in an application have isolated. There is no point in taking segmentation past the level of detail required to identify those elements. It is the process that partitions the image pixels into non-overlapping regions such that: Each region is homogeneous, i.e., uniform in terms of the pixel attributes such as intensity, colour, range, or texture. To understand the concept using mathematical representation here $\{R_i\}$ is a segmentation of an entire image $R$ if:

1. $R = \bigcup\limits_{j=1}^{n} R_j$ the union of all regions covers entire $R$

2. $R_i \cap R_j$ For all $i$ and $j$, $I \neq j$ there is no overlap of the regions

3. $P(R_i)$ for $i = 1, 2... n$, $P$ is the logical uniformity predicate defined over the points in the set $R_i$

4. $P(R_i \cup R_j)$ =false, for $I \neq j$ and $Ri$ and $Rj$ are neighbouring regions.

5. $Ri$ is a connected region, $i = 1, 2... n$

All pixels must be assigned to regions. Each pixel must belong to a single region only. Each region must be uniform. Any merged pair of adjacent regions must be non-uniform. Each region must be a connected set of pixels.

## Several Predicate Examples

1. $P(R)$ =True, if $|g(x1, y1) - g(x2, y2)| <= \varepsilon$ for all$(x1, y1)$, $(x2, y2)$ in R

2.   P(R) =True, if T1<=g(x, y) <=T2 for all (x, y) in R where T1and T2are thresholds that define the region.

3.   P(R) = True if If (j,k)-f(m,n)I≤ Δ and false otherwise

where (j,k) and (m, n) are the coordinates of neighbouring pixels in region R., This predicate states that a region R is uniform if (and only if) any two neighbouring pixels differ in grey-level of no more than Δ.

4.   P(R) = True if If(j,k)-$\mu_R$I≤Δ and false otherwise

where f (j, k) is the grey-level of a pixel with coordinates (j, k) and $\mu_R$ the mean grey level of all pixels in R.

Several different segmentation techniques could be used to come up with similar results. The methods typically vary in speed, accuracy and robustness. In the following section, various segmentation methods studied:

## Clustering Based Methods

Clustering is a process of grouping the unlabeled sets into the clusters such that similar patterns occur in one cluster. The grouping can categorise as hard clustering or fuzzy clustering. In hard clustering boundaries of groups are clearly defined. But in some cases, borders cannot be defined, and a pixel can belong to more than one group. Fuzzy c means (FCM) is an unsupervised clustering model that can apply to a wide range of problems in chemistry, agriculture, zoology, image analysis and medical diagnosis. The K-means algorithm is another method for segmentation of clusters (Avati, A., Jung, K., Harman, S., Downing, L., Ng, A., & Shah, N. H., 2018). It takes cluster centres based on random selection or some heuristic then allocate every pixel in the image to the group that reduces the distance between the pixel and the cluster centre after this again calculates the cluster centres by averaging all of the pixels in the group repeat this process up to no pixel changes.

## Watershed Methods

Watershed segmentation uses the analogy from topography by interpreting the gradient map of an intensity image as height values get lines which appear to be ridges. If the contours were a terrain, falling rain would find the way from the dividing lines towards the connected catchment basin. These dividing lines are called watersheds. The watershed segmentation has proven to be a powerful and fast technique for both contour detection and region-based segmentation. In principle, watershed segmentation depends on ridges to perform a proper segmentation, a property which often fulfilled in contour detection where the boundaries of the objects expressed as ridges. For region-based segmentation, it is possible to convert the edges of the objects into ribs by calculating an edge map of the image (Kashyap, R.,2019a). A Watershed usually implemented by region growing based on a set of markers to avoid severe over-segmentation. Different watershed methods use slightly different distance measures, but they all share the property that the watershed lines appear as the points of the distance between two adjacent minima. The success of watershed segmentation relies on a situation where the desired boundaries are ridges. Unfortunately, the standard watershed framework has minimal flexibility in optimised parameters. As an example, there exists no possibility to smooth the edges. However, recent progress allows regularization of the watershed lines with an energy-based watershed algorithm (water snakes), the improved work based on partial differential equations which easily allow regularisation of the watersheds (Guleria, P., &Sood, M.,2014).

Moreover, the method is flexible about several optimisation parameters. As an example, it could enable optimisation of the Euler number to avoid internal holes inside the phases. Furthermore, it would be desirable to develop methods which could optimise the number of markers in addition to the already implemented location of the watersheds.

## Segmentation Based on Prior Knowledge

Segmentation can view as the job of partitioning the actual image into foreground thing or objects along with background regions. Since the concept of an object is subjective and applied primarily based segmentation, in general, isn't well defined. Also, even when the thing of interest is good to know, segmentation is challenging (Kashyap, R.,2019b). It is so since in the imaging process, the actual inherent properties of the inspected object could be corrupt due to being able to noise, occlusion, illumination conditions, plus more. General syntactical assumptions, for instance, continuity and smoothness involving edges and homogeneity of semantic regions, should thus be complemented with apriori semantical information on the objects to be segmented.

The nature of prior understanding varies, depending on the features that distinguish the thing of interest from its surroundings. Colour distribution, texture, motion and form or their combinations are generally used to characterise the parts of interest given the entire scene. The mix of such high amount visual cues with the low-level image features yields a useful segmentation framework. However, the partitioning of the image into meaningful regions is usually a preliminary step towards image understanding. The next step is identifying the segments depending on their internal qualities and interrelations. Only then, one may have an intelligent say within the world depicted through the camera. The interleaving top-down, along with bottom-up processes, are most often an incompatible stream.

A possibly more powerful claim stems from the point that in most real-life applications in the least some knowledge comes in advance. Consider, for example, the images acquired using medical imaging devices, for instance, Magnetic Resonance Imaging (MRI), Computed Tomography (CT), positron emission tomography (PET) and Ultrasound etc. There is certainly much information within the patient (age, girl or boy, medical history, physical conditions); on the actual imaged organ along with tissue; on the expected pathologies along with the standard, healthy states plus on the imaging modalities used along with their limits. Medical imaging analysis problems are generally severe, but the solutions should be as reliable as it can be. Mathematical modelling involving prior information as well as incorporation in segmentation frameworks is an active field involving research. The main issues raised in combining the information about the anticipated object appearance with the actual image info. This thesis advisees a variational way of region-based segmentation that allows a convenient way to integrate information from several sources in a coherent manner.

## Variational Models Based

Intensive image processing research within the last few two decades went up to new insights concerning the nature of pictures. Modern segmentation techniques adopted these fresh concepts. The most important observation is that the piecewise smooth purpose can approximate the image. The essence of the inspection, made by Mumford and Shah is that an organic image is composed of homogeneous regions (Kashyap, R.,2019c). The image segments, along with their delimiting border, obey the Gestalt basic principle of minimal description length. About annually later, Perona, along with Malik, suggested the actual anisotropic diffusion regarding image denoising, a same good concept involving piecewise smoothness. Realise that image denoising, as well as edge detection along with integration, was the objectives of the Mumford-Shah framework likewise. These image processing tasks are in many senses supporting to image segmentation.

Partitioning of the actual image into semantic regions is equivalent to the detection of the closed contours that will bind them. The fundamental assumption behind the region based segmentation techniques is that significant image regions are homogeneous about their colour or perhaps texture. The Mumford-Shah functional was the foundation of the most region-based segmentation frameworks. Prominent methods are the works of Zhu along with Y000uille, Paragios, along with Deriche and Chan, along with Vese.

Traditional ways to segmentation consider the correspondence of the image edges with the object boundaries. Several image filters suggested for side detection. The detection of the prominent image gradients must be followed by a new grouping process to secure a coherent edge map which is compatible with picture contours. The current curve methods originated through the snakes of Kass, Witkin and Terzopoulos suggest an elegant solution to the challenge of edge group. The main underlying principle was the construction of a cost function that will impose the alignment of the segmenting contour with the local maxima of the image gradients while maintaining its smoothness. The contour evolution determined by PDEs produced from the first variation of the function. The classical snake's approach was elaborated through the introduction of the actual balloon term using Cohen and Cohen that controls the direction of the contour propagation. The geodesic snakes using Caselles, Kimmel along with Shapiro and using Kichenassamy, Kumar, Olver, Tannenbaum and Yezzi suggested an essential modification of the actual edge-based segmentation functions in connection with the anisotropic diffusion period of Perona along with Malik. The foundation of the thesis is a new unified functional that is composed of edge-based terms as well as a fidelity term good piecewise-smoothness assumption.

## Histogram Based Methods

Histogram-based methods are very efficient when compared to other image segmentation methods because they typically require only one pass through the pixels. In this technique, a histogram computed from all of the pixels in the image, and the peaks and valleys in the histogram are used to locate the clusters in the image. Colour or intensity can use as the measure. A refinement of this technique is to recursively apply the histogram-seeking method to clusters in the image to divide them into smaller groups. It is repeated with smaller and smaller clusters until no more clusters formed (Bathaee, Y., 2018). One disadvantage of the histogram-seeking method is that it may be challenging to identify significant peaks and valleys in the image. In this technique of image classification, distance metric and integrated region matching are familiar. Histogram-based approaches can also be quickly adapted to occur over multiple frames while maintaining their single pass efficiency. The histogram can be done in various fashions when various structures considered. The same approach that taken with one frame can apply to multiple, and after the results merged, peaks and valleys that were previously difficult to identify are more likely to be distinguishable (Kashyap, R.,2019d).

## Edge Detection Based

Edge detection is a well-developed field on its own within image processing. Region boundaries and edges are closely related since there is often a sharp adjustment in the intensity of the region boundaries. Edge detection techniques have therefore used as the base of another segmentation technique. The edges identified by edge detection are often disconnected to segment an object from an image; one needs closed region boundaries; the desired edges are the boundaries between such objects (Kashyap, R.,2019e). The local pixel intensity gradient defines the Edge-based segmentation technique boundary of an image or aside. An estimation of the first-order derivative of the image function is called a slope. The magnitude of the gradient for a given image $f(x,y)$ can calculate. Edge-based techniques are fast in computation, and usually, in this approach, a priori information about image content is not required. The more general problem of this approach is that often, the edges do not enclose the object completely. In this segmentation technique, the direction and magnitude can present as images. A post-processing step of linking or grouping edges is required to structure closed boundaries neighbouring regions.

## Partial Differential Equation-Based Methods

Using a partial differential equation (PDE) based method and solving the PDE equation by a numerical scheme, one can segment the image. Curve propagation is a widespread technique in this category, with numerous applications to object extraction, object tracking, stereo reconstruction, etc. The central idea is to evolve an initial curve towards the lowest potential of a cost function, where its definition reflects the task addressed. As for most inverse problems, the minimisation of the cost function is non-trivial and imposes certain smoothness constraints on the solution, which in the present case can be express as geometrical constraints on the evolving curve.

## Parametric Methods

Lagrangian techniques based on parameterising the contour according to some sampling strategy and then evolve each element according to the image and internal terms. Such techniques are fast and efficient. However, the original purely parametric formulation, is generally criticised for its limitations regarding the choice of sampling strategy, the intrinsic geometric properties of the curve, topology changes, addressing problems in higher dimensions, etc. Nowadays, efficient discretised formulations have been developed to address these limitations while maintaining high efficiency. In both cases, energy minimisation is generally conducted using a steepest-gradient descent, whereby derivatives computed.

## Level Set Methods

Segmenting images with the level set method (LSM) was introduced at the end of the 1980s and was based on previous work on moving curvatures. Since then several variants and improvements have come up. Some of the upgrades aimed at speeding up the processing. Other methods have strength related to specific challenges like noise and broken edges. In the level set method, the curve is represented implicitly as a level set of a two dimensional (2D) scalar function referred to as the level set function which usually defined on the same domain as the image (Gallege, L. S., &Raje, R. R., 2017). The level set defined as the set of points that have an equal function value. It is worth noting that the level set function is different from the level sets of images, which sometimes used for image enhancement. The sole purpose of the level set function is to provide an implicit representation of the evolving curve. Instead of tracing a curve through time, the LSM evolves a curve by updating the level set function at fixed coordinates through time (Kashyap, R.,2019f). This perspective is similar to that of a Eulerian formulation of motion as opposed to the Lagrangian formulation, which is analogous to the parametric deformable model. A useful property of this approach is that the level set function remains a valid function while the embedded curve can change its topology.

## MANUAL SEGMENTATION

The pixels on the same intensity array could manually talk about, but this is a very time-consuming method in the event the image is significant. A better choice is always to mark the contours of the objects. It might be done discretely through the keyboard, giving higher accuracy, but low speed or it may do with the particular mouse with more top speed but less accuracy. The manual techniques all have in common the amount of time spent in tracing the items, and human resources are very pricey. Determining algorithms can also utilise geometrical figures like ellipses to close the boundaries of the objects. It has done a lot of medical reasons, but the approximations may not be excellent.

## INTERACTIVE SEGMENTATION

Olabarriaga and Smeulders have investigated interactive segmentation of medical images about segmentation tasks, both semi-automatic and interactive refers to algorithms that require some form of user input. From the viewpoint, interactive

*Table 1. Difference between semi-automatic and interactive segmentation method*

| Criteria | Semi-automatic | Interactive |
|---|---|---|
| Segmentation process Role of user Manipulation / Input Performance requirements | Fire and forget Initialisation and parameterisation Direct or indirect Moderate | Iterative Steering and correcting Indirect Fast (real-time response) |

segmentation varies from semi-automatic segmentation from the role of the person and thus from the algorithmic requirements, especially concerning the computation times plus the interface used regarding human-computer-interaction.

In distinction to semi-automatic segmentation, an interactive segmentation puts the person into an essential role throughout the segmentation task. When it's in semi-automatic segmentation, the person input is typically useful for initialisation of some automatic algorithm. Interactive segmentation, the segmentation is usually an iterative process where short answers are generated from every user input to present the principal user feedback on the effect produced by the algorithm based on the current parameters derived from the input data. It allows the person to evaluate the impact and to react onto it directly. As a result, an interactive segmentation algorithm must be fast enough to enable such real-time suggestions (Buriro, A., Crispo, B., & Conti, M., 2019). A well-known example, just for this class of segmentation algorithms in 2D will be the live-wire algorithm. Besides the already discussed requirements, the process connected with interactive segmentation additionally poses requirements for the visualisation of advanced beginner results and for the human-computer-interaction, that happen to be both essential to have an intuitive and efficient use of an interactive segmentation method.

## AUTOMATIC SEGMENTATION

Fully automatic segmentation will be challenging to implement due to the high complexity and variation of pictures. Most algorithms have to have some a priori information to execute the segmentation, and for a means to be automatic, this a priori information must be available to the particular computer. They needed a priori information could, for instance, be noise level and the probability of the objects having an exclusive distribution.

# SEMIAUTOMATIC SEGMENTATION

Semiautomatic segmentation combines the use of both manual and automatic segmentation by giving some initial information regarding the structures; to proceed with programmed methods. Interactive image segmentations try to find the "golden path" between fully automatic image segmentation and fully manual user drawing. They all try to balance between the user's ability to specify initial hints and the computer's ability to complete them automatically.

Active contours methods allow the user to draw an initial contour that must be either fully encapsulated by an object or to enclose the thing entirely. Some of the particular implementations reduce interaction with the user, click inside the object that translated into a drawing of the small circle. The "in or maybe out" decision was made in the specific implementation since all implementations have a very "balloon terms propagation speed" that is pre-configured to be either positive or maybe negative. Drawing the initial contour can be deemed giving "loose hints" on the algorithm. If an individual wants to offer specific contour points, he's got no way to do so.

In the graph cut method, an individual also uses "loose hints", this time by drawing thick brush marks inside and away from the object. "Lazy Snapping" additionally suggest user editing and also placement of command points, but just for "fine-tuning" the borders instead of as principal segmentation guidance. Furthermore, the initial drawing is just not very user-intuitive: this method doesn't fit for a user who wants something similar to the known "manual interaction", that is, to "roughly sketch" the thing and let the machine do the rest.

In the domain of computer vision, segmentation could be the process of partitioning an image into different meaningful parts. Medical imaging can be an essential source connected with anatomical and functional information and is particularly indispensable for diagnosis and treatment method of disease. However, massive amounts connected with high-resolution three-dimensional spatial along with temporal data, are not adequately processed along with utilised with conventional visualisation techniques. It is generally insufficient or perhaps inefficient for physicians to only aesthetically inspect the professional medical image data compiled from MRI, CT, and PET along with modalities. The role connected with medical imaging is expanding along with the medical image analysis community has become preoccupied with the challenging problem of producing quantification algorithms that take advantage of the information inside the flood of image data.

Among the principal tasks of professional medical image analysis usually are image segmentation, registration, and matching. Medical image investigation directly impacts applications, for example, image data fusion, quantitative and occasion series analysis, biomechanical modelling, generating anatomical atlases, visualisation, virtual and increased reality, instrument along with patient localisation along with tracking, etc.. Medical images, for illustration, are analysed to see the detailed design and organisation connected with anatomic structures that allows enabling a medical expert to analyse medical images for evaluating relationships between structural abnormalities along with deformations and several functional abnormalities along with diseases. In radiotherapy, medical image analysis is vital for allowing the delivery of the necrotic dose of radiation with a tumour with minimal collateral problems for healthy tissue.

With the medical image segmentation, these essential parts often correspond to different organs, tissue groups, pathologies, or perhaps other biologically applicable structures. These regions of interests (ROIs) segmented by using some similar characteristics in medical images, such as purity, colour, texture, sizing, shape, location, along with local statistical features, etc. Medical image segmentation has an array of applications in professional medical research, such as computer-aided surgery, medical diagnosis, pathological investigation, surgical planning. Accurate segmentation connected with medical images is a critical step in the medical image investigation. The theme of this thesis is to develop some new strategies on medical picture segmentation. This chapter begins using the motivation of this thesis, then the downsides in medical picture segmentation are introduced, and several existing solution strategies on such complications are reviewed. Eventually, the importance of the project was presented with, followed by is designed and objects of this thesis and achievement on professional medical image segmentation. Finally, this chapter concludes with the outline of the argument.

## MOTIVATION

In medical imaging research, segmentation is generally the first step which allows later quantitative dimensions, diagnosis and cures planning and modelling regarding anatomical structures. Medical imaging technologies, like CT, MRI in addition to PET, have been widely given to various therapeutic techniques. Compared to conventional medical diagnosis, they feature a non-invasive yet powerful way to investigate the internal structures and actions of human figures. With the help of such technology, doctors can acquire multi-dimensional information like 2-D slices, 3-D volumetric images on a region of interest, which facilitates the overall performance of both qualitative in addition to quantitative analysis. This analysis supplies invaluable information for diagnosis as well as surgical planning; therefore, may relieve the pains to the patients to some extent.

Medical image segmentation is usually the first step of most analysis procedures already stated. It is also a crucial step that determines a final result of the full application since other analysis entirely relies upon the data out of this step. For case in point, to build some 3-D volumetric model from several medical images, segmentation in 2-D images needs to be as accurate as is possible; otherwise, the amount of the reconstructed model will probably be wrong, and visualisation of this model will possibly be meaningless. A subsequent medical control and analysis step occasionally include quantification, registration, creation and computer-aided diagnosis. ROI sometimes include brain, bone houses, vessels, soft tissues, etc.

Medical image segmentation plays an essential role for example, in the application of cardiac diagnosis, offered the segmentation regarding cardiac tissues throughout consecutive slices, volumetric models of the heart and bloodstream can be reconstructed by only modelling the blood flow inside, doctors can pinpoint one's heart problem and measure the risk quantitatively. Visualisation regarding heart can additionally aid doctors for making assessments (Guleria, P., &Sood, M., 2014). The segmentation with the various organs or tissues is vital to medical decision makings, such since disease classification in addition to disease risk examination. The segmentation results provide the foundation in addition to the prerequisite for focus on separation, feature removal, and quantitative rating. Also, contemporary medical imaging techniques like CT, MRI and PET often have a large number of images which produce medical imaging research a tedious and struggle. Therefore, it is necessary to develop unsupervised image analysis methods throughout medical images. Apart from this interactive approach with fast processing is also required for processing medical images. The proposed work can be motivated by the requirement to offer unsupervised, correct and robust image segmentation methods throughout the routine clinical situation.

## CHALLENGES IN MEDICAL IMAGE SEGMENTATION

Recently, various medical image segmentation approaches have proposed, and many significant improvements have obtained. However, as a result of shortcomings in healthcare imaging systems, medical images can contain different varieties of artefacts. These artefacts can affect the product data and befuddle the pathology. Some objects can mitigate by magnetic imaging technology, and some require post control. In clinical research, the common phenomenons created are noise, intensity inhomogeneity, and partial volume effects that happen to considered as the open problems in medical image segmentation. There are numerous techniques to segment a photo into regions which might be homogeneous. Not each of the methods is suitable for medical image analysis because of complexity and inaccuracy. There's no standard image segmentation technique that may produce satisfactory results for all imaging applications similar to brain MRI, brain cancer diagnosis, and so forth. Optimal selection of features, tissues, brain and non–brain elements thought as main limitations for brain image segmentation. Accurate segmentation over the full field of view is another interruption. Operator direction and manual thresholding are generally other barriers to segment brain image. During the segmentation treatment verification of benefits is another cause of difficulty.

Image segmentation will be the problem of removing foreground objects from the background in an image. It is among the most fundamental issues in computer vision and possesses many new types of research throughout the years. As the easy use in computers increase as time passes, reliable image segmentation needed in more and more application, in the industrial, medical and also personal fields. Fully automatic segmentation continues to be an open problem due to a wide variety of possible objects' mix, and so apparently the use of human "hints" is inevitable. Interactive image segmentation provides, therefore, become more and more popular among research nowadays. The goal of interactive segmentation would be to extract object(s) from a background in an accurate way, using user knowledge in a way that requires minimal conversation and minimal reply time. This thesis will indeed start by describing general strategies to categorise segmentation approaches, continues with a thorough survey of existing contour-based interactive image segmentation techniques, and ends by introducing a whole new combined editing and also segmentation tool.

Image segmentation is a crucial problem with image analysis, along with image understanding. It is also an essential problem in computer vision and pattern recognition. The active contour models (ACM) are the most successful techniques in image segmentation, and the fundamental idea of ACM is to evolve a curve as outlined by some certain constraints to extract the required object. These prevailing active contour models categorised as an edge-based and region-based both types have their unique paybacks and negatives, and the choice between them to use in applications determined by the different characteristics with the images. The model builds an edge-based function using image edge facts, which can generate the contour on the object boundaries. The edge-based role in line with the image gradient can take a look at the right limitations, for the images with intense noise or maybe a weak edge (Kashyap, R., 2020).

Conversely, a region-based model uses statistical information to develop a region, stopping function which could prevent the contour evolution between distinct areas. Compared to the edge-based model, this model can do better for images with blurred ends. The region-based model is not sensitive to the initialisation of the level set function and can recognise the object's restrictions. Region-based models are preferred for image segmentation because they provide an improvement over the edge-based model in a few aspects; it has limitations. The regular region-based models which proposed in binary images with the assumption that every single image region can be homogeneous, do not operate correctly for images with intensity inhomogeneity and it is sensitive to the preliminary contour, and the evolving curve may trap into regional minima. Also, the Chan–Vese (CV) method isn't suitable for quick processing because, in each iteration, the standard intensities inside and beyond contour should end up computed, which improves the computation time. The classic region-based models which proposed in the binary images, do not work effectively if the goal image contains intensity inhomogeneous regions in it. The local binary fitted (LBF) model by embedding nearby image information and can segment images with intensity inhomogeneity, which is much more accurate as opposed to planned procedures. The fundamental idea is to introduce the Gaussian kernel function, although it portions well the images with intensity inhomogeneity. It got high computational time complexity. Therefore, the segmentation process takes a significant time compared to old segmentation procedures. Zhang proposed an active contour method motivated by local image fitting (LIF) energy, which provides the same segmentation results and contains less time complexity compared to LBF model. Reinitializing the particular level set function to some signed distance function (SDF) throughout the evolution used for maintaining stable growth and being sure desirable results. From a practical viewpoint, the re-initialisation process is often somewhat convoluted and costly. The region-based LSM uses a function to eliminate the need associated with re-initialisation and regularisation work well under the high-intensity inhomogeneity problem. It has better results in comparison with other methods. It utilises both edge and the spot information to segment an image into no overlapping spot and based on controlling the evolving curve in through membership degree in the current pixel being inside or outside the active contour. It executes through signed pressure function that uses the local information in the image. The proposed method will segment imaging with intensity inhomogeneity and put on MR images to show the reliability, effectiveness, and robustness in the algorithm.

## Noise

Noise is often a common phenomenon inside medical images. In all of the imaging procedures utilising x-ray or gamma photons, the vast majority of image noise manufactured by the random characteristics on the photons distributed within the image. It is generally designated quantum sound. Severe noise can easily significantly affect the sharpness of the images. It can cover and slow up the visibility of specific features within the image, thereby impact the segmentation effects. Some popular methods of general solutions to noise removal procedures in computer vision listed inside Table 2. These kinds of techniques can efficiently reduce noise, but a number of them still have space for improvement. For example, the anisotropic nonlinear diffusion filtering is usually dominant in minimising the noise in homogeneous places and reducing the diffusivity in the edges of an image. However, the iteration amount of the anisotropic diffusion model is unknown.

149

*Table 2. Noise removal filters*

| Methods | Description |
|---|---|
| Mean filter | The filter reduce noise by updating on-line of a pixel depending on a notion with the average of grey level values inside a spatial neighbourhood |
| Median filter | The filter reduce noise by updating on-line of a pixel-based with a notion of centre of grey level values inside a spatial neighbourhood |
| Gaussian smoothing filter | The noise photograph is convolved with a Gaussian kernel, then updating on-line of a pixel depending on a weighted spatial local community |
| Anisotropic diffusion filter | It reduces noise in flat regions and the diffusivity at the edge of an image through the use of an anisotropic diffusion modelling |
| Total variation model | A total variation model features two terms which denote the actual constant in small areas as well as a set of hooked upsets for local community smoothing. |
| Local adaptive filter | The noise is estimated inside a moving window, only by computing and adjusting the spectrum just a local window |
| Transform domain | It attempts to extract the image from the noise inside a frequency domain only using a threshold |
| Wavelet thresholding | The value regarding pixels is updated using the weighted average with the samples where the actual neighbourhood is similar to the area with the current pixel |

If the iteration number is usually significant, the edge is going to be significant blurred. If the iteration number is generally small, the noise is going to retain. Therefore, the anisotropic diffusion model could be improved by routinely estimating the time number. Medical images tend to suffer much far more noise than realistic images to do the character of the acquisition devices. It poses significant troubles to any picture segmentation technique. So that noise can reduce, and many devices raise the part volume that is usually, the average acquisition with a thick slice. It brings about blurring the edges between the objects, which make decisions very, very hard for automatic equipment. Fig.1 shows an example of MRI with noise, and without having noise, removal of noise is very important for medical image segmentation.

## Intensity Inhomogeneity

Intensity inhomogeneity is recognised as a smooth spatially varying perform which alters the strength inside originally homogeneous regions. The bias field causes the common trend of density inhomogeneity within the MRI. The Bias field signal is often a low frequency and also smooth signal that will corrupt MR images, especially those created by old MRI devices. Image processing algorithms like segmentation, texture analysis or even classification that utilise grey level prices of image pixels is not going to produce satisfactory effects. A pre-processing step

*Figure 1. Left Image: MR image with noise, Right Image: normal MRI image*

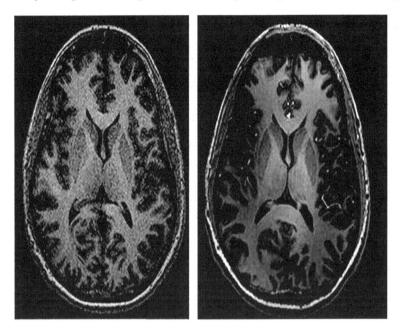

can be correct for the bias field sign before submitting harmful MRI images for such algorithms. Fig.2 shows an example of an MR image with and without the bias field. Compared with the normal MR image, the middle section of the density inhomogeneity picture is darker compared to the surrounding areas that are often misclassified as an additional part of the tissue. Therefore, the additive bias field need to removed as a way to improve the segmentation exactness. Some existing denseness inhomogeneity correction methods listed within Table 3.

*Figure 2. Images with intensity inhomogeneity*

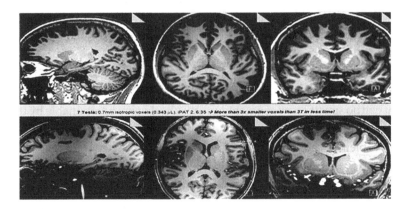

*Table 3. Intensity inhomogeneity correction methods*

| Methods | Description |
| --- | --- |
| Phantom based | Inhomogeneity filter estimated with a uniform phantom, then scaling and smoothing of the acquired phantom images |
| Multi-coil | The less inhomogeneous image is achieved using combining both area coil and human body coil |
| Special sequence | It achieved by using a specific pulse sequence to discover the inhomogeneity field |
| Filtering | It utilises low-pass filter to part ways the low consistency artefact (assuming while density inhomogeneity) from the original image |
| Surface fitting | A parametric area is fitted to a few image features that contain density inhomogeneity |
| Segmentation based | The density inhomogeneity estimated by using a modified fuzzy c-means algorithm |
| Histogram based | It operates upon image intensity histograms |

## AIMS AND OBJECTIVES

### Correct Segmentation

Image segmentation suffers from incorrect results, many methods have developed for accurate results, but some methods take so much time for computation, and some method gives over segmented results. The globally optimal geodesic active contour (GOGAC) is one of the best methods based on energy, but it stuck in local minima and gave incorrect results. Here microarray images have attracted much attention because of the inability of creating correctly segmented spots. Fig 3 presents the actual segmentation result image obtained when using the GOGAC. If segmented result will be incorrect, and it will give for further analysis of the image, then surely it will give wrong results because it will affect the whole process like information extraction, analysis, quantification and evaluation, the aim is to get better and accurate result so that correct analysis must generate through segmentation.

### Interactive Segmentation

Interactive image segmentation involves small user interaction to include user intention for the segmentation process and is also an active research area nowadays because it can do satisfactory segmentation results that are unattainable by the actual state-of-the-art automatic image segmentation algorithms. This thesis considers the identical problem of how can interactively segment some foreground objects out from its surrounding qualifications. The goal should be to develop an intelligent image segmentation method with tools that let users to interactively segmentation

*Figure 3. Segmentation results of GOGAC method*

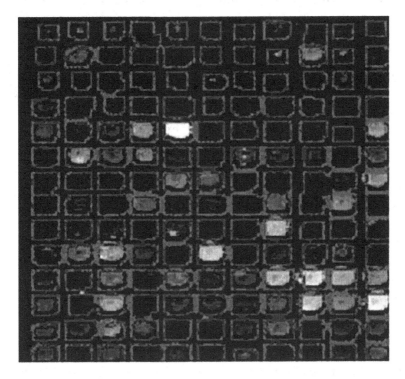

with small amount of intuitive interactions. Here the problem with traditional methods is each time, the technique gives different result because of the initialisation of contour location is different, and it gives the wrong analysis result. The other objective is to develop an effective segmentation method which is independent of the selection; it will reduce the complexity of the processes. An excellent interactive image segmentation method demands are: (1) given clear user input, the algorithm really should produce automatic segmentation that reflects anyone intent; (2) the algorithm should be efficient so that it can provide instantaneous visual feedback.

## Fast Segmentation

Image segmentation will be the front stage of numerous works in impression processing, such as object orient compression based on these kinds of requirements, a good impression segmentation algorithm must have the following about three advantages: (1) quickly speedy, (2) functional condition connectivity, and (3) proper condition matching. The spot growing method provides good segmentation results, but the swiftness is slow. The k-means and the watershed methods are fast, but needs improvements by comparison; the proposed method can achieve the goals associated with high efficiency as well as better performance as well. The result is related to k-means fragmented as well as compress the segmenting result will waste an excessive amount of resource for us all to record these boundaries. The proposed method takes advantage within the k-means and these watershed methods inside the system reliability period (Tiwari S., Gupta R.K., & Kashyap R., 2019). However, it ought to say the dependability is worse compared to the region growing method. The image segmenting algorithm as the front-stage processing associated with image compression and that is the fast swiftness, the excellent appearance connectivity of segmenting result, and the superb condition matching.

## MEDICAL IMAGING MODALITIES

Medical imaging has made a significant side of the bargain of medicine, including the creation of several different imaging modalities from the aspect of diagnostic radiology. The most crucial and commonly used noninvasive imaging techniques include X-ray, CT, MRI, and also PET. Due to different imaging theory, graphic medical modalities are delicate to different tissue properties. For instance, in X-ray and even CT, a region of reduced transmission corresponding to some part of the fascination, the dense tissues could be shown clearly (Kashyap, R., & Piersson, A. D., 2018).

Nonetheless, the image quality is going to be miserable when looking at soft tissues. As opposed, the MR photographs provide an excellent distinction between various kinds of soft tissues. Nonetheless, it can merely demonstrate the physiological structures but does not illustrate the physical processes. PET image can provide metabolic information utilising tracing this blood vessel flow activity; the resulting nuclear medication image tells physicians in regards to the biological activity in the organ or the actual vascular system of which nourishes it, for instance, tumour, metastasis, as well as an infection (Shukla R., Gupta R.K., & Kashyap R., 2019). It is widely believed these different medical graphic modalities provide distinct yet complementary information which is conducive to reduce the density overlap and improve the segmentation accuracy.

### X-Ray

X-ray is a standard medical imaging modalit the task of producing the actual X-ray image. The individual placed between the X-ray tube and also silver halide film. Next, the X-ray passed by the body hit the actual silver halide film and also turns it darker. The more X-ray perm0eates, the more shaded areas inscribed on the actual film. X-ray is widespread for disease verification. However, the disadvantage will be the high level of radiation emitted that may cause diseases, for instance, cancer.

## Computed Tomography

Computed tomography is a medical imaging procedure that functions using computer-processed X-rays to create tomographic images. Fig.4 shows the strategy of generating CT perception. The scanner device includes a moving table and a revolving X-ray pipe. Then the CT scanner collects emits X-ray in the 360∘ arcs regarding the patient. Finally, the CT image might reconstruct from quite a few X-rays. In medical imaging, CT images are generally widespread for diagnostic together with therapeutic purposes in several medical disciplines. Even so, similar to X-ray, the high dosage of radiation may harm the natural areas.

## Magnetic Resonance Imaging

MRI may be a popular method all through medical imaging, which can produce top quality images with the interior of the body. Fig 5 shows the device of the MRI scanning device.

Inside of first step, the affected individual placed inside of a static magnetic field. Next, the magnetised proton (spinning H nuclei) within the patient aligns with this particular field like sharp compass needles. In the second step, the scanning functioning controlled from the central computer, which specifies the style of the gradient, third radio frequency (RF) waveforms, and timings for being used. Subsequently, this record from the central computer passes for the waveform

*Figure 4. Computed tomography scanner systems*

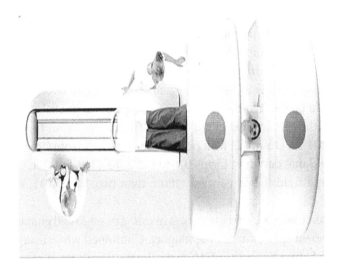

*Figure 5. MRI scanning systems*

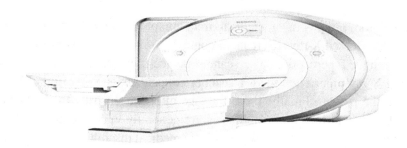

generator, which outputs this specific signal and passes the crooks to be amplified and delivered to the coils. Additionally, the RF pulsed emitted from the RF coil bombard this specific magnetised nucleus, causing the crooks to flip around. The nuclei absorb this RF energy and as well enter a fired upstate. When the magnet is turned off, excited nuclei resume normal state and present off of the RF power which reflect the number of protons inside of a slice of muscle tissue. Different tissue absorbs, and supplies turn off different various RF energy. The RF strength given off is acquired with the receiver coil and resulted in images (Waoo, N., Kashyap, R., & Jaiswal, A.,2010) which turns into an electronic digital signal by way of great analogue to the electronic converter. Finally, the digital signal delivered to an image processor in addition to the image is displayed using a monitor. Some diverse MRI modalities typically are shown in Fig. 6.

While using the generation of this magnetic field, the MR scanner could be classified as eternal, normal conducting in addition to superconductivity. The strongest long term magnets might develop a field close to at least one Tesla that much less compared to normal conducting in addition to superconductivity. The superconductivity is possible to obtain close to 24. 5 Tesla at a niobium-tin superconductor. Comparing while using the permanent and usual conducting, take advantage of superconducting electromagnets current is entirely applied once for the wires, this can form inside a closed-loop and let the current over oneness magnetic field to remain a problem indefinitely. According to the intensity of around unity magnetic field, the MR scanner could be classified as numerous types. 1) Low field that is less than 0. 5T (tesla), 2) Mid field that is certainly from 0. 5T to at least one. 0T, 3) High field that certainly forms 0 T to aid 2.0 T (1.0 T, 1.5 T, 2.0 T generally used), Ultra-high field that is certainly more than two. 0T (3. 0T, several. 7T, 7T usually used).

The individualised patient framework gives all of us on-board guidance to optimise any time the patient spends inside the magnet. Combined while using the increased signal that can help noise ratio of 4G*, the image excellent is clear and sharp to

*Figure 6. (A) T2W (B) T1W (C) and post-contrast T1W axial images (D) T2W (E) flair and (F) post-contrast T1W coronal images*

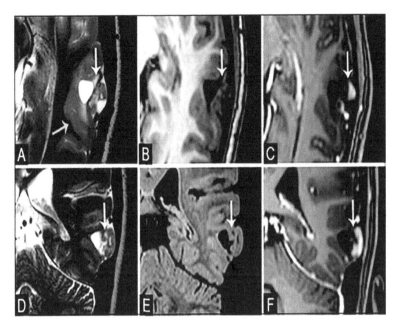

the edges of the specific 50 x 50 returning button 45 cm division of view. Ultra high-density coils are as well as the highest channel adjustments ever offered. Ultra-lightweight coils incorporate seamlessly to complement ample anatomic insurance coverage, for example merging head, brain, and body and spine coil elements to make a neurovascular array. This 3T technology is an exciting new conclusion for patients via the hospital matches. Up to 20% increase because of the unique RF style with around 128 RF programmers. CT-like comfort, along with dependable 1.5 Tesla high-field durability. So its head out and feet first for most of the exams. The Siemens Magnetom Espree could be the world's first start out bore, 1.5 Tesla MRI technique and Turville Most of these MRI & Rays Oncology Center were one of several primary diagnostic image resolution centres inside the nation to provide patients with the luxury of this new technological innovation.

The Espree has an ultra-short 1. 25 m (4') length as well as a 70 cm (over 2'3") with this report diameter, providing a more and more spacious opening to accommodate claustrophobic, large, extremely young, and older patients. Nearly 60% of exams inside Espree can execute with the patient's head outside the scanner.

Using a whole new Siemens technological innovative named total image resolution matrix (TIM), scans can be executed faster with a lot more precise results with no patient repositioning, leading to shorter exam predicaments. The signal-to-noise

*Figure 7. MRI scanner with 1.5 Tesla ultra high field*

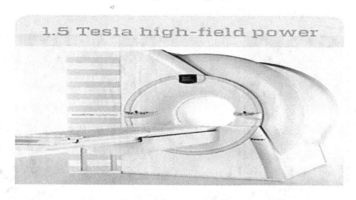

*Figure 8. MRI scanner with 3 Tesla ultra high field*

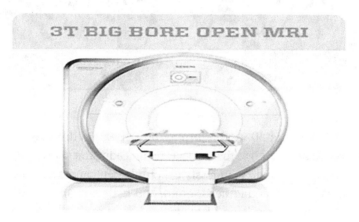

percentage of MR image is proportional to the potency of the leading over unity magnetic field. Some types related to the MR scanner usually shown in Figure 7 and 8.

The RF coil is critical equipment in MRI method. It can broadcast the RF indication towards the patient as well as receive the return signal from the patient. Fig 9 and 10 show two kinds of RF coils (surface coil and volume coil) that are most frequently present in the MRI. The surface coil usually provides an excellent signal to noise ratio but produces severe thickness inhomogeneity. The quantity coil exhibits a lesser amount of inhomogeneity but provides a weak signal to noise ratio. Hence, the two models of reels are top-rated together with specialised medical.

While comparing with all the X-rays and CT, MRI provides four advantages. In the first place, it reveals fine information on anatomy, because MRI gives a wealth of facts of human tender tissue anatomy. Secondly, it is relatively safe since it is noninvasive, and doesn't involve ionising radiation, for example, X-rays. Thirdly,

*Figure 9. RF surface coils of MRI scanner system*

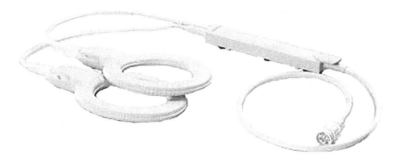

*Figure 10. RF volume coils of MRI scanner system*

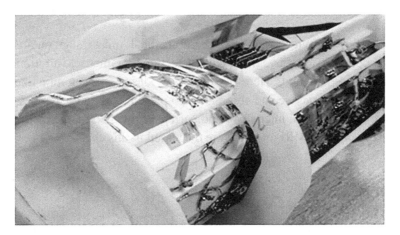

they've got better characterise and discrimination about the physical and biochemical houses such as regular water, iron, fat, bloodstream, etc. Fourthly, it depends and flexible to generate many kinds regarding high contrast photographs for different utilises by altering RF, gradient pulses, as well as carefully choosing serenity timings. The rich anatomy information supplied by MRI has got an indispensable tool in health care prognosis, radiation and medical operation planning.

## Positron Emission Tomography

PET is often an imaging modality about diagnosing and discovering the stages of various kinds of cancer, including lung, intellect and neck, heart and brain this is the nuclear medicine image resolution technology that creates a three-dimensional graphic or picture regarding functional process techniques. Fig.15 shows the PET system. In the first place, the patient could inject with isotope tracer. The abnormal tissues absorb the tracer for the higher rate in comparison with healthy tissues, producing tracer concentration higher in diseased tissue. Next, the positron emission occurs in the event the proton-rich isotope (Unstable Father or mother Nucleus) decays. A Proton decays with a Neutron, a Positron or a Neutrino. After travelling a shorter distance (3-5mm), the positron offered encounters an electron from the surrounding environment. Next both the particles merge as well as "annihilate" 1 a different, emitting γ rays in opposite directions each which can be picked up as a result of γ camera. In the end, the computer reconstructs the radioactivity into 3d images of body or area along with beyond normal tracer uptake.

## CONCLUSION

In this chapter, a review and critique of medical image segmentation using clustering, compression, histogram, edge detection, parametric, variational model and level set-based methods. Here also discuss modes of segmentation like manual, semi-automatic, interactive and automatic. To present current challenges, aim and motivation for doing fast, interactive and correct segmentation, the medical image modalities X-ray, CT, MRI and PET are discussed in this chapter.

## REFERENCES

Anderson, C. W. (1987, January). Strategy learning with multilayer connectionist representations. In *Proceedings of the Fourth International Workshop on Machine Learning* (pp. 103-114). Morgan Kaufmann. 10.1016/B978-0-934613-41-5.50014-3

Avati, A., Jung, K., Harman, S., Downing, L., Ng, A., & Shah, N. H. (2018). Improving palliative care with deep learning. *BMC Medical Informatics and Decision Making*, *18*(4), 122. doi:10.118612911-018-0677-8 PMID:30537977

Bathaee, Y. (2018). The artificial intelligence black box and the failure of intent and causation. *Harvard Journal of Law & Technology*, *31*(2), 889.

Buriro, A., Crispo, B., & Conti, M. (2019). AnswerAuth: A bimodal behavioral biometric-based user authentication scheme for smartphones. *Journal of Information Security and Applications, 44*, 89-103.

Gallege, L. S., & Raje, R. R. (2017, April). Parallel methods for evidence and trust based selection and recommendation of software apps from online marketplaces. In *Proceedings of the 12th Annual Conference on Cyber and Information Security Research* (p. 4). ACM. 10.1145/3064814.3064819

Guleria, P., & Sood, M. (2014). Data Mining in Education: A review on the knowledge discovery perspective. *International Journal of Data Mining & Knowledge Management Process, 4*(5), 47–60. doi:10.5121/ijdkp.2014.4504

Kashyap, R. (2019a). Security, Reliability, and Performance Assessment for Healthcare Biometrics. In D. Kisku, P. Gupta, & J. Sing (Eds.), Design and Implementation of Healthcare Biometric Systems (pp. 29-54). Hershey, PA: IGI Global. doi:10.4018/978-1-5225-7525-2.ch002

Kashyap, R. (2019b). Sensation of Deep Learning in Image Processing Applications. In A. Hassanien, A. Darwish, & C. Chowdhary (Eds.), *Handbook of Research on Deep Learning Innovations and Trends* (pp. 72–96). Hershey, PA: IGI Global. doi:10.4018/978-1-5225-7862-8.ch005

Kashyap, R. (2019c). Big *Data Analytics Challenges and Solutions*. doi:10.1016/B978-0-12-818146-1.00002-7

Kashyap, R. (2019d). Geospatial Big Data, Analytics and IoT: Challenges, Applications and Potential. In H. Das, R. Barik, H. Dubey, & D. Roy (Eds.), *Cloud Computing for Geospatial Big Data Analytics. Studies in Big Data* (Vol. 49). Cham: Springer. doi:10.1007/978-3-030-03359-0_9

Kashyap, R. (2019e). Big Data and Global Software Engineering. In M. Rehman, A. Amin, A. Gilal, & M. Hashmani (Eds.), *Human Factors in Global Software Engineering* (pp. 131–163). Hershey, PA: IGI Global. doi:10.4018/978-1-5225-9448-2.ch006

Kashyap, R. (2019f). Deep Learning: An Application in Internet of Things. In H. Purnomo (Ed.), *Computational Intelligence in the Internet of Things* (pp. 130–158). Hershey, PA: IGI Global. doi:10.4018/978-1-5225-7955-7.ch006

Kashyap, R. (2020). Applications of Wireless Sensor Networks in Healthcare. In P. Mukherjee, P. Pattnaik, & S. Panda (Eds.), *IoT and WSN Applications for Modern Agricultural Advancements: Emerging Research and Opportunities* (pp. 8–40). Hershey, PA: IGI Global. doi:10.4018/978-1-5225-9004-0.ch002

Kashyap, R., & Piersson, A. D. (2018). Impact of Big Data on Security. In G. Shrivastava, P. Kumar, B. Gupta, S. Bala, & N. Dey (Eds.), *Handbook of Research on Network Forensics and Analysis Techniques* (pp. 283–299). Hershey, PA: IGI Global. doi:10.4018/978-1-5225-4100-4.ch015

Shukla, R., Gupta, R. K., & Kashyap, R. (2019). A multiphase pre-copy strategy for the virtual machine migration in cloud. In S. Satapathy, V. Bhateja, & S. Das (Eds.), *Smart Intelligent Computing and Applications. Smart Innovation, Systems and Technologies* (Vol. 104). Singapore: Springer. doi:10.1007/978-981-13-1921-1_43

Tiwari, S., Gupta, R. K., & Kashyap, R. (2019). To enhance web response time using agglomerative clustering technique for web navigation recommendation. In H. Behera, J. Nayak, B. Naik, & A. Abraham (Eds.), *Computational Intelligence in Data Mining. Advances in Intelligent Systems and Computing* (Vol. 711). Singapore: Springer. doi:10.1007/978-981-10-8055-5_59

Waoo, N., Kashyap, R., & Jaiswal, A. (2010). DNA nano array analysis using hierarchical quality threshold clustering. In *Proceedings of 2010 2nd IEEE International Conference on Information Management and Engineering* (pp. 81-85). IEEE. 10.1109/ICIME.2010.5477579

Chapter 7

# Image Processing Approaches and Disaster Management

**Surendra Rahamatkar**
*Amity University, Raipur, India*

## ABSTRACT

*This chapter presents the relevance of picture handling to distinguish different sorts of harm. For areal-type harm, 1) edge extraction, 2) unsupervised arrangement, 3) texture examination, and 4) edge improvement are suitable to distinguish harmed zone. For liner-type harm, it is hard to improve the permeability of harm partition by picture preparing. Likewise, the impact of overlaying office information to help staff to discover harm at an extraction is described.*

## INTRODUCTION

Disasters are disruptive events that cause deprivation, injury, hardship, suffering, and even death. Thousands of people are affected every year due to natural disasters. It results in a large amount of physical destruction and loss of lives. Natural disasters are large scale meteorological or geological events that have enough power to destroy nature, infrastructure, human being, and property. Some major types of natural disasters are hurricanes, tornadoes, earthquakes, droughts, floods, landslide, wildfires, etc. Storms and floods are the most common types of disaster. Every year, these types of disasters witnessed in certain parts of the world that have such an adverse effect on human and wildlife. In developing countries like India, disasters much more pronounced. Some of the types of natural disasters are more likely to occur in certain parts of the world. For instance, areas near rivers or lake have the maximum chances of witnessing floods. But one cannot say when and where the

DOI: 10.4018/978-1-7998-0182-5.ch007

natural calamity can occur and cause massive destruction. Some of the disasters can reduce to a certain extent by using disaster management techniques. This chapter deals with the disaster management techniques to be applied after analysing images captured from the satellite.

## Natural Disaster Image Capturing Methods and Tools like Satellite

Natural disasters caused in the different regions can be detected by the satellite of high resolution to capture the image and process it later to find out the destruction caused in the particular area. Ørsted, Denmark's first satellite, was launched on February 23, 1999, into a polar, low Earth orbit to provide the first near-global set of high precision geomagnetic observations since the Magsat mission of 1979–1980 (Neubert et al., 2001). The satellite used for a different number of purposes. Some of the types include navigation, weather, communication, earth observation, and research satellites. The satellite data is beneficial for analysts to detect specific measures required for different purposes (Pichuzhkina & Roldugin, 2016). There are many advantages of using satellite for disaster situation: They can provide a rapid and accurate view of a disaster situation of large geographical dimension. The data can be used to detect the destruction and bring it to a significant concern. They can also provide the data on "the restricted areas" such as disaster occurring in a region where the entry should be prohibited. Satellite provides highly valuable information in disaster condition. Some of the times, this is the only option and necessity for retrieving any information. Scientists, Computer scientists, geologists have put a lot of effort in research to predict the place, time, occurrence, and severity of the disaster. Different data mining models have proposed for the prediction purpose. Along with this, researchers have been focusing on the disaster management and analysis of the needs of victims (Goswami, Chakraborty, Ghosh, Chakrabarti & Chakraborty, 2018). Data collected from the satellites, remote sensors, government bodies, geological departments before, during, and after the disaster.

## Natural Disaster in India

India faces a variety of natural disasters every year. Rivers cover India on the three sides and Himalayas on the top. Due to this, India is more immune to floods. Recently we have seen how Kerala was profoundly affected by floods. Every year, natural calamities hit India with increasing frequency (Goswami, Chakraborty, Ghosh, Chakrabarti & Chakraborty, 2018). Cyclones, floods, and earthquakes are frequent. In June 2013, Kedarnath and Badrinath were affected by devastating floods and landslides. Below table shows disaster list from the previous 15 years:

*Table 1. Natural calamities in different parts of India*

| Disaster Type | Year | Origin |
|---|---|---|
| Earthquake | 2001 | Gujarat |
| | 1999 | Chamoli |
| Floods | 2007 | Bihar |
| | 2005 | Mumbai |
| | 2018 | Kerala |
| Landslides | 2014 | Pune |
| | 1998 | Malpa |
| Tsunami | 2004 | Indian ocean |
| Cyclones | 2010 | Andhra Pradesh |
| | 2018 | Orissa |
| | 2011 | Tamil Nadu |
| | 2012 | Tamil Nadu |

Asia tops the list of disasters. Below image shows the pie chart of crashes occurring in different continents. In India, the National Disaster Management Authority (NDMA) is the body that handles disaster management. Prime minister is the chairman of NDMA.

## TASKS RELATED TO DISASTER MANAGEMENT

The categories of functions that need to be carried out in the disaster management system can state as:

- **Prediction**: These tasks include the prediction of natural disaster in a particular area so that the preventive measures can take; the inhabitants of the place can be alerted for their safety. The prediction tasks include estimating the magnitude of the earthquake, an intensity of cyclone, or any other calamity.
- **Detection**: These tasks include detecting the damage or destruction of the particular region caused due to any natural calamity that occurred in that area. The management authority, observatories detect the location of the disaster and communicate with the proper authority (Goswami, Chakraborty, Ghosh, Chakrabarti & Chakraborty, 2018).

- **Disaster Management Strategies**: These tasks include strategies, adequate planning, and adequate communication to detect and manage the affected areas. The aims and objectives of the management system are to Shift animals and people to a safer area, rescue people on time, repair of the damage and provide proper first aid.

## Remote Sensing in Natural Disaster

Remote sensing is a tool which is used to obtain a piece of information about a specific object or region from a distance without going near it. It is a general definition of remote sensing. It is a growing technology which has a large number of applications. It is a tool to monitor the earth surface condition by using high-resolution imagery captured by the satellite remote sensing. Remote sensing has a variety of applications in certain areas like watching the growth of a region, the study of agriculture, water life, vegetation, forestry, managing the water resources. It is, in fact, necessary for developing countries (Ghaffarian, Kerle & Filatova, 2018).

Remote sensing has the following advantages:

- Data can obtain at a regular time interval, which enables to monitor the changes.
- Full area covered in Inaccessible areas like mountains; forests covered quickly through satellite remote sensing.
- This method is cost and time efficient.

Now one of the significant uses of this technology is in disaster management. As we know, in recent years, due to different calamities, there has been tremendous damage to the urban and rural areas of different parts of the world. Advancement in the remote sensing technology has made it possible to capture the destruction of a particular area without even having to visit the place. Because of its ability to obtain a large area in a given time, satellite remote sensing is a potent and advanced tool to monitor the condition of the earth (Joyce, Belliss, Samsonov, McNeill & Glassey, 2009). High-resolution pre and post event images which are being captured by the satellite remote sensing for the last few years is handy for disaster management as it can detect the damage caused in buildings, vegetation area due to calamities.

# A REMOTE SENSING IMAGE PROCESS METHOD OF SUPERVISED CLASSIFICATION UNDER GRID ENVIRONMENT

On the base of considering and breaking down the Globus Toolkit2.4 stage and remote detecting innovation, this article utilizes the matrix stage Globus Toolkit2.4 and the Bayesian grouping to construct a remote detecting picture process strategy for an administered arrangement under the lattice condition. This technique can give a favoured way to deal with the order of a remote detecting picture. Remote detecting innovation advanced during the 1960s, yet the flying remote detecting innovation utilized in military surveillance in the mid-twentieth century. It has used in topography structural designing and other non-military personnel zones since the start of 1920. The remote detecting innovation got a full scope of uses at present, yet the remote detecting information is colossal and complex, with the advancement of data innovation and sensor innovation, spatial goals. Otherworldly goals and transient goals of remote detecting picture expanded incredibly, so the measure of processing step by step instructions to manage this information rapidly has turned into a significant issue in the remote detecting region. Customarily, the remote detecting picture preparing frameworks are remaining solitary structures, the fundamental model concentrated model, and both of the information and handling arranged in a single machine (Kashyap, R., 2019a). This preparing mode isn't in similarity with the opening, disseminated and arranges necessities. The matrix gives a conveyed domain to remote detecting picture handling. The lattice joined the web as a super PC whose centre may be "the web is a PC". Because of the full utilisation of the system assets, when managing the remote detecting information, parallel preparing can spare additional time. IT not exclusively can accomplish the number juggling parallel, however information parallel. This paper joined with the order of remote detecting information and Grid figuring innovation, presented a remote detecting information preparing technique dependent on Grid condition that can enormously improve the handling speed. But the Grid innovation is still in the phase of research, with the advancement of research, and it will broadly utilize in the remote detecting information process.

## SATELLITE IMAGE PROCESSING ON DISTRIBUTED COMPUTING ENVIRONMENTS

Satellite picture preparing assumes a crucial job for research advancements in Astronomy, Remote Sensing, GIS, Agriculture Monitoring, Disaster Management and numerous different fields of study. Be that as it may, handling those satellite pictures requires a lot of calculation time because of its mind-boggling and enormous preparing criteria. It appears a hindrance for ongoing essential leadership. To switch the activity quicker, appropriated registering can be a reasonable arrangement. As of late, Cluster and Grid are two most well-known and incredible appropriated frameworks to serve for superior parallel applications. GRASS GIS (Geographical Resources Analysis Support System) is an open source programming/apparatus, which has been utilized to process the satellite pictures. Inside GRASS, various modules have created for handling satellite pictures. Building up the strategy, which empowers to run GRASS GIS condition for satellite pictures handling on appropriated registering frameworks, is the principle concerning the issue.

Furthermore, two distinctive usage approaches for allocated are talked about for two diverse programming stages. The GRASS module is utilised to process 13 different vegetation records for the satellite pictures. Vegetation Index (VI) is the real arrangement of markers for vegetation. NDVI (Normalized Difference Vegetation Index) is one of them. Where, RED and NIR represent the ghostly reflectance estimations gained in the red and close infrared locales, individually. Other vegetation files are inferred, utilising different strategies for separations and difference (Tiwari S., Gupta R.K., & Kashyap R., 2019). The GRASS condition, and disintegrates the objective pictures in lines and dispatches the calculation of columns to various labourer forms. Specialist procedures are free from GRASS; they run the calculation and send back the column insightful outcome to ace procedure. The model module executed utilising MPI on a PC group framework and Nico-G on a Grid framework. The significant target of this exploration is to give the Remote Sensing client a smaller model for Grid, and MPI programming as GRASS GIS circulated preparing. Furthermore, these sorts of research will combine the Remote Sensing or GIS with High-Performance Computing people group

## A New Tool for Classification of Satellite Images Available from Google Maps

Efficient Implementation in Graphics Processing Units It builds up another parallel execution of the k-implies unsupervised bunching calculation for item realistic preparing units (GPUs). Further, assess the presence of this recently created calculation in the undertaking of grouping (in unsupervised design) satellite symbolism accessible from Google Maps motor. With a definitive objective of assessing the characterisation accuracy of the recently created calculation, we have investigated the accord or understanding in the order accomplished by our usage and an elective execution of the forecast accessible in business programming. Our trial results directed utilising satellite pictures acquired from Google Maps motor over various areas around the Earth demonstrate that the arrangement understanding between our parallel form and the k-implies calculation accessible in business programming is exceptionally high. Likewise, the GPU adaptation (created utilising the CUDA language available from NVidiaTM) is a lot quicker than the sequential one (speedup over 30), in this way showing our proposed execution takes into consideration bigger scale preparing of high-dimensional picture databases, for example, those accessible in the Google Maps motor depicts another apparatus which enables an unpracticed client to perform unsupervised order of satellite pictures acquired using Google Maps by methods for the notable k-implies bunching calculation, which can be trailed by spatial postprocessing dependent on the lion's share casting a ballot (Shukla R., Gupta R.K., & Kashyap R., 2019). The grouping stage has been executed in parallel utilising item realistic handling units, which are particular equipment cards that are these days generally accessible in standard PCs. The identical variant of the k-implies calculation executed in NVidiaTM GPUs utilising the process brought together gadget design (CUDA)4–is demonstrated to be more than multiple times quicker than the sequential adaptation. This opens the path for energizing new advancements and possibilities in proficient preparing of vast databases of satellite pictures, for example, those accessible from Google Maps motor and utilized in this work for showing In the action, it built up another parallel execution of the k-implies grouping calculation with regards to satellite picture handling utilizing NVIDIATM GPUs. The forecast has been actualised utilising CUDA and tried using an as of late created framework for data extraction and investigation of picture informational indexes from Google Maps motor. The calculation has been assessed as far as its concurrence with business programming in a similar setting and furthermore dissecting the speedup concerning the (streamlined) sequential execution of the same code. The primary commitments of this investigation can be outlined as pursues: The strategy prevailing with regards to acquiring a decent understanding in order concerning business programming. • The GPU usage got a critical speedup over the enhanced sequential rendition, consequently supporting enormous scale tests in the Google Maps motor.

## Contribution of Satellite Symbolism

Greece Thessaly is a locale of low alleviation in Greece where several Neolithic settlements/tells called modules were built up from Early Neolithic period until Bronze Age. Multi-sensor remote detecting was connected to the examination zone to assess its capability to distinguish Neolithic settlements. Also, various types of advanced rise models utilised, for example, SRTM, DEM built by the introduction of shapes from topographic maps, DEM developed by aeronautical photographs and DEM developed by Aster pictures, where can be distinguished as little differentiating spots inside the height example of the characteristic variety of the land surface (Shukla R., Gupta R.K., & Kashyap R., 2019). A scope of picture preparing systems, for example, shading composite, head segments examination, decorrelation extend, trailed by visual understanding, were initially connected to the hyperspectral symbolism to recognise the settlements and approve the aftereffects of GPS reviewing. The subsequent stage was to gather otherworldly marks of these tell destinations, to associate them inside the equivalent ghostly scope of the distinctive sensor frameworks lastly to continue with their factual investigation. Different channels were connected to all pictures to investigate the high ghostly and spatial fluctuation of the settlement designs, for example, Sobel 3*3 right inclining and Laplace channel. Order of the considerable number of pictures utilising distinctive hard and delicate classifiers and utilisation of vegetation list pursued (Kashyap, R., 2019b). To adapt to the troubles of pixel-based strategies, object–arranged order procedures additionally connected to Ikonos symbolism to group advice as per their shape and geometry. Furthermore, advanced channels were connected to each DEMto recognise the settlements. In the wake of approving the outcomes with accurate height information, we closed which of them are progressively dependable either for general topographic investigations of the region or all the more explicitly for the recognition of the settlements. The last advance was the use of fluffy calculations for the characterisation of the likelihood of settlement presence. Even though there are specific challenges experienced in the characterisation of archaeological highlights created by a comparable parent material with the encompassing scene, the aftereffects of the exploration recommended an alternate reaction of every sensor to the discovery of the Neolithic settlements, as per its unearthly and spatial goals. Also, the coordinated utilisation of remote detecting symbolism and the computerised rise models created a significant upgrade to the plan of a prescient model of the Neolithic settlements of Thessaly by consolidating the phantom, spatial and topographic properties of the tells. ASTER pictures demonstrated to be the most solid and productive for the identification of Neolithic settlements. Conversely, Landsat pictures did not create attractive outcomes, for the most part, because of the late spring obtaining the date of it. The high spectral capacities of HYPERION, particularly in the wake of blending it with the high goals pictures of Ikonos, appear to have an expanded potential for identifying as well as for laying out the specific highlights. The picture forms that demonstrated to be progressively successful were the spatial sifting, the procedure of de-relationship extend and the radiometric upgrade. Moreover, the consequences of the investigation of DEMs, particularly the utilisation of the three distinct channels to SRTM DEM, demonstrated to be very promising.However, Providence of remotely detected information advances the difficulties of how to process the information and how to break down it as quickly as time permits. With the agreement to Grid similarity heterogeneous registering sources, a Grid domain worked for the handling of remotely detected pictures. Recognising proper applications for innovation to evaluate the wellbeing and security of scaffolds is a significant issue for extension proprietors around the globe. Customarily, thruway extension conditions have been checked through visual examination strategies with auxiliary lacks being physically distinguished and characterised by qualified architects and auditors. It requires more prolonged investment to handle harm, regardless of whether genuine injuries are centred around. Since the time has come devouring to identify damage by human eyes, it is compelling to apply picture preparing. At the point when there is a bizarre climate, or a seismic tremor happens, proper emergency the executives are required, including making data accessible by distinguishing and holding onto the fiasco circumstances. For instance, a street manager should rapidly get a handle on a street debacle and, in light of the nearness/nonappearance of catastrophe, make acceptable courses in the hazardous situation to the general population to give help to the harmed zone. Secure traffic wellbeing for street clients, and make appropriate crisis fixes on significant courses to immediately revive the streets by evacuating snags (Kashyap, R., 2019c). At a genuine tremor, it sets aside more extended effort to handle harm by office assessment watch, regardless of whether we disregard little harm and spotlight on actual harm. In such a circumstance, remote detecting innovation can assume vital jobs. For Areal-type damage,

1. Edge extraction,
2. Unsupervised grouping,
3. The surface investigation, and
4. Edge upgrade is proper to distinguish harmed zone (Kashyap, R., & Gautam, P., 2015, November) for Liner-type harm, Edge extraction is done to recognise the damaged parcel by picture handling, the kind of calculation which is highlight extraction calculation. Highlights Extraction In highlight extraction calculation Textural Analysis, Spectral Extraction and Geometric Extraction additionally done.

## Co-Event Methodology for Texture Analysis

The picture examination strategy chose the CCM technique the utilisation of shading picture includes in the noticeable light range gives extra picture trademark includes over the conventional dark scale portrayal. The CCM philosophy built up comprises of three noteworthy scientific procedures. The RGB pictures of leaves are changed over into Hue Saturation Intensity (HSI) shading space portrayal. When this procedure finished, every pixel guide is utilised to create a shading co-event network, bringing about three CCM lattices, one for every one of the H, S and I pixel maps. (HSI) Space is, likewise an excellent shading space since it depends on human shading recognition. Electromagnetic radiation in the scope of wavelengths of around 400 to 700 nanometers is called noticeable light because the human visual framework is delicate to this range. The shade with the wavelength of light and power demonstrates the sufficiency of a fire.

In conclusion, immersion is a segment that measures the "colourfulness" in HSI space. Shading spaces can be changed, starting with one area then onto the next effectively. Satellite symbolism investigation can be in all respects comprehensively be characterized into two to be specific, Pixel-based picture arrangement and item based picture characterization old style pixel-based picture order naturally arranges all pixels in a picture into land spread classes or topics in a pixel by pixel way. Ordinarily, multispectral information is utilized, and the ghostly example present inside the data for every pixel used as the numerical reason for the arrangement. The traditional pixel-based strategies are least separation/closest neighbour, parallelepiped and most extreme probability classifiers. Among the division techniques, picture thresholding strategy is a standout amongst the essential approach because of its straightforwardness, heartiness, and high exactness. Thresholding technique can into two classifications: The main class incorporates strategies that locate the ideal edge utilising picture histogram examination. The subsequent classification includes procedures that determine the absolute limit utilizing target capacities. The objective is to find the definite limit in pictures, yet the obstruction of every one of these techniques is the multifaceted nature of figuring (Kashyap, R., 2019d). Picture Segmentation procedures can fall into the accompanying classifications: Edge-based, Threshold-based, Region-based, Neural Network based, Cluster-based, and Hybrid. Image division dependent on thresholding is one of the most established and fantastic strategies since the limit worth partitions the pixels in such a way that pixels having force esteem not as much as edge has a place with one class while pixels whose power worth is more prominent than side has a home with another type. Division dependent nervous recognition endeavours to determine picture by recognising the edges between various areas that have an unexpected change in power worth are separated and connected to frame shut locale limits. Locale based strategies divide a picture into multiple districts that are comparable as indicated by a lot of some predefined conditions. The Neural Network based picture division procedures detailed in writing can predominantly group into two classifications: managed and unsupervised techniques. Regulated strategies require a master human contribution to the division. General, this implies human specialists are cautiously choosing the preparation information that is then used to fragment the pictures. Unsupervised techniques are semi or completely programmed. Client mediation may be fundamental sooner or later in the process to improve the execution of the method. However, the outcomes ought to be pretty much human autonomous. An unsupervised division strategy consequently parcels the pictures without administrator intercession (Kashyap, R., 2019e).

Nonetheless, these structures executed utilizing application explicit from the earlier information at configuration time, for example, anatomical, physical or genetic information. Grouping is an unsupervised learning procedure, where one has to know the number of bunches ahead of time to characterize pixels. A similitude condition described among pixels, and after that, comparable pixels are assembled to shape clusters. For the momentum inquire about the pictures are sourced from the open source information base give by Digital Globe, a satellite imaging firm. These pictures provided as a piece of their exertion towards salvage and restoration in the fallout of the Nepal tremor.

## IMAGE PROCESSING IN REMOTE SENSING

The primary purpose of using image processing techniques is to extract the information from an image and make it visually more enhanced to obtain a bright look and details. The image represented in digital form hence called digital image used for extraction of information the images obtained from cameras, sensors, satellite, etc. Remote sensed data, i.e., the data collected from the satellite after processing gives a clear understanding of the earth's surface (Yang & Fang, 2016). Different types of processing techniques are developed to build a remote sensing application. The image first obtained needs to be geometrical, radiometrically improved before analysis. Before applying specific processing techniques, the different types of correction are done to remove atmospheric, geometric errors. After removal of error, the remotely sensed image goes through a series of steps for analysing. For example, if we have to calculate the urban growth, the pre and post images of that area, captured in the satellite are taken and processed individually using different types of techniques to calculate the percentage growth in that place. Similarly, there are many applications of image processing and remote sensing. Below explains the various image processing techniques for satellite captured image.

## IMAGE PROCESSING TECHNIQUES FOR IMAGE ANALYSIS

Digital image processing is a technique which is used to manipulate an image as per needed by the individual application. It widely used for processing of remotely sensed data in the digital form. Certain types of preprocessing required in the obtained image, it is a collection of specific hardware and software which combines to form Image processing system (Singh & Nair, 2018). For the extraction of meaningful information from remotely sensed data, it is required to apply different image processing techniques. Remote sensing images represented in the digital form where the digital number of a pixel represents the resolution of an image.

*Figure 1. Sciences related to image processing*

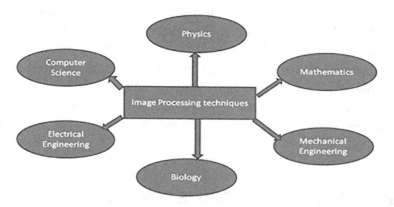

Image analysis systems can provide categories:

(i)   Pre-processing stage
(ii)  Image Enhancement
(iii) Image Transformation
(iv) Image Classification and Analysis.

*Figure 2. Steps of image processing*

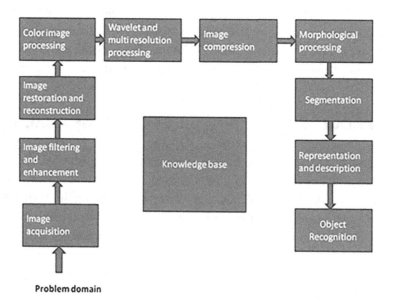

## Pre-Processing Stage

Pre-processing functions are applied in an image to reduce the geometric errors, atmospheric errors, radiometric errors to avoid any distortion and to obtain the information effectively both qualitatively and quantitatively from an image (Firozjaei, Daryaei, Sedighi, Weng & Alavipanah, 2019).

## Image Enhancement

The visual interpretation of image enhancement, different enhancement techniques are applied in an image. There are four types of image enhancement techniques: radiometric improvement, spatial enhancement, spectral enhancement, geometric enhancement.

### Radiometric Enhancement

It is a technique that improves the contrast between features of the surface of the earth by altering the image based on pixel value. A tone mapping algorithm was applied to enhance the dark and bright regions in an image. It resulted in revealing the minor details of the shadowed area.

### Spatial Enhancement

Spatial enhancement techniques deal with the spatial frequency of an image. The way the grayscale value changes in an image from one side to other defines the spatial frequency. Spatial filters are used in this method to enhance, sharpen, or smooth the edges of the objects in an image (Lenti, Nunziata, Estatico & Migliaccio, 2016). Low pass filters used for noise reduction whereas high pass filters used for sharpening of the sides.

### Spectral Enhancement

The process of creating a new spectral band from the available groups, these techniques is used to extract the appropriate information for analysis (Kashyap, R.,2020).

### Geometric Enhancement

Geometric enhancement is done to enhance the geometric detail of an image. In this type, the new pixel values calculated based on its neighbouring pixels. This type of enhancement deals with smoothing, sharpening, edge detection, and improvement (Firozjaei, Daryaei, Sedighi, Weng & Alavipanah, 2019).

## Image Segmentation

Image segmentation is a critical process of digital image processing. As the name segmentation, it is a technique used to segment the image into parts having similar features and properties. Segmentation is the critical task of image processing. It has several applications. For example, in medical imaging, it is used as a tool for describing the anatomical structure as needed. In remote sensing, it can use for landscape change detection, land cover classification. The different types of segmentation techniques are:

- Region-based Segmentation
- Edge-based Segmentation
- Threshold-based Segmentation
- ANN-based Segmentation
- Fuzzy based Segmentation

## Image Classification

Image Classification is considered to be a very complicated step for machines. Classification systems consist of a database of existing patterns and compare the detected object with the designs and classify the object to a particular group. The classification includes image sensors, processing, segmentation, object detection, feature extraction, and object classification (Waoo, N., Kashyap, R., & Jaiswal, A., 2010). Image classification is an essential and challenging task in various applications such as biomedical, robot navigation, vehicle navigation, remote sensing. Classification of image classification techniques are:

1. Supervised training
2. Unsupervised training
3. Object-based classification

*Figure 3. Steps for image classification*

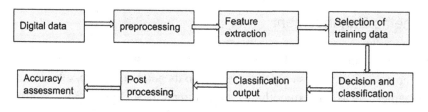

Some classification techniques are:

Artificial Neural Network (ANN): ANN is an artificial intelligence method which consists of different layers. Each layer consists of a set of neurons. The sheets are connected among themselves by the weighted connections. Performance and accuracy of ANN depend on the number of inputs and the structure of the network. Computation rate is high, but the training time is significant.

Decision tree- Decision tree is a hierarchy based method which calculates class membership by partitioning datasets repeatedly. It is a simple method, and the computation efficiency is high, it becomes complicated when specific values not decided.

Support Vector Machine (SVM)- SVM builds a set of hyperplanes in the space of classification. Functional separation achieved in this case. This method provides excellent generalisation capability; there is no problem of overfitting, Complexity reduced in this case.

## Image Processing for Disaster Analysis

Recently, disaster detection has been the most coveted and exciting field of research due to the increased number of disaster and loss of lives. The changes have observed by researchers caused due to natural disaster using sensors (Chen, Chen, Huang, Ciou & Zhang, 2015) and image processing techniques (URABE & SAJI, 2009). Since failure can occur at any place and at any time, an automated process can be used to do the following: image discovery, processing, detection of the damage as calculated from the image. The Joint Research Centre of the European Commission (JRC) deals with the assessment of the pre and post-disaster image analysis both outside and inside the European Union. An Analysis of both the images by which analysts measure the extent and severity of damage caused due to disasters (Bielski, Gentilini & Pappalardo, 2011).

When the team is alerted to any calamity, the following steps carried out as quickly:

1.  Identify the location and the type of disaster as informed by the online alerting system.
2.  Download the image before the disaster.
3.  Download the post image of disaster.
4.  Process both the images to find the affected areas and the extent of the damage (Bielski, Gentilini & Pappalardo, 2011)

*Figure 4. Flow chart for the damage detection process*

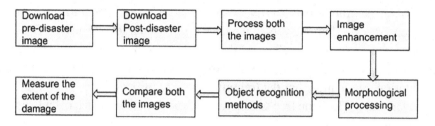

## Download Pre and Post Image

Pre and post-disaster image downloaded for analysis of the damage caused in that particular region.

## Pre-Processing

Pre-processing functions are applied to remove the geometric, radiometric, atmospheric errors.

## Image Enhancement

There are different types of enhancement techniques as described in the above segment, which can apply in an image for enhancing the features of the image for better evaluation.

## Morphological Processing

The different types of morphological processes are:

- Erosion: Shrinks the object by the use of a structuring element.
- Dilation: dilates the object by the use of a structuring element.
- Opening: the erosion of an object followed by dilation
- Closing: dilation of an object followed by erosion.

Based on the needs, a particular technique is applied.

## Object Recognition Method

Different types of object recognition and feature extraction algorithms Used for feature extraction in disaster assessment. The usefulness of deep CNN's with domain-specific fine tuning to effectively detect the level of damage from images. They were calculating the damage caused in the buildings after the disaster (Win & Aung, 2018).

## Compare Both the Images and Measure the Extent of the Damage

The pre and post images of the disaster separately processed by applying the above steps and the results observed are compared to calculate the difference. The size of damage depends upon the change in an image after the disaster. The occurrence of natural disasters such as earthquakes, floods, and cyclones is on the rise leading to the increased awareness of the impact of catastrophic events. In this case, we have focused on the damage caused in the buildings due to earthquakes. It takes a very long time to grasp the loss at high magnitude earthquake. In that case, Remote sensing technology can play crucial roles. It becomes complex for an Individual to detect these things manually (Kashyap, R., & Piersson, A. D., 2018). The fact that the manual analysis of an image may take a lot of time and effort, we have tried to apply different image processing techniques to detect the information in an image obtained from remote sensing.

## METHODOLOGIES

The solution to our problem revolves around the analysis of images obtained before and after the calamity, which can provide an approximate comparison between the two images. This comparison gives the percentage of damage to the buildings due to the earthquake.

The steps of the process are given below in detail:

## Image Acquisition

It involves the gathering of two types of images, one before the damage and another after the image. The Satellite image of a particular region is downloaded and considered where we have to detect the destruction after the calamity. The image downloaded is ready for further Processing. After the image has obtained, different methods of processing can be applied to the image to perform the many various vision tasks required. The same process used in both the images and the results between the two images calculated.

## Image Pre-Processing: Bilateral filter

There are many image pre-processing techniques. These used for noise removal, contrast, enhancement, and illumination equalization. For noise removal, we use various filters such as median filter, Wiener filter, Gaussian filter, etc. For contrast, enhancement, and illumination, we can use contrast stretching. Apart from these, many other techniques are available. Here we have used a bilateral filter. The bilateral filter is a type of filter which is used to smooth images while preserving edge. How it formulated is: a weighted average of its neighbors replaces each pixel. It converts any input image to a smoothed version. It removes most noise and fine details but preserves the sharp edges without blurring

## Detect Vegetation

For the detection of vegetation region in an image, the following series of steps is carried out by converting RGB to Grayscale then bilateral image turned to grayscale image.bit). The grayscale image luminance value ranges from 0-255. Thresholding process is used here for the detection of vegetation area. The most straightforward Implementation of the threshold method used, which gives a binary image as an output. The binary image consists of two colours: black, which represents background and white represents foreground (Kashyap, R., & Gautam, P.,2016). It is a type of segmentation technique that separates two regions based on a parameter known as intensity threshold. It sets the values as '0' of a pixel whose intensity is less than the threshold value and '1' for the pixel whose brightness is higher than the threshold value. Therefore the two regions can be distinguished as black and white regions.

## Morphological Operation: Opening

The opening can describe the erosion of an image followed by dilation by the same structuring element. Opening removes small objects from the foreground (usually taken as the bright pixels) of an image, placing them in the background. Hence, the opening is used here for morphological noise removal. For the detection of buildings, we need to remove the vegetation area. In the above image, the white region showing the vegetation area set to the backdrop.

## Image Segmentation

Image segmentation is a critical process of Digital image processing. As the name segmentation, it is a technique used to segment the image into parts having similar features and properties. It is the very first step in the image analysis. Here, in our

*Figure 5. Images after thresholding*

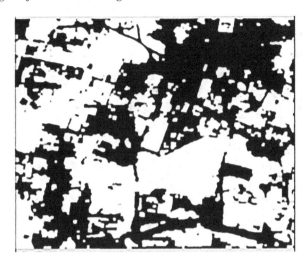

project image segmentation techniques are used to divide the image into different parts (Kashyap, R., & Rahamatkar, S.,2019a). In our project, the main concern is to detect the buildings and avoid the other region. The vegetation area already set as background by use of the segmentation technique threshold method which separates the image into two parts, the vegetation region therefore easily divided (Kashyap, R., & Rahamatkar, S.,2019b). Now we need to separate the buildings and roads for which mask is used to separate them by using colour invariants.

*Figure 6. Vegetation area set as background*

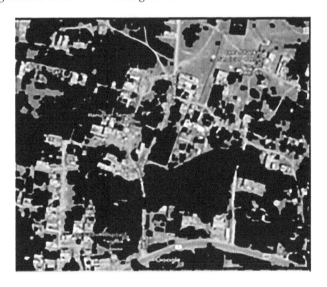

*Figure 7. Segmentation result*

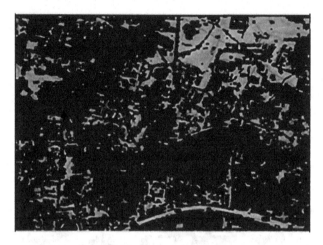

## Polygon Detection

The polygon detection is used to detect the number of buildings in an image. It is an object detection method in which a shapefile included in the code which consists of then different shapes of the polygon this file, therefore used for the detection of the buildings (Kashyap, R., & Gautam, P., 2017).

*Figure 8. Buildings detected result of polygon detection*

## Result and Discussion

After applying all the processing techniques, after the last step polygon detection, the number of buildings is obtained, and the comparison between the number of buildings in the pre-image and the post image is used to measure the destruction caused. The change in the numbers of buildings gives the devastation caused on the premises. Table 2, shows the building count before and after the earthquake for three samples of images.

## ADVANTAGES OF IMAGE PROCESSING TECHNIQUES

Firstly we will talk about the benefits of satellite images over ground observation: Satellite images give a compact view of the region, a permanent record kept, and the information can be accessed whenever needed.It is cost and time effective, spectral and the spatial resolution. At a time a large area is covered and interpreted. Now, as far as the visual interpretation considered, it becomes complex and a tedious job for an individual to interpret the image manually. Suppose a person needs to calculate urban growth in a region if he calculates manually it becomes time taking and complicated work. So due to these complexities, image processing techniques came into the role. Time is a significant fact due to image processing techniques; it becomes easy for a person to analyze the image in reduced time. There are different processes and steps to follow for processing and examining an image, as discussed earlier. Efficiency is another factor. Sometimes crafty things manually don't provide high accuracy. So once the model set for a particular task, it will work for the image analysis and will give the efficient answer.

Now, as far as disaster management considered: Remotely sensed images keep a record of the destruction in an area. The disruption in a larger area can be analysed at a time and can report to the respective government, which becomes a difficult task if the destruction is calculated personally by visiting the place. There will be a record of natural hazards taking place in a specific region. Because of the documents, the

*Table 2. Number of building collapse*

| S.No | Buildings Detected before Earthquake | Structures Detected after Earthquake | No of Buildings Collapsed |
|------|--------------------------------------|--------------------------------------|---------------------------|
| 1 | 4,428 | 3,267 | 1,161 |
| 2 | 12,546 | 9,389 | 3,157 |
| 3 | 9,892 | 7,247 | 2,645 |

dangers with its intensity and magnitude can predict, and the area will declare as the high alert. As said, prevention is better than cure; it gives a chance for people to understand the risk in the surrounding areas and to escape from the region for their survival.

## CONCLUSION

Natural calamities like earthquake, landslides, and floods cause severe destruction to the environment and damage to human life and property all over the world — the study of recurrence of the earthquakes, forest fires, landslides, floods needed for effective preventive measures. Remote sensing technology helps in the disaster management process through detection of disaster-prone areas, safe alternate routes, future scenario predictions, and alerting people before any calamity. Post-disaster satellite data collected can help in the disaster recovery, fast settlement, and damage claim. Image processing techniques are a great advantage to the disaster management process. Satellite images obtained are processed to find out sufficient information. Therefore Remote sensing technology, GPS, along with the processing techniques has proved a powerful tool for monitoring of disaster.

## REFERENCES

Bielski, C., Gentilini, S., & Pappalardo, M. (2011). Post-Disaster Image Processing for Damage Analysis Using GENESI-DR, WPS and Grid Computing. *Remote Sensing*, *3*(6), 1234–1250. doi:10.3390/rs3061234

Chen, M., Chen, C., Huang, M., Ciou, J., & Zhang, G. (2015). Design of Unmanned Vehicle System for Disaster Detection. *International Journal of Distributed Sensor Networks*, *11*(4), 784298. doi:10.1155/2015/784298

Firozjaei, M., Daryaei, I., Sedighi, A., Weng, Q., & Alavipanah, S. (2019). Homogeneity Distance Classification Algorithm (HDCA): A Novel Algorithm for Satellite Image Classification. *Remote Sensing*, *11*(5), 546. doi:10.3390/rs11050546

Ghaffarian, S., Kerle, N., & Filatova, T. (2018). Remote Sensing-Based Proxies for Urban Disaster Risk Management and Resilience: A Review. *Remote Sensing*, *10*(11), 1760. doi:10.3390/rs10111760

Goswami, S., Chakraborty, S., Ghosh, S., Chakrabarti, A., & Chakraborty, B. (2018). A review on application of data mining techniques to combat natural disasters. *Ain Shams Engineering Journal*, *9*(3), 365–378. doi:10.1016/j.asej.2016.01.012

Joyce, K., Belliss, S., Samsonov, S., McNeill, S., & Glassey, P. (2009). A review of the status of satellite remote sensing and image processing techniques for mapping natural hazards and disasters. *Progress In Physical Geography: Earth And Environment, 33*(2), 183–207. doi:10.1177/0309133309339563

Kashyap, R. (2019a). Sensation of Deep Learning in Image Processing Applications. In A. Hassanien, A. Darwish, & C. Chowdhary (Eds.), *Handbook of Research on Deep Learning Innovations and Trends* (pp. 72–96). Hershey, PA: IGI Global. doi:10.4018/978-1-5225-7862-8.ch005

Kashyap, R. (2019b). Computational Healthcare System With Image Analysis. In C. Chen & S. Cheung (Eds.), *Computational Models for Biomedical Reasoning and Problem Solving* (pp. 89–127). Hershey, PA: IGI Global. doi:10.4018/978-1-5225-7467-5.ch004

Kashyap, R. (2019c). Machine Learning, Data Mining for IoT-Based Systems. In G. Kaur & P. Tomar (Eds.), *Handbook of Research on Big Data and the IoT* (pp. 314–338). Hershey, PA: IGI Global. doi:10.4018/978-1-5225-7432-3.ch018

Kashyap, R. (2019d). Medical Image Segmentation and Analysis. In C. Chakraborty (Ed.), *Advanced Classification Techniques for Healthcare Analysis* (pp. 132–160). Hershey, PA: IGI Global. doi:10.4018/978-1-5225-7796-6.ch007

Kashyap, R. (2019e). Big Data and High-Performance Analyses and Processes. In A. Voghera & L. La Riccia (Eds.), *Spatial Planning in the Big Data Revolution* (pp. 45–83). Hershey, PA: IGI Global. doi:10.4018/978-1-5225-7927-4.ch003

Kashyap, R. (2020). Applications of Wireless Sensor Networks in Healthcare. In P. Mukherjee, P. Pattnaik, & S. Panda (Eds.), *IoT and WSN Applications for Modern Agricultural Advancements: Emerging Research and Opportunities* (pp. 8–40). Hershey, PA: IGI Global. doi:10.4018/978-1-5225-9004-0.ch002

Kashyap, R., & Gautam, P. (2015, November). Modified region based segmentation of medical images. In *Proceedings of International Conference on Communication Networks* (ICCN) (pp. 209–216). IEEE. 10.1109/ICCN.2015.41

Kashyap, R., & Gautam, P. (2016). Fast level set method for segmentation of medical images. In *Proceedings of the International Conference on Informatics and Analytics*. ACM. 10.1145/2980258.2980302

Kashyap, R., & Gautam, P. (2017). Fast Medical Image Segmentation Using Energy-Based Method. In V. Tiwari, B. Tiwari, R. Thakur, & S. Gupta (Eds.), *Pattern and Data Analysis in Healthcare Settings* (pp. 35–60). Hershey, PA: IGI Global. doi:10.4018/978-1-5225-0536-5.ch003

Kashyap, R., & Piersson, A. D. (2018). Impact of Big Data on Security. In G. Shrivastava, P. Kumar, B. Gupta, S. Bala, & N. Dey (Eds.), *Handbook of Research on Network Forensics and Analysis Techniques* (pp. 283–299). Hershey, PA: IGI Global. doi:10.4018/978-1-5225-4100-4.ch015

Kashyap, R., & Rahamatkar, S. (2019a). Medical Image Segmentation: An Advanced Approach. In S. Paul, P. Bhattacharya, & A. Bit (Eds.), *Early Detection of Neurological Disorders Using Machine Learning Systems* (pp. 292–321). Hershey, PA: IGI Global. doi:10.4018/978-1-5225-8567-1.ch015

Kashyap, R., & Rahamatkar, S. (2019b). Healthcare Informatics Using Modern Image Processing Approaches. In B. Singh, B. Saini, D. Singh, & A. Pandey (Eds.), *Medical Data Security for Bioengineers* (pp. 254–277). Hershey, PA: IGI Global. doi:10.4018/978-1-5225-7952-6.ch013

Lenti, F., Nunziata, F., Estatico, C., & Migliaccio, M. (2016). Conjugate Gradient Method in Hilbert and Banach Spaces to Enhance the Spatial Resolution of Radiometer Data. *IEEE Transactions on Geoscience and Remote Sensing, 54*(1), 397–406. doi:10.1109/TGRS.2015.2458014

Neubert, T., Mandea, M., Hulot, G., von Frese, R., Primdahl, F., Jørgensen, J., ... Risbo, T. (2001). Ørsted satellite captures high-precision geomagnetic field data. *Eos (Washington, D.C.), 82*(7), 81–88. doi:10.1029/01EO00043

Pichuzhkina, A., & Roldugin, D. (2016). Geomagnetic field models for satellite angular motion. *Keldysh Institute Preprints*, (87-e), 1-25. doi:10.20948/prepr-2016-87-e

Shukla, R., Gupta, R. K., & Kashyap, R. (2019). A multiphase pre-copy strategy for the virtual machine migration in cloud. In S. Satapathy, V. Bhateja, & S. Das (Eds.), *Smart Intelligent Computing and Applications. Smart Innovation, Systems and Technologies* (Vol. 104). Singapore: Springer. doi:10.1007/978-981-13-1921-1_43

Singh, K., & Nair, J. (2018). A Literature Review On Satellite Image Data Enhancement Using Digital Image Processing. *International Journal on Computer Science and Engineering, 6*(7), 1114–1119. doi:10.26438/ijcse/v6i7.11141119

Tiwari, S., Gupta, R. K., & Kashyap, R. (2019). To enhance web response time using agglomerative clustering technique for web navigation recommendation. In H. Behera, J. Nayak, B. Naik, & A. Abraham (Eds.), *Computational Intelligence in Data Mining. Advances in Intelligent Systems and Computing* (Vol. 711). Singapore: Springer. doi:10.1007/978-981-10-8055-5_59

Urabe, K., & Saji, H. (2009). Detection of Road Blockage Areas after Earthquake Disaster in Mountainous Districts Using Aerial Images. *Journal Of Japan Association For Earthquake Engineering*, 9(4), 26–38. doi:10.5610/jaee.9.4_26

Waoo, N., Kashyap, R., & Jaiswal, A. (2010). DNA nano array analysis using hierarchical quality threshold clustering. In *Proceedings of 2010 2nd IEEE International Conference on Information Management and Engineering* (pp. 81-85). IEEE. 10.1109/ICIME.2010.5477579

Win, S., & Aung, T. (2018). Automated Text Annotation for Social Media Data during Natural Disasters. *Advances In Science. Technology And Engineering Systems Journal*, 3(2), 119–127. doi:10.25046/aj030214

Yang, G., & Fang, S. (2016). Improving remote sensing image classification by exploiting adaptive features and hierarchical hybrid decision trees. *Remote Sensing Letters*, 8(2), 156–164. doi:10.1080/2150704X.2016.1239282

# Chapter 8
# Artificial Intelligence and Machine Learning Algorithms

**Amit Kumar Tyagi**

iD https://orcid.org/0000-0003-2657-8700

*School of Computing Science and Engineering, Vellore Institute of Technology, Chennai, India*

**Poonam Chahal**

iD https://orcid.org/0000-0002-2684-4354

*MRIIRS, Faridabad, India*

## ABSTRACT

*With the recent development in technologies and integration of millions of internet of things devices, a lot of data is being generated every day (known as Big Data). This is required to improve the growth of several organizations or in applications like e-healthcare, etc. Also, we are entering into an era of smart world, where robotics is going to take place in most of the applications (to solve the world's problems). Implementing robotics in applications like medical, automobile, etc. is an aim/goal of computer vision. Computer vision (CV) is fulfilled by several components like artificial intelligence (AI), machine learning (ML), and deep learning (DL). Here, machine learning and deep learning techniques/algorithms are used to analyze Big Data. Today's various organizations like Google, Facebook, etc. are using ML techniques to search particular data or recommend any post. Hence, the requirement of a computer vision is fulfilled through these three terms: AI, ML, and DL.*

DOI: 10.4018/978-1-7998-0182-5.ch008

# INTRODUCTION ABOUT ARTIFICIAL INTELLIGENCE& MACHINE LEARNING

Computer Vision is a subdivision of computer science which is integrated with the usual mining, analysis and consideration of constructive information. In simple words, computer vision means "How machines can/ a machine sees/ solves problems without a human-being". In the past decade, this area is too popular and has still attracted several research communities to develop machines better than human being (in terms of work-efficiency, thinking-level or solving problems). For example, Sophia is a recent and enhanced robot which is being developed by the Hong Kong based company Hanson Robotics. It is the first robot to come to get the Saudi Arabia citizenship in 2016. So, it can be said that the computer vision domain is the becoming the upcoming field of research that can solve various problems related to virtualization. The computer vision has been expanding and emerging with the new and advanced technologies or concepts (like Blockchain, Internet of Everything, etc.) and applications that utilize different computer vision techniques. Among all existing technologies (in recent years), over a hundred applications/ many organizations have moved to the practice and execution of Artificial Intelligence techniques.

Machine Learning techniques required in their business/ to give boost to the aim of computer vision. Hence, to fulfil the vision of smart worlds/ requirements, artificial intelligence, and machine learning allows tools/ applications to become more accurate (in terms of values) in predicting results (without being explicitly programmed). For artificial intelligence algorithms, several inferences, rules and logic that were used in the systems which were created using traditional techniques of Artificial Intelligence are not meeting the today's requirement of the changing world. In divergence, systems that focus on the analysis and detection the patterns that are existing in dataset for classification, clustering, regression, are becoming the overriding system of AI. In addition to the existing mechanisms, the domain of AI can be further taken into the form of three main groups like Artificial Slight intellect, Artificial Overall Intelligence, and Artificial Super Intelligence. On the other way round there are numerous categories of existing techniques of Machine Learning (ML) algorithms used in fulfilling the objective of computer vision like supervised (regression, decision tree, random forest, classification) and unsupervised (Clustering, Association Analysis, Hidden Markov Model (HMM), etc.) and semi-supervised. In simple words, computer vision is the science and technology of machines that a machine sees (without a human-being). Computer vision is an exploration extent that comprises numerous methods to approach several graphic problems. In recent years, over a hundred applications/ many organizations have been replaced by Artificial Intelligence, Deep Learning and other Machine Learning techniques to give boost to the aim of computer vision. Hence, to fulfil the vision of smart worlds/ requirements, artificial intelligence, and machine learning allows tools/ applications to become more accurate (in terms of values) in predicting results (without being explicitly programmed).

## BACKGROUND

### Artificial Intelligence (AI)

It is a division of Computer Science which tracks technology, i.e., generating the computers or machineries that behave as intelligent and rational as human beings. In general, the definition of Artificial Intelligence includes the designing and creation of systems that can understand the human intelligence and behave accordingly in an environment provided. It will include the learning, planning etc. to behave the system rationally. AI not only creates the intelligent systems or expert systems but it also expand to the biologically observable. In addition to this the father of AI named as John McCarthy, "The science and engineering of creating intellectual machines, specifically intellectual system programs".

In other words, Artificial Intelligence (AI) is a means of constructing a computer, a robot controlled by computer, or software that contemplates intelligently, similar to a human/individual. Artificial Intelligence accomplish its aims by deeply studying the structure and thinking process of an individual brain to find out the ways of learning, planning, decision capability, and taking action in a particular situation. In the previous years, Artificial Intelligence has increased acceptance due to growing people's curiosity in numerous novel research domains like big data, Blockchain technology etc., because of the enhancement in the speed of generation of data, its huge size and its various varieties. The use of AI also helps in businesses by making the use of the techniques of business intelligence embedded with the AI techniques. In an organization, the tools, methodologies used to enhance their business processes in real world when combined with the AI tools, give better results.

In the domain of computer science, where programming perspective is very strong and allied, AI deals with the searching, planning, learning, computational linguistic, etc. It also includes the representation of knowledge in the knowledge base or production system y considering the characteristics of the problem to be solved and all the possible issues related to the same. In general, the knowledge base constructed for the intelligent system should be systematic and it should have a control strategy and motion. By motion, it means that whenever a rule is selected to be applied while solving a problem it should cause the current state to be enhanced in the state space search. The control strategy should be designed like that the same rule is not be selected again and again, the rule selection should be based on the learning mechanism which is to be embedded in the system that can access the knowledge base.

The knowledge base is basically the collection of facts and rules. The facts act as the terminating statements for a problem which can be solved by applying various rules. So, to solve a particular problem we should be able to define the problem, its input, its output, the set of rules/facts, its cost of computation to find the efficiency of the system. There are various applications of AI like computer vision, creation of expert system, computational linguistic, Natural Language Processing (NLP), Machine Learning (ML), etc. Hence, an Artificial Intelligence (AI) method that exploits knowledge, which is used to characterize:

- The knowledge apprehensions generalizations that segment properties, are grouped together, rather than being acceptable distinct representation.
- It can be tacit by people who must make available it. For numerous programs, most of the data comes inevitably from interpretations.
- In numerous AI domains, how the people comprehend the similar people must source the knowledge to a program.
- It can be simply adapted to precise faults and reproduce changes in actual circumstances.
- It can be extensively used even if it is inadequate or imprecise.
- It can be used to aid stunned its own issues or problems by serving to slender the variety of options.

## Data Mining

In general terms, Data Mining is a process to finding several new patterns in huge collection of data sets using numerous techniques like classification, clustering (Tyagi &Tyagi, 2014), regression, etc. to predict future trends (see figure 1). In old days (from 1990 to 2010), data mining techniques was used quite a lot. But, when the revolution in smart technology enters, a lot of data is being collected at server side (for all organisations). In other words, data mining was used in past decades to discover hidden pattern/ information/ unknown facts from a data. These hidden patterns play an essential role in increasing profit for organisation. On the other hand, a lot of data has been produced by several (integration of internet connected devices together) Internet of Things (via machine to machine/ device to device communication). But available traditional data mining tools were not sufficient to handle this data or finding hidden patterns. So, a new term "Machine Learning" was created by Arthur Samuel (Anderson, 1987) and the definition of Machine Learning as "ML is a field of study that gives computers the capability to learn without being explicitly programmed". Today's era the domain of Machine learning is being used

*Figure 1. An overview of tasks and main algorithms in data mining*

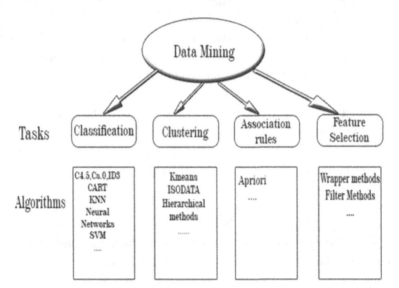

in several applications like e-healthcare, retail, defence, etc., to make some useful decision (prediction). For that, it works on indicative based learning, instance based learning, neural network (i.e., based supervised, unsupervised and semi-supervised learning) (refer figure 3).

In recent days (or in the past decade), data mining technique have been used in analysing of data. Generally, Data mining can be directed or undirected data mining. The data mining techniques based on directed approach extracts the data from the past records to detect the existing patterns that gives a particular framework for the outcome of the problem which includes clustering, regression, prediction, classification etc. Whereas, the undirected data mining extracts the data through the similar records for detecting the patterns that are hidden using the association rules, clustering etc.

Generally, Data Mining never aspect for precise goal, but it continuously emphases on extracting novel or hidden knowledge considering semantics. Data mining is achieved on following kinds of databases, i.e., Relational databases, Advanced Data bases, Data warehouses, and material repositories, Object-oriented concepts and object-relational databases,, Heterogeneous with legacy databases, Transactional and Spatial databases (considering space), Multimedia with streaming database, Text mining, Text based data storage, and Web information mining (Tyagi, 2019). So, Data Mining techniques can be summarized as:

- **Classification:** This technique classifies the data based on different classes. It is mainly used to invent the class tag for new samples of data.
- **Clustering:** Clustering analysis technique to identify data similarities by projecting the data on n-dimensional space.
- **Regression:** Regression analysis finds the relationship between variables by identifies the possibility of a definite variable, given the existence of additional variables.
- **Rules based on Association:** This technique creates the connotation between diverse items in the system of rules. It determines a concealed pattern in the data set.
- **Outlier recognition:** This technique is used to uncover the unexpected pattern or unexpected behavior from the dataset. It is used in several areas/domain, such as invasion detection, deception or fault uncovering, etc. Alternative name for outlier recognition is outlier investigation or outlier mining.
- **Sequential based Patterns:** It works on transactional data bases and assistances to determine the like patterns or drifts occur in transaction data sets for firm passé of time.

In conclusion, Data Mining is all round amplification the precedent and envisaging the prospect based on analysis. It aids in mining of treasured information from huge volume of data. It is the method of mining knowledge from data. Data mining (Guleria & Sood, 2019; Bathela, 2018) (term introduced by Gregory Piatetsky-Shapiro, in KDD-1989 workshop, as "knowledge discovery in databases" first workshop of same topic) includes Business Considerate, Data Considerate, Data Grounding, Exhibiting, Progression, and Distribution. Some of significant Data mining techniques are: Categorization, Classification, Clustering, Regression, Association rules, Outlier analysis, and Sequential patterns (as shown is figure 1). For implementation, the protuberant data mining tools used are Weka, R Tool and Oracle server based Data mining. Data mining technique benefits organisations/ companies to get knowledge-based information to progress their revenue (with reference to their products). The bid of data mining techniques has been implemented in numerous businesses such as insurance, education, communication, manufacturing, banking, retail, ecommerce, service providers and many more.

## Machine Learning

Machine learning algorithms are frequently characterized as supervised or unsupervised. Supervised algorithms require a data analyst or scientist with machine learning techniques aids to run both effort and anticipated outcome. Further, to furnish the response about the correctness of estimates while training the algorithm.

*Figure 2. Process of machine learning*

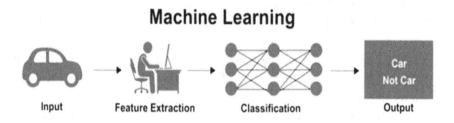

Data Scientists works on extracting the features that will help in prediction. The feature extraction then leads to the training of data set so that the system designed can learn to give the desired output. This needs deep learning which is based on unsupervised learning techniques that come under the umbrella of neural network. The unsupervised learning techniques are used in many applications like image recognition, natural language generation, computational linguistic etc.

Hence, figure 2 discusses the method of machine learning, i.e., in Machine Learning (ML) is done using past data (including human intervention), for example, IBM Watson, Google search algorithm, email spam filer, etc. Whereas, figure 3 explains machine learning algorithms in terms of inductive based learning, instance based learning, genetic algorithms, neural networks and Bayesian approaches.

Hence in general, Machine learning is a subdivision of artificial intelligence, where as deep learning is a subdivision of machine leaning (Tyagi, 2019). Whereas data mining are tools or techniques used in old days to refine or process data, but fails to refine or process large amount of data (and different format of data), so we sued machine learning. Today various organizations like Google, Facebook etc.,

*Figure 3. Classification of main machine learning algorithms*

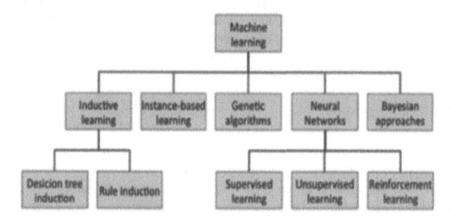

are using Machine Learning techniques to search particular data or recommend any post/ finding friends or finding respective picture of a user. Hence, the requirement of a computer vision is fulfilled by these three terms, i.e., by AI, ML, and DL. Now due to the recent development in technologies and integration of millions of internet of thing's devices, a lot of data is being generated everyday (known as Big Data). This is required to analysis for improving growth of several organizations or in applications like e-healthcare. Here, data mining or machine learning techniques/ algorithms used to analysis this Big Data for producing a decision for future (or for prediction purpose). Hence, this section discusses about artificial intelligence, data mining and machine learning as introduction in brief. Now next section of this chapter will discuss several raised problems in artificial intelligence and machine learning.

## PROBLEMS WITH ARTIFICIAL INTELLIGENCE (AI) AND MACHINE LEARNING (ML)

There are numerous branches occur of Artificial Intelligence (AI), which are: Logical AI, Pattern detection, Common intellect Knowledge and interpretation, Ontology, Heuristics, Genetic Programming, etc. The mentioned branches are only some to be named here and AI does not restrict to only these but extends to many more. Moreover this, even all branches are not discovered yet, even though AI, ML and DL have several problems in it. Now some problem in AI (area-wise), ML is being discussed here as:

### Problems That Occur in Artificial Intelligence

Intelligence does not infer perfect considerate; every intellectual being has inadequate perception, retention and computation. AI looks to comprehend the computations essential from intellectual behaviour and to yield computer systems that revelation intellect. Characteristics of intelligence studied by AI comprise perception, communicational using human dialects, reasoning, planning, learning and retention. The following queries are to be well-thought-out before we move advancing:

- Fundamental norms about intelligence?
- Techniques used for problem solving using AI?
- How to model Level of human intelligence?
- When and How to realize that an intelligent program has been built?

To solve the above mentioned problems/issues AI can be amended a lot using machine learning and other methods in near future.

## Problems of Machine Learning

Deep learning techniques are in infancy stage. They require large amount of data-sets (properly structured and arranged) to provide precise answers to existing questions. An Organization occupied on a realistic machine learning appliance requires to devote time, assets, and take extensive threats. Artificial Neural Network (ANN) requires millions of parameter, whereas a training set (in ANN) uses millions of records (i.e., used as input for processing). While an association is accomplished of retention the training dataset sample and providing answers with 100 percent correctness, but this accurateness may become useless when we collect/ receive new data. This process is called over-fitting (or overtraining) and one popular limitation of deep learning techniques.

1.  **Problem based on Black Box:** The initial phase of machine learning fitted to moderately modest, superficial methods. For example, a tree algorithm based on decision acts firmly according to the convention its superior skilled it: "if something is oval and green, there is a probability P it is a cucumber". These forms were not very good at recognizing a cucumber in a image, but at slightest everybody knew how they effort. Deep Learning algorithms are diverse. They construct a hierarchical demonstration of data layers which them to construct their own perceptive. After analyzing this huge amount of data-sets, neural networks can discover how to identify cucumbers with good precision. But here the difficulty is that machine learning engineers/data scientists do not recognize "how they received these results"? In summary this problem is called a black box problem.

Artificial Intelligence controller appreciated the input (the data that the algorithm works) and the output (the resolution it makes). While the engineers are able to appreciate "how a single prediction was made"? Here, it is a lack of lack of transparency, interpretability. Generally, it is very complicated to appreciate "how the whole model works"? As discussed in, one of popular limitations of deep learning (a subset of AI and ML) is: we do not know that how a neural network reaches at a particular solution. It is impossible to look inside of it to see how it works (called black box problem). It is a major barrier in the growth of other AI applications like provides efficient formulas for medicine (in medical-care), or automatic assessment of credit rating. Now thing, what if an algorithm's analysis comes incorrect? How will a car producer explain the performance of the autopilot when a deadly calamity occurs? How will a bank reply a customer's grievance? By many researchers (which has done previously), we find that artificial intelligence causes fright and other unconstructive passion in people (or human-being). Most of the People are anxious of an object seeing and behaving "almost like a human" (i.e., this phenomenon is known as "uncanny valley").

2.  **Talent Deficit:** A data scientist can understand machine learning good but he/ she can not have sufficient knowledge of software engineering. Knowing every areas/ subject knowledge is a big problem now days. There are few (at the near end of 2017, there were approximate 300,000 researchers, educationist, academicians, practitioners, industrialist working with AI globally, according to). Apart that, who are skilled one require serious artificial intelligence research. For top companies like Google, Amazon, etc., machine learning engineers and data scientists are pinnacle precedence choices. In area of machine learning, there are lot of incentives and good salaries given to talented people who know how to work with machine learning. Several organisations are doing brain drain with the help of organising job fair, etc.

3.  **Data is Paid:** To train a machine learning prototype, we require massive data. However, it is not a difficulty anymore, since everybody can work to accumulate and process petabytes of information. While storage space may be inexpensive, it needs time to gather a enough quantity of data. But, retailing ready-sets of data is costly. There are also issues of a diverse nature. Preparing data after pre-processing for training of any algorithm is a complex task (takes a lot of time). Using algorithms like classification, clustering, regression, etc., we prepare meaningful data. Also, we require to accumulate data compilation methods and reliable formatting. Then, we have to decrease data with characteristic sampling, record sampling, or aggregating sampling. We require to divide the data and scaling of the same needs to be done. It is a composite task that requires highly knowledgeable engineers and time. So even if we have unlimited disk storage available, the process is too costly. On another side, if attempt to use individual data, people will begin facing extra challenges like leaking of their information/ knowledge (or defending their isolation), trust, protection, etc. Individual data and big data actions have also become more complicated, dangerous and expensive with the foreword of novel regulations defending individual data, like the well-known European General Data Protection Regulation (Mrakovic & Vojnomic, 2019), HIPAA (Marcos & Garcia, 2019; Benett & Verceler, 2018).

4.  **Based on Technology:** The Alphabet Inc. (former Google) bids TensorFlow, whereas Microsoft liaises with Facebook emerging Open Neural Network Exchange (ONNX). The systems constructed by them are overloaded with data generated in each business across the world. Although the environments created are novel like the very primary version of TensorFlow available in 2015 February, PyTorch, which is a remarkable library released in 2016. In

today's era of technology the solutions required for problem solving needs too much of efforts and contemplation to build a product and make it ready for release to the outside world. This requires time to achieve the promising and efficient results. In general, the development of the code for any machine language algorithm is also complex and needs intelligence so that the machine can perform the desired task. In addition to this the learning is also complex and it requires the coding in the form of layers which helps the machine to get trained to perform the task as required. Further, the working on AI project is a high hazard, high recompense innovativeness. We require to be persistent, plan prudently, reverence the challenges of advanced technology, and find people who really comprehend machine learning and are not demanding to vend and vacant ability.

Now days using machine learning-based strategies in computer vision is an extremely critical issue (due to rising of several critical challenges in ML). For example, object acknowledgment and image grouping, colossal advancement has been made in applying deep learning systems. Then again, there are a few discussions with regards to the explanations behind the high achievement of the profound learning-based techniques, and about the restrictions of these strategies. Hence, this section discusses several problems raised in AI and ML in the previous decade. Now next section will deal with some real world's examples with respect to AI and ML in detail.

## Artificial Intelligence and Machine Learning: Real World's Examples

Artificial Intelligence is a method of constructing a computer, a robot controlled by the computer, or software contemplates intelligently, similar to a human who can contemplate intelligently. As deliberated in preceding sections, area or field of Artificial Intelligence is firm to define, since it is used in many other domains now days. For example, Google (search engine which searches results as per user query), Wikipedia (used for getting outcomes in brief), etc. Artificial Intelligence (AI) is firm to define, because intelligence is firm to define in the primary place. Artificial Intelligence is not natural- living, it is a constructed machine made by human which is running on code. AI systems can make decisions that take into account numerous factors, such as how an individual brain functions (in dissimilar scenarios). In modest terms, "robot" is not a synonym for Artificial Intelligence. Artificial Intelligence is a reference to the software that establishes intelligence, however robots deduce a physical component, a shell which conveys out the decisions made by the AI engine overdue it. Not all AI desires a robot to carry out its functions, i.e., an AI desires to envisage an incident/decision earlier occurring, but not all robots desire accurate AI to power its functionality.

As we nurture and together this technology evolves, the definition of AI also gets variations. In fact, John McCarthy, who invented the term "Artificial Intelligence" in 1956 (Albert et. al., 2018), focussed that "as soon as it works, no one demands it AI anymore". Today's many of the rules- and logic-based systems that were earlier considered Artificial Intelligence are no extended classified as AI. In contrary, systems that analyse and detect patterns in data (using machine learning) are becoming a fragment of Artificial Intelligence. Hence, the level of AI can be fragmented down into three key categories.

1. **Artificial Narrow Intelligence:** Narrow AI (or weak AI) is the only method of Artificial Intelligence that humankind has attained so far. This is virtuous at performing a solitary task, such as playing chess or Go, making procurement suggestions, sales forecasts and weather predictions. Computer vision and computational linguistic are in the present stage narrow AI. Speech and image detection are narrow AI, even if their developments seem enthralling. Even Google's transformation engine, Self-driving car skill, etc., is a system of narrow AI. In over-all, narrow AI works within a very inadequate framework, and cannot take on errands beyond its field. Narrow AI (or weak AI) does not mean incompetence. On additional side, it is so decent at routine jobs, both physical and cognitive. It is narrow AI which is intimidating to substitute (or rather displace) numerous human jobs. And it is slight AI that can explore required patterns and associations from data that would take years for people to find. But, it is still not individual-level AI (i.e., contented/ part of Artificial General Intelligence).

2. **Artificial General Intelligence:** General AI (individual-level AI or robust AI) is the kind of Artificial Intelligence that can comprehend and reason its environment as an individual would. General AI has constantly been subtle. In the previous decades, we are using it in escalate the miracles, i.e., behind the individual brain or to know concealed patterns in individual brain. This is very hard to define (or achieve) each and every action of human being (how we perceive input the things form the environment, disguise between numerous unrelated opinions and memories) by general AI. Also, the competence of general AI is firm to define. Humans might not be able to process and work on data as fast as computers, but they can contemplate abstractly and design, resolve problems at a wide-ranging level without going into the specifics. They can revolutionize, come up with opinions and thoughts that have no superiority. Several inventions like ships, telescopes, telephone, concepts such as gaming,

graphics, e-mail, social media, and virtual reality, has been done by humans which cannot be done by computers. It is very firm to make a computer which can invent things that are not available which is possible only by human's by making the use of brain only.

3. **Artificial Super Intelligence:** According to a scholar from University of Oxford, AI expert Nick Bostrom, when AI develops much smarter than the best human brains in essentially each field, including technical creativity, general knowledge and social aids, we have attained Artificial Super Intelligence (ASI). ASI is even indistinct (vague) than AGI at this point. By some accounts, the remoteness between AGI and ASI is very short. It shall occur in few months, weeks, or maybe the blink of an eye and will continue at the speed of light. What happens then, no one (i.e., human-being) knows for sure. Some scientists such as Stephen Hawking see the development of full artificial intelligence as the potential end of humanity. Even in previous decades, several movies have made to show such reality/ on such incidents. On other side, Google's Demis Hassabis (founder of DeepMind, 2010), believe the shrewder AI gets, the improved humans will develop at saving the environment, curing illnesses, discover the universe, and at thoughtful themselves (Powel & Hodson, 2017).

Some other applications of Artificial intelligence are Expert System, Planning, learning, Machine Learning, probability based learning, computational linguistic, Theorem Proving, virtual reality, Symbolic Mathematics, animation, Game Playing, semantic similarity, Natural Language Processing, uncertainty dealing, Robotics, etc. Apart that, some applications of machine learning are weather forecasting, healthcare, sentiment analysis, fraud detection, and e-commerce, etc.

## TYPES OF ARTIFICIAL INTELLIGENCE AND MACHINE LEARNING ALGORITHMS

There are a lot of benefits of AI in in today's life for a human life. AI has reduced work load and increase productivity and serving better for good for humanity. In summary, AI is using several algorithms to serve or perform human's work. On the another side, some benefits of machine learning are powerful processing, better decision making and predication, quicker processing, accurate results/ decisions, affordable data management, inexpensive services to users and analysing complex (large) big data. Hence, such services or benefits are provided by using several learning algorithms like supervise, unsupervised and re-enforcement techniques. Each learning technique will be discussed in this section in detail (Horowitz, 2018).

## Artificial Intelligence Algorithms

Artificial Intelligences being used in an extensive range of applications today, for example, Google Search, Facebook's News Feed. Google Search practices AI to find or to give reply to individual query by searching among huge amount of data (on web i.e. WWW). Also, the News Feed practices machine learning to engrave every member's feed. For example, if any person stops reading or scrolling or liking a post posted by any friend, then using machine learning technique the News feed will show more activities related to that friend as compared to activities that were shown earlier. Any software used for any kind of machine learning needs the statistical and predictive analysis for detecting the hidden patterns in the dataset of the user and then further uses these patterns in feeding the news. AI and ML are also emerging as an array of applications in enterprise domain like customer relation management (CRM), supplier chain management (SCM), human resource management (HRM, business intelligence (BI) etc. CRM basically uses the machine learning models to read the emails for responding the sales team on time regarding the delivery of any product or service. BI uses the models of machine learning to identify the significant points in their business processes and decisions which can impact the profit of an organization. HRM uses the models of machine learning to detect the characteristics of their employees, their training, development program so that they work to the best of their knowledge. Machine learning algorithms/techniques also play an important role in automation like it creates the self- identifying and driving car to reduce man work/efforts. Neural Networks which include machine learning with deep learning helps in determining the optimal and rational solution/action for steering a car round the road to avoid any kind of accidents. This technology is called virtual assistant which is also gained by machine learning. Smart assistants combine numerous deep learning models to construe natural speech, fetch in appropriate context, i.e., similar to a user's personal plan or formerly defined predilections and take an accomplishment, like booking an aircraft or pulling up driving directions. Hence, AI practices all machine learning and deep learning technique to do any kind of processing. In AI some algorithms are A*, AO*, production, heuristic search, etc., but these algorithms are used to detect an optimal/rational solution. Apart that, AI uses all knowledge algorithms like supervised and unsupervised listed in figure 4. Also, it practices the significant deep learning techniques like Convolutional Neural Networks (CNNs), Back-propagation, Recurrent Neural Networks (RNNs), and Reinforcement Learning (RL).

*Figure 4. Structure of machine learning techniques and algorithms*

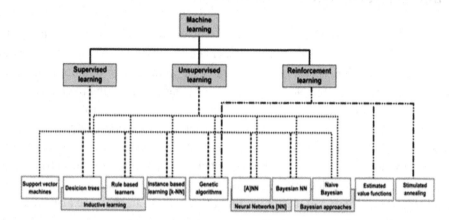

## Machine Learning Algorithms

As discussed there are many applications/ uses of machine learning techniques, hence there exists variety of machine learning algorithms. They vary from the fairly simple (less time complexity) to the highly complex (high time complexity). The class of machine learning algorithm includes categorizing an association, i.e., among two variables and using that association to make predictions about imminent data points. Some of the most commonly used techniques are:

- **Decision trees:** The decision tree is a hierarchical representation of a problem solving technique. It uses observations about firm actions and finds an optimal path for receiving an outcome that is desired.
- **K-means clustering:** This is type of clustering which forms the clusters depending on the value of k provided by the user. The cluster specifies a group of data points that are similar in characteristics.
- **Neural networks:** It includes machine leaning with deep learning methods that utilizes huge amounts of training data to detect association among various variables. This association helps in learning of the process which manages the incoming data in near future. The types of Neural Networks are Artificial Neural Network (ANN), Convolution Neural Network (CNN), Recursive Neural Network (RNN), Deep Neural Network (DNN) and Deep Belief Network (DBN).

- **Reinforcement Learning:** This area of deep learning includes methods which iterate over various steps in a process to get the desired results. Steps that yield desirable outcomes are content and steps that yield undesired outcomes are reprimanded until the algorithm is able to learn the given optimal process. In unassuming terms, learning is finished on its own or effort on feedback or content based learning.

In next section each machine learning algorithms (Burio et al. 2019) is been discussed in details (with respect to supervised learning and unsupervised learning).

## SUPERVISED LEARNING

### Decision Trees

A tree or hierarchical representation based on decision is a sustenance tool that aids the use of a tree-like hierarchical structure or form of decisions and their feasible cost, with chance-event effect, foundation costs, and utility role. From the analysis point of big business view, a decision tree is the least number of yes/no questions that one has to request, to measure the probability of creation an accurate decision. As a technique, it allows us to move in the direction of the difficulty in an ordered and methodical way to attain at a logical conclusion (Galley & Raje, 2012).

### Naive Bayes Classification

Naive Bayes classifiers are an intimate of straightforward probabilistic classifiers build on pertaining Bayes' theorem with vigorous (naive) eccentricity supposition among the characteristics. The characteristic representation is the equation, i.e., with P(A|B) which is known as posterior probability, P(B|A) which is called as likelihood, P(A) which is called as class prior probability, and P(B) which is called as predictor prior probability. Nearly of real world examples of Naive Bayes Classification are:

- Finding of an email marked as spam.
- Classifying the articles of news article based on technology, politics, or sports.
- To do sentiment analysis of a text which finds its polarity?
- Software based on face/image recognition.

## Ordinary Least Squares Regression

When we have consequence with statistics, we need linear regression for prediction. Here, least square is a technique for accomplishment linear regression. Linear regression is the mission of appropriating a straight line through a given set of points. There are manifold probable conducts to do this, so here "ordinary least squares" plan used, i.e., we can illustrate a line, and then for every of the data points, calculate the vertical remoteness among the point and the line, and append these up; the built-in line would be the solitary where this addition of distances is as minute as achievable (see figure 5).

## Logistic Regression

It is type of regression based on logistics (or logit regression) is a influential numerical way of modelling a binomial effect more than one explanatory variables. It is the method in which relationship among the categorical variable which is dependent and more than one independent variables by approximating probabilities using mathematical function based on logistic, which is the collective logistic distribution (see figure 6). It is used to approximate the values which are discrete in nature (Binary values like 0/1, yes/no, true/false) based on known set of autonomous variable (s). In simple words, it estimates the probability of result of an event by correcting data to a logic function. Note that it estimates the probability, its outcome values always lays in range of 0 and 1 (as expected) (Turner, 2019).

*Figure 5. Ordinary least squares regression*

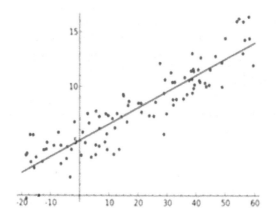

There are many real world applications of regressions such as:

- Scoring of credit
- accomplishment rates measurement of crusades used for marketing
- Recognising the revenues of a firm service or product
- Forecasting of weather

For example, if a puzzle needs to be solved and then there exist two possibilities wither the puzzle is solved or remains unsolvable. Now envisage that we are being specified with diverse range of puzzles/ quizzes in an effort to understand which subjects we are decent at. The result to this study would be like a trigonometry based problem of tenth grade and so we are likely to solve it to the extent of 70%. Whereas the question from history related to grade five then the possibility of solving reduces to 30% (Avati et. al., 2018).

## Support Vector Machines (SVM)

It is a dual classification algorithm. For example, for set of two kinds of points in a agreed N dimensional space, SVM constructs (N-1) dimensional hyper-plane to different the known N points into two groups. Suppose we have some points of two different types that can be separated linearly. By using SVM a straight line can be constructed which divides the two types of points as shown in figure 7.

*Figure 6. Regression with logistic concept*

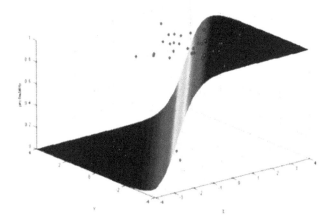

*Figure 7. Support vector machine (linear classification)*

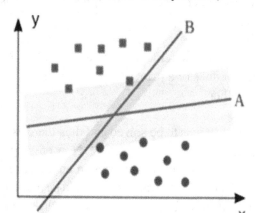

In the past decade, various complex problems have been solved efficiently with less time and space complexity using SVMs. The classification method used in SVM is highly remarkable and attained from the domain of data mining. In the algorithm of SVM the data items are plotted in N dimensional space where, N is the count of features that have been extracted from the data points. The SVM classification is shown in Figure 8.

In Figure 8 the data points are clustered and now the line is to be created that actually separates the data points so that the classification of two groups is done. The line constructed is the major division between the two types of data types to show two groups.

*Figure 8. Support vector machine showing classification*

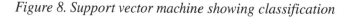

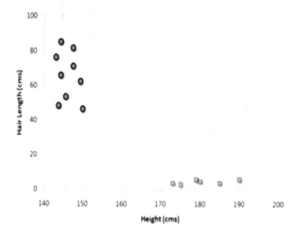

*Figure 9. Support vector machine showing two groups*

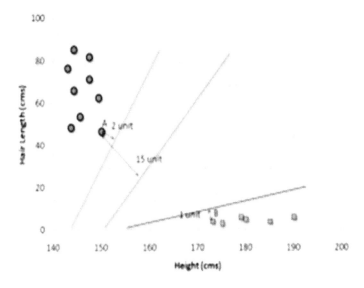

In figure 9, the black line is constructed which separates the data into two contrarily classified groups. This black line is the classifier created by SVM. Whereas, the red lines on either side of the black line is the one on which the user tests the classification done by SVM.

## kNN (k- Nearest Neighbors)

It can be used for the problems based on classification and regression. K-nearest neighbors is a modest algorithm that stores all accessible cases and classifies novel cases by a common voting of its neighbors k. The case being allocated to the class is most communal amongst its nearest neighbors k measured by a function based on distance. These distance functions can be Euclidean, Manhattan, Minkowski and Hamming distance. First three functions are continuous function and fourth one (Hamming) is based on categorical variables. If $K = 1$, then the case is simply allocated to the class of its nearest neighbor. It is important to note that choosing the value of K is also a challenging task while implementing the kNN modeling. Also, kNN is extensively used in industry problems based on classification.

*Figure 10. k- nearest neighbors (KNN)*

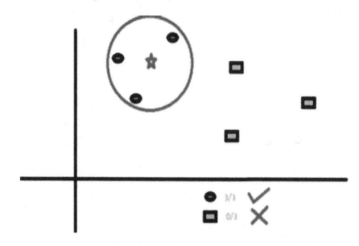

## k-Means

It is a unsupervised algorithm to resolve clustering based problem, i.e., it is using simple process to classify a assumed data-set through a firm number of clusters (assume k-clusters). It is to be noted that data points privileged a cluster may be homogeneous or heterogeneous (for peer groups).Figure 11 shows approximately shapes like ink blots. Using these shape and feast, the different clusters/ categorization can be determined which are present in a given data-set.

*Figure 11. An example of k-means showing constructed clusters*

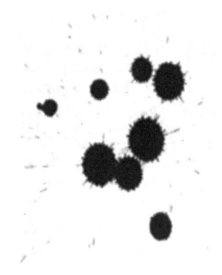

*Figure 12. Process of setting value of k used in k-means algorithm*

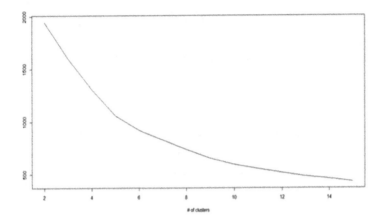

## Process Used by k-Means to Construct the Cluster

1. k-means input value of k which is number of points for each cluster also called as centroids.
2. Each data point constructs a cluster with the minimum distance from centroids, i.e., k clusters.
3. Each cluster centroid is determined based on existing members of the cluster. Here we have novel centroids.
4. After finding new centroids, step 2 and 3 are repeated. Again, the closest distance for each data point from new centroids is calculated using any distance formula and the data points get associated with new k-clusters. This process is repeated until merging occurs i.e. centroids remains fixed or does not change.

## Random Forest

Random Forest (RF) is based on assembly of decision trees thus called as "Forest". To classify a novel object based on characteristics, each tree gives arrangement, i.e., the tree "votes" for individual class. The forest selects the classification having the maximum votes covering all the trees available in the forest. In RF, each and every tree is constructed as follows:

1. If the numeral of cases in the training set is N, then sample of N cases is taken at random but with replacement. This sample will be the training set for growing the tree.

2.   If there are M input variables, a number m<<M is specified such that at each node, m variables are selected at random out of the M and the best split on these m is used to split the node. The value of m is held constant during the forest growing.

3.   Each tree is grown to the largest extent possible. There is no pruning.

## Ensemble Approaches

Ensemble approaches are learning algorithms that creates a classifier based on the set of data points and then categorize novel data points by considering a prejudiced vote of their forecasts. The innovative ensemble technique is based on averaging Bayesian, but more current established algorithms comprise error-correcting output coding.

## UNSUPERVISED LEARNING

Clustering is the undertaking of collecting a set of substances in a way that substances in the similar group (also called as cluster) are alike to each other as compared to those in previous groups. Every algorithm used for clustering algorithm is diverse as shown in figure 14.

*Figure 13. Ensemble learning algorithms (ELA)*

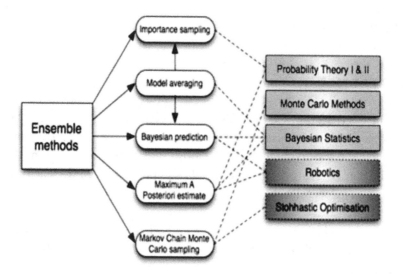

*Figure 14. Examples of clustering algorithms*

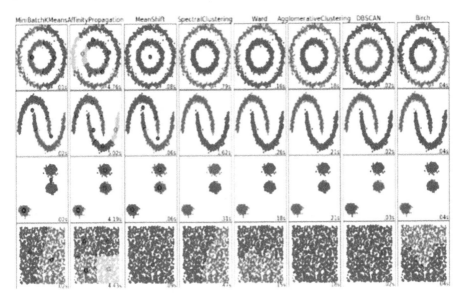

*Few algorithms used for Clustering are:* Connectivity-based, Centroid-based, Density and Probabilistic based, Dimensionality Reduction based, neural networks based, Deep Learning based.

## Principal Component Analysis (PCA)

It is a statistical process that utilizes an orthogonal alteration to change a set of annotations of probably associated variables into a dataset of standards of linearly non-associated variables are known as principal components as shown in figure 15.

Few of the appliances of PCA comprise compression of image/ videos, abridge data for relaxed learning, imagining etc. For all the applications the knowledge related to a domain is actually significant while selecting that the execution is to go frontward with PCA or still carried out with other available techniques. It is also found that PCA is not appropriate in cases where datasets are noisy i.e. the data points have elevated variance.

## Singular Value Decomposition (SVD)

It is a representation of actual matrix that is complex in nature, for example, m * n representing multiplication of two matrices m and n and the result is stored in matrix M, then the decomposition exist as $M = U\Sigma V$. In which U and V are the matrices are unitary and $\Sigma$ is the matrix which represents diagonal.

*Figure 15. Principal component analysis (PCA)*

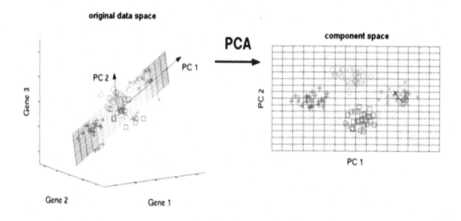

*Figure 16. Singular value decomposition (SVD)*

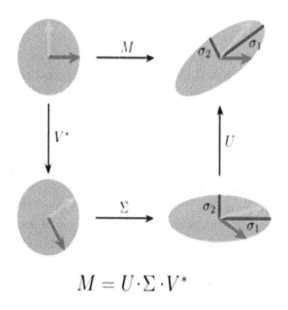

$$M = U \cdot \Sigma \cdot V^*$$

Generally, PCA is a modest appliance of SVD. In the field of computer vision, to identify and filter a face, PCA and SVD are used in order to signify faces as a linear mixture of "Eigen-faces", then dimensionality decrease is done, and then counterpart faces to individualities via modest techniques. This technique provides a modest way to identify any image as compared to other existing traditional or modern methods.

## Independent Component Analysis (ICA)

ICA is a numerical method for skimpy concealed factors that lie behind groups of random variables, dimensions, or signals. It defines a generative prototype for the experiential multivariate data, i.e., for a huge database of samples. In this prototype, the data variables are presumed to be linear combinations of approximately unidentified latent variables as shown in figure 17. The latent variables used are presumed to be non-Gaussian and communally independent (also known as independent elements of the experiential data).

Generally, ICA is also connected to PCA (like SVD). But, ICA is additionally influential method which is accomplished of detecting the underlying factors of emerged from various sources when the traditional methods does not provide the desired outcome. Today's ICA is used in numerous domains showing its appliances like digital formed images, document based, economic calculation sign and dimensions of psychometrics, etc.

*Figure 17. Independent component analysis (ICA)*

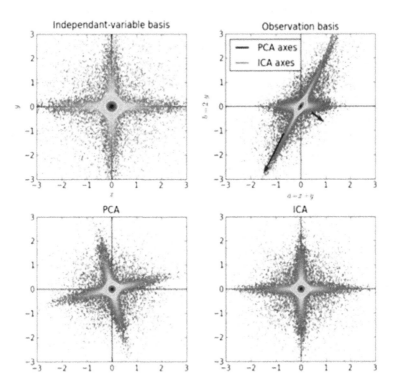

# HOW ARTIFICIAL INTELLIGENCE AND MACHINE LEARNING WILL INFLUENCE BUSINESS/ IT INFRASTRUCTURE IN FUTURE

Till now, we have been uses of AI and ML algorithms in various applications like medical-diagnosis, weather forecasting, etc. Using machine intelligence, cities, transportation, manufacturing, etc., are getting more productive (also smarter). Artificial Intelligence is also using its intelligence (in form of its subsets like machine learning and deep learning) in several uses cases like future of insurance, and future on market (e.g., social media market, e-commerce, integrating chat-bots, automation in industry (operation, accounting, payroll/ HR automation, etc.), business). Such industries/ areas are getting a huge growth with integration/ use of AI. The organisation/ company can use machine learning to up-sell the right product, to the right customer, at the right time. In simple words, machine learning is about understanding data and statistics, and Artificial Intelligence has to fulfil this demand using its intelligence (e.g., manufacturing of 1 million of BMW cars in one year using automation systems). As discussed in (Tyagi, 2019), Internet of Things (IoTs) and machine learning are going to change future, these are technologies which will be used together for produces prediction, i.e., IoTs will generate a lot of data (i.e., Big Data, and machine learning or artificial intelligence will make prediction for future (after applying efficient analysis methods/ tools).

Also in future, AI-assisted robots will be there to perform tasks or serve human being. In areas like medical-care, robots can help patient to move, live more as younger, etc. In general, Artificial intelligence is a type of automation where machines can "outwit people on every dimension". But, AI can make a major impact in the enterprise as discussed before also, i.e., particularly with any mission with adequate data that has a "set of inputs that map to a set of outputs". On another side, machine learning algorithms have been available since many decades (but got more attention in 20's century), they have also attained new popularity as Artificial Intelligence (AI). Hence, some future enhancements using machine intelligence (AI and ML together) will be like deeper personalization, self-driving cars, automatic translation, smarter investment opportunities, better medical diagnosis, number plate detection, instance segmentation, etc.

Today's in medical care system, we require patients at little risk for difficulties to outpatient conduct, preserving hospital beds and the consideration of medical staff. For that, scientists are recommending to use several algorithms to doctors. The neural network is giving far better results than any of the other methods. But, note that without the extra care of a patient, hospital's patient records may changes, i.e., outcomes could have been received different (called "explainability" problem). In summary, we do not want to create systems that aids us with medical dealings,

*Table 1. Undeveloped research issues in ML on big data*

| Elements | Parameters | Issues |
|---|---|---|
| **Big Data** | Volume | • cleaning and condensing big data<br>• Huge scale dispersed characteristic extraction<br>• Workflow organization and job development |
| | Velocity | • factual time online wisdom for streaming data |
| | Variety | • Multi-view knowledge for diverse multimedia data<br>• Multimedia neural semantic annotations |
| | Veracity | • Assessing data reliability<br>• information with changeable or denying data |
| | Value | • comprehensible ML for resolution support<br>• Multi-user supportive decision maintain based on big data testing |
| **User** | Labeling | • multitude sourced vigorous learning for real large scale data Annotation |
| | Assessment | • widespread assessment method for ML (e.g., usability-based method) |
| | Privacy | • confidentiality protecting dispersed ML |
| | User Interface | • envisaging big data<br>• intellectual user interfaces for interactive ML<br>• Declarative ML |
| **Domain** | Information | • integrating general field knowledge (e.g., ontology, first-order logic (FOL), business rules) in ML |
| **System** | Infrastructure | • Novel infrastructure that seamlessly afford decision sustain based on factual time investigation of huge amount of assorted and unpredictable data.<br>• wide-ranging big data middleware |

transportation possibilities and profitable opportunities to detect out after the statistic that these systems do not actually work, i.e., they give/ make errors when they needed most (in cases of human lives and happiness). Hence, a lot of research is required (also on-going) by research community to fix that problem. Table 1 provides some undeveloped research concern in machine earning with big data.

In current following are the areas where subset of AI like ML and Deep Learning is being applied. Some of these areas are included here:

- **Computer Vision:** AI is used for dissimilar applications as vehicle plate identification on which number is written and also in facial recognition.
- **Information Retrieval:** ML and DL learning techniques are used in applications like searching by search engines, text matching and search by finding similarity, and image filtering.

- **Marketing:** ML learning technique is used in automated email marketing and target identification.

- **Diagnosis in medical domain:** ML and DL learning techniques are used in this area, i.e., in applications like cancer recognition and anomaly recognition, etc.

- **Computational Linguistic:** To identify handwritten languages by machine (using its intelligence), we refer machine learning and deep learning techniques.

- **Others:** ML and for applications like opinion mining, sentiment analysis, online Advertising, etc.

In summary, Artificial intelligence, is intelligence done by machines to learn "how a human being things and react"? In simple words, it creates some intelligent machines which work and react like humans. Hence, AI is used in several applications like Speech recognition, Text matching, semantic similarity, Learning, computational linguistic, robotics, Planning, and Problem solving, etc. Now in next section, this chapter will be concluded with some essential remarks.

## CONCLUSION

This chapter discusses about Artificial Intelligence and its sub-related areas, algorithms and their uses in various applications like Natural image processing, Speech recognition, Learning, Planning, and Problem solving, etc. In this chapter, we find that AI is a technique which enables machines to mimic human behavior, for example, IBM Deep Blue chess, and Electronic game character. Whereas, Machine Learning (ML) is a technique which uses statistical methods, enabling machines to learn from their past data (including human intervention), for example, IBM Watson, Google search algorithm, email spam filer, etc. On another side, deep learning (also a sub-set of AI) is a subset of ML composing algorithms that allow a model to train itself (without human intervention) and perform tasks for example, Alpha Go, Natural Speech Recognition, etc. Hence, the aim of this chapter is to study algorithms/ techniques used in artificial intelligence and machine learning. It also focuses on the application areas like virtual reality, image processing, robotics, automation, weather forecasting, etc. In modest terms, this chapter also explains the goals of a computer vision. This chapter aims to showcase the latest advances and trends in computer vision/ AI and machine learning algorithms for various applications. This chapter shows that methods involved in AI usages in machine learning techniques, which are analogous to data mining and predictive modelling, as both the techniques require searching and mining through data to look for hidden patterns and regulating program actions accordingly. Hence, machine learning techniques include cases like fraud discovery, spam sieving, network security threat recognition, predictive conservation and constructing news feeds, etc.

Apart above discussion, we also found that un-scalability and centralization, non-dynamic and uniform data structure are the biggest limitation in existing analysis algorithms (supported by ML, and DL learning techniques). Using this big data (collected from Internet of things/ machine communication), data mining, machine learning techniques are able to identify hidden trends and associations. Several benefits of AI are: providing cost reduction, quicker, better verdict making, new goods and services, product recommendation, and fraud discovery. AI uses data mining, machine learning techniques to make machine intelligent which used metrics to measure performance of respective machine (or used algorithms). Data mining algorithms are measures using accuracy, reliability, and usefulness. Some other evaluation metrics for data mining tasks are: cross-validation, holdout technique, arbitrary sub-sampling, k-fold cross authentication, leave one out technique, bootstrap, confusion matrix, Receiver Operating Curves (ROC). Also, there are several metrics for association rule mining like Support, Confidence, Lift, Succinctness and Conviction. Some metrics like confusion matrix, Receiver Operating Curves (ROC), precision call etc., are also used in machine learning techniques.

## REFRENCES

Albert, J. R. G., Orbeta, A. C. Jr, Paqueo, V. B., Serafica, R. B., Dadios, E. P., Culaba, A. B., & Bairan, J. C. A. C. (2018). *Harnessing government's role for the Fourth Industrial Revolution*. Academic Press.

Anderson, C. W. (1987, January). Strategy learning with multilayer connectionist representations. In *Proceedings of the Fourth International Workshop on Machine Learning* (pp. 103-114). Morgan Kaufmann. doi:10.1016/B978-0-934613-41-5.50014-3

Avati, A., Jung, K., Harman, S., Downing, L., Ng, A., & Shah, N. H. (2018). Improving palliative care with deep learning. [PubMed]. *BMC Medical Informatics and Decision Making*, *18*(4), 122. doi:10.118612911-018-0677-8

Bathaee, Y. (2018). The artificial intelligence black box and the failure of intent and causation. *Harvard Journal of Law & Technology*, *31*(2), 889.

Bennett, K. G., & Vercler, C. J. (2018). When Is Posting about Patients on Social Media Unethical "Medutainment"? [PubMed]. *AMA Journal of Ethics*, *20*(4), 328–335. doi:10.1001/journalofethics.2018.20.4.ecas1-1804

Buriro, A., Crispo, B., & Conti, M. (2019). AnswerAuth: A bimodal behavioral biometric-based user authentication scheme for smartphones. *Journal of Information Security and Applications*, *44*, 89–103.

Gallege, L. S., & Raje, R. R. (2017, April). Parallel methods for evidence and trust based selection and recommendation of software apps from online marketplaces. In *Proceedings of the 12th Annual Conference on Cyber and Information Security Research* (p. 4). ACM. doi:10.1145/3064814.3064819

Guleria, P., & Sood, M. (2014). Data Mining in Education: A review on the knowledge discovery perspective. *International Journal of Data Mining & Knowledge Management Process*, *4*(5), 47–60. doi:10.5121/ijdkp.2014.4504

Horowitz, M. C. (2018). *Artificial Intelligence, International Competition, and the Balance of Power*. Texas National Security Review.

Kumar, A., Tyagi, A. K., & Tyagi, S. K. (2014). Data Mining: Various Issues and Challenges for Future A Short discussion on Data Mining issues for future work. *International Journal of Emerging Technology and Advanced Engineering*, *4*(1), 1–8.

Marcos-Pablos, S., & García-Peñalvo, F. J. (2019). Technological Ecosystems in Care and Assistance: A Systematic Literature Review. [PubMed]. *Sensors (Basel)*, *19*(3), 708. doi:10.339019030708

Mraković, I., & Vojinović, R. (2019). Maritime Cyber Security Analysis–How to Reduce Threats? *Transactions on Maritime Science*, *8*(1), 132–139.

Powles, J., & Hodson, H. (2017). Google DeepMind and healthcare in an age of algorithms. [PubMed]. *Health and technology*, *7*(4), 351–367. doi:10.100712553-017-0179-1

Sergeev, A., & Del Balso, M. (2018). *Horovod: fast and easy distributed deep learning in TensorFlow*. arXiv preprint arXiv:1802.05799

Turner, J. (2019). Controlling the Creators. In *Robot Rules* (pp. 263–318). Cham: Palgrave Macmillan; doi:10.1007/978-3-319-96235-1_7

Tyagi, A. K. (2019). Building a Smart and Sustainable Environment using Internet of Things. In *Proceedings of International Conference on Sustainable Computing in Science, Technology and Management (SUSCOM)*. Amity University Rajasthan, Jaipur - India. Available at SSRN: https://ssrn.com/abstract=3356500 or http://dx.doi.org/ doi:10.2139srn.3356500

Tyagi & Rekha. (2019). Machine Learning with Big Data. In *Proceedings of International Conference on Sustainable Computing in Science, Technology and Management (SUSCOM)*. Amity University Rajasthan. Available at SSRN: https://ssrn.com/abstract=3356269 or http://dx.doi.org/ doi:10.2139srn.3356269

Wei, W. A. N. G. (2018). *Prediction of protein-ligand binding affinity via deep learning*. Academic Press.

## KEY TERMS AND DEFINITIONS

**Artificial Intelligence:** Artificial intelligence (AI) deals with the creating of machines with the mind. The creation of machines that can work better than human.

**Computer Vision:** AI is used for dissimilar applications as vehicle plate identification on which number is written and also in facial recognition.

**Data Mining:** In general terms, data mining is a process of finding several new patterns in a huge collection of data sets using numerous techniques like classification, clustering, regression, etc. to predict future trends.

**Information Retrieval:** ML and DL learning techniques are used in applications like searching by search engines, text matching and search by finding similarity, and image filtering.

**Machine Learning:** Machine learning (ML) is the branch of computer science that comes under the umbrella of Artificial Intelligence. ML deals with the learning of machines to perform various tasks that can be done better than human beings.

**Neural Networks:** It includes machine learning with deep learning methods that utilizes huge amounts of training data to detect association among various variables.

**Reinforcement Learning:** This area of deep learning includes methods which iterates over various steps in a process to get the desired results. Steps that yield desirable outcomes are content and steps that yield undesired outcomes are reprimanded until the algorithm is able to learn the given optimal process. In unassuming terms, learning is finished on its own or effort on feedback or content-based learning.

# Chapter 9
# Application of Content-Based Image Retrieval in Medical Image Acquisition

**Vinayak Majhi**

 https://orcid.org/0000-0003-0805-1219
*North-Eastern Hill University, India*

**Sudip Paul**

 https://orcid.org/0000-0001-9856-539X
*North-Eastern Hill University, India*

## ABSTRACT

*Content-based image retrieval is a promising technique to access visual data. With the huge development of computer storage, networking, and the transmission technology now it becomes possible to retrieve the image data beside the text. In the traditional way, we find the content of image by the tagged image with some indexed text. With the development of machine learning technique in the domain of artificial intelligence, the feature extraction techniques become easier for CBIR. The medical images are continuously increasing day by day where each image holds some specific and unique information about some specific disease. The objectives of using CBIR in medical diagnosis are to provide correct and effective information to the specialist for the quality and efficient diagnosis of the disease. Medical image content requires different types of CBIR technique for different medical image acquisition techniques such as MRI, CT, PET Scan, USG, MRS, etc. So, in this concern, each CBIR technique has its unique feature extraction algorithm for each acquisition technique.*

DOI: 10.4018/978-1-7998-0182-5.ch009

## INTRODUCTION

Content-based image retrieval (CBIR) is a handy Image searching system that searches for images by image content. Image content means the color, shape, texture, or other information which can get from an image directly. It has been one of the most exciting areas of research in the field of computer vision science since last ten years. CBIR is also known as query by image content (QBIC) and content-based visual information retrieval (CBVIR) (Karthikram & Parthiban, 2014). This application is a solution to the image retrieval problem, the problem of finding an image in a vast database. Nowadays, in medical system images are widely used like Magnetic Resonance Imaging (MRI), Computed Tomography (CT) Scan, Positron Emission Tomography (PET), Ultrasonography (USG). CBIR considered as one of the most efficient ways to access the visual data. In the year of 2002, The Radiology Department of the University Hospital of Geneva generates near about 12,000 pictures per day. The aggregate sum of cardiologic picture information created in the Geneva University Hospital was around 1 Terabyte (TB) in 2002 (Müller, Michoux, Bandon, & Geissbuhler, 2004). In the case of the centralized medical system in any Health organization, a considerable amount of image is scanned and stored every day. To retrieve this data, CBIR is a very efficient process. It analyzes the image by color, texture, shape and space relationship of objects, etc. rather than keywords, tags and set up feature vectors of an image(Müller et al., 2004).

Standard Boolean based queries used for searching purpose in any case, with the rise of enormous picture databases, the conventional content-based inquiry experiences the accompanying constraints: Manual tag require a lot of time and are costly to execute (Waoo, N., Kashyap, R., & Jaiswal, A., 2010). Increasing numbers of Images in a database proliferates. It isn't practical to physically explain all tags of the picture content for a large number of pictures because of the following reasons (Erickson, 2009).

1. Manual tags neglect to manage the disparity of subjective observation. The textual portrayal isn't adequate for delineating personal inspection. Ordinarily, a medicinal picture more often than not, contains a few attributes, which pass on specific data. In any case, extraordinary radiologists can do distinctive translations for an obsessive zone. To catch all information, ideas, considerations, and affections for the substance of any pictures is practically unthinkable.

2. The contents of medical images are hard to be adequately descriptive in words. For instance, irregular natural shapes can only with significant effort communicated in textual structure. However, individuals may hope to look for pictures with comparable substance dependent on the models they give.

These issues limit the plausibility of text-based look for medicinal image recovery. The improvement of CBIR is required to upgrade the massive development in the volume of images and the broad application in therapeutic fields. In the late 1970s, models were first commented on with text and afterward sought to utilize a text-based methodology from conventional database management frameworks. It is troublesome for the traditional text-based techniques to help an assortment of subordinate assignment inquiries. This procedure likewise neglected to keep up the massive size of the database. Along these lines, this framework did not work effectively. In 1992, the National Science Foundation of the United States suggested a productive and natural approach to speak to and list visual data. It based on specific properties of the image which has a place with that image. The expression "Content-Based Image Retrieval" may begin in this period. IBM brought the central business arrangement of CBIR; they named it as Query by Image Content (QBIC) (Flickner et al., 1995). In this framework shading rates, shading format, texture, shape, area, color format, color gradient, and different keywords utilized (Datta, Joshi, Li, & Wang, 2008).

All through the improvement of the mechanical framework, there are a few strategies for CBIR have created. Every single frame explicitly created for its seeking reason. An image can be characterized in numerous ways, as per the mechanism, we can recover different information from those images (Shapiro & George, 2002). For this reason, distinctive kinds of image recovery mechanisms utilized like,

- Pattern-Based Image Retrieval System.
- Texture-Based Image Retrieval System.
- Colour Based Image Retrieval System.
- Shape-Based Image Retrieval System.

All these methods have its unique characteristics to identify particular feature form an unknown image. Features of an image are like the key to the CBIR system. But it is the same image then there may be different types of elements based on the information on a particular model. We can consider only a single specific type to identify a set of image matching with its color, pattern, texture, or shape, and we will try to match that identifier for unknown images. Here we will discuss these four primary CBIR technique and its mechanism of identifying a particular feature based query system.

## Pattern-Based Image Retrieval System

Pattern-based methods are seeking reason based on the apparent element of an image. In the cutting edge times, an object tracking and segmentation forms are most crucial job in Pattern Based Image Retrieval (PBIR) system because these two procedures bewildered the fundamental issues of Content-Based Image Retrieval (CBIR) framework. It is likewise an essential advance in image pattern acknowledgment, image investigation, and Personal Computer (PC) vision methods (Dharani & Aroquiaraj, 2017). Image segmentation is the way toward assigning a digital image into different portions or sets of pixels (Kaur & Kaur, 2014).

It considers chiefly the designs of the image for finding a comparable gathering of pictures from the various image database (Dharani & Laurence Aroquiaraj, 2017). The basic of PBIR system is to extract feature from the query image. The extracted feature then use as a reference feature for finding the pattern from the Image database. The following block diagram will show the methods of PBIR system.

## Texture-Based Image Retrieval System

Texture defines different properties like smoothness, coarseness, and consistency. From the nearness of solitary shading, auxiliary homogeneity can't be delineated and may require different powers communication inside a locale. To recognize comparable shading objects like the sky, grass, and so forth. Texture similitude is the better alternative. Be that as it may, useful texture examination is tough to accomplish. Texture recovery performed by portioning an image whose texture investigation must do into several texture districts and after that play out every locale examination independently however appropriate segmentation isn't simpler to accomplish and because of this image recovery procedure may influence (Mehta, Mishra, & Sharma, 2011).

Recovery based on different texture sections is typically delicate with over and under segmentation. On the one hand, spatial changes in texture appearance can make unique textures be part into little portions that are over-segmentation. Then again, the segmentation calculation can erroneously consolidate together small areas of various surfaces is under-segmentation (Kashyap, R. and Tiwari, V., 2017).

*Figure 1. Block diagram of PBIR system*

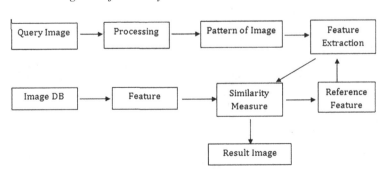

With these issues may happen when some texture in the image, albeit critical in size when joined together, is dissipated over the image and in this way lost. A case of this wonder is an aerial perspective on the town in a luxuriously vegetated territory, in which both vegetation and building are comprised of various yet little texture patches. A single point has no texture. In case the surface is described in the repeat territory, the texture information of a spot in the image is passed on by the repeat content of a zone of it. Gabor limits are usually used in texture examination to get this information. There is also verification that clear cells in the primary visual cortex can exhibit by Gabor limits tuned to recognize unmistakable presentations and scales on a log-polar system (Rubner & Tomasi, 1999).

The process of Texture-Based Image Retrieval System has two distinct steps (Regniers, Da Costa, Grenier, Germain, & Bombrun, 2013).

1.  Feature extraction: the step where each fix of the database defined by a limited arrangement of descriptors called features.
2.  Similarity measurement: consists in measuring the similarity between two images based on the set of textural features.

The varieties of appearance both inside a similar texture and crosswise over various surfaces in an image, both individual textures and multi-textured models best depicted by appropriations of descriptors, instead of by personal descriptors (Kashyap, R., & Gautam, P., 2016). It is proposed a compelling usage of this standard

*Figure 2. Texture-based image retrieval. Image searching by a zebra texture from the database (a) Zebra texture block extracted from an image of the image contains zebra (b) Matched images at least 10% of same texture (Rubner & Tomasi, 1999)*

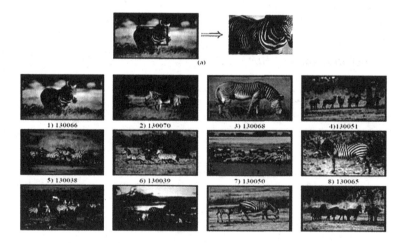

by supplanting image segmentation with a grouping of comparative texture descriptors into reduced, however nitty-gritty and adaptable texture marks (Regniers et al., 2013). Figure 2: Texture-based image retrieval. Image searching by a zebra texture from the database (a) Zebra texture block extracted from an image of the image contains zebra (b) Matched images at least 10% of same texture (Rubner & Tomasi, 1999)

## Colour Based Image Retrieval System

In regular CBIR framework, the visual substance of the pictures in the database is extricated and described by future multidimensional components. Colors generally utilized in Image Retrieval System. Figures digital map might consider as a two-dimensional array where the exhibit cells relate to the picture pixels and the qualities put away in the cells to the estimations of color-intensity, in the event of a grayscale picture. A color picture comprises of three single-color images that compare to the colors Red, Green, and Blue by making capacity from the discrete estimations of intensity to the number of pixels with the personal esteem (Varshney & Soni, 2011).

## Colour Histogram

Colour is the most natural element of a picture and to portray colors by, and large histograms embraced. Histogram techniques have the benefits of quickness, the low interest of memory space. Color highlights are the most vital components empowering human to perceive pictures. For arranging pictures, color highlights can give amazing data, and they utilized for picture recovery, so color based picture recovery is generally utilized strategy. Color highlights of the pictures are commonly spoken to by color histograms. Before using color histograms, be that as it may, we have to choose and measure a color space demonstrate and pick a separation metric (Luo & Crandall, 2006). Histogram also applied into two different color models, one is Red, Green, Blue (RGB) color model, and another is Hue, Saturation, Value (HSV) color model. Both contain the information about the color of an image, but the type of storing the data is different.

Histogram can also be categorized into two different types one is Local, and another is Global color histogram — the comparisons of these two histograms given below.

## Shape-Based Image Retrieval System

The shape is an essential and most dominant element utilized for image classification, ordering, and recoveries. Shape data removed using the histogram of edge recognition methods for shape highlight extraction is a primary descriptor, Fourier descriptor, format coordinating, quantized descriptors, and so forth. Different procedures for

*Table 1. Colour model comparison*

| RGB Model | HSV Model |
|---|---|
| Red, Green, Blue, these three primary color used | Image attribute of Hue saturation and value used |
| Most easy to extract feature. | Compared to RGB quite challenging to extract feature. |
| Each pixel value contains 0 – 255 different gradient of each primary color so total 16777216 color variation can do. | The hue value range from 0-255. |

*Table 2. Local and global color histogram comparison (Narwade Manoorkar & Kumar, 2016)*

| Local Colour Histogram | Global Colour Histogram |
|---|---|
| To generate a color histogram, we need to segmentize the image into different color blocks. | In the case of the global color histogram, the whole image analyzed with single color histogram. |
| In the comparison between two images, we consider histogram to calculate the quadric distance between the region of one image and the same region in the other image. | The quadric distance is measured using a single color histogram. |

*Figure 3. Flowchart of color based image retrieval system (Chaudhari & Patil, 2012)*

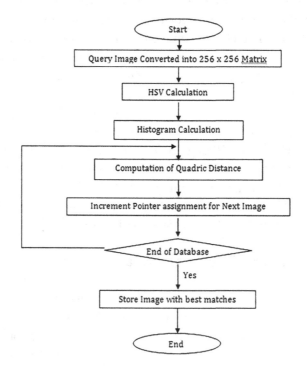

*Figure 4. RGB and HSV conversion of the same Image (Narwade Manoorkar & Kumar, 2016)*

shape includes removal are a rudimentary descriptor, Fourier descriptor, format coordinating, quantized descriptors, and so forth. Shrewd edge location beats a considerable lot of the more up to date calculations that have created in the business (Shirazi, Khan, Umar, Naz, & AlHaqbani, 2016).

The capacity to recover by shape is maybe the most apparent necessity at the fundamental level. In contrast to the surface, the way is a genuinely all-around defined idea, and there is extensive proof that their shape perceives regular articles. Various highlights usual for article shape (yet free of size or introduction) processed for each item personality inside each put away the image. Queries are then replied by registering a similar arrangement of highlights for the question image and recovering those put-away images whose highlights most intently coordinate those of the inquiry. Two primary sorts of the shape include generally utilized, worldwide highlights, for example, perspective proportion, circularity and minute invariant and neighborhood highlights, for example, sets of sequential limit fragments. Elective strategies proposed for shape coordinating have included versatile twisting of formats, the examination of directional histograms of edges separated from the image, and shocks, skeletal portrayals of item shape that can look at utilizing graph matching techniques. Queries to shape recovery frameworks are figured either by distinguishing a model image to go about as the inquiry or as a user-drawn sketch (Marques, 2001).

There are two types of the procedure has been explicitly completed offline and online. In the offline process, Image highlight database has built through one of the predominant element of the image, for example, shape extraction by utilizing Canny Edge Detection (CED) calculation. In the online procedure, Graphical User Interface (GUI) for the client cooperation has created through which client can associate with the framework for the recovery of their ideal images from the image database. For the recovery process, the likeness correlation strategy has done between online client inquiry image and disconnected image include a database(Tiwari S., Gupta R.K., & Kashyap R.,2019). After examination, coming about images are filed and recovered dependent on their position (Shirazi et al., 2016).

*Figure 5. Flowchart of offline and online process of shape-based image retrieval (Ramamurthy & Chandran, 2011).*

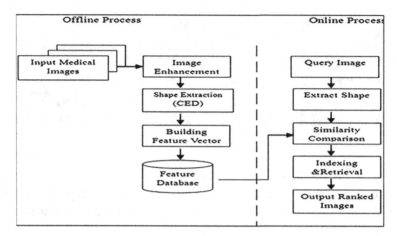

Algorithm: For detecting edges using Canny Edge Detection Algorithm (Ramamurthy & Chandran, 2011)

**Step 1:** Smoothing: Image smoothing with a two dimensional Gaussian. Much of the time the calculation of a two dimensional Gaussian is expensive, so two one dimensional Gaussians approximate it.

**Step 2:** Finding Gradients: Take the gradient of the image this shows changes in intensity, which demonstrates the nearness of edges. It gives two outcomes, the angle in the x bearing and the slope in their heading.

**Step 3:** Non-maximal suppression: Edges will occur at points where the gradient is at a maximum. The magnitude and direction of the slope computed at each pixel.

**Step 4:** Edge Threshold: The method of the threshold used by the Canny Edge Detector referred to as "hysteresis." It makes use of both a high threshold and a low threshold.

**Step 5:** Thinning: Using interpolation to find the pixels where the norms of the gradient are local maximum.

The following Figure (a) and (b) depicts the results of before and after feature extraction of the work for a brain image.

*Figure 6. Sample edge detected brain image (Ramamurthy & Chandran, 2011)*

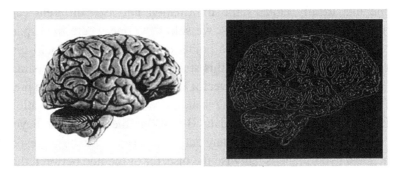

## Use of Machine Learning in CBIR System

The execution of CBIR has been restricted by a few issues, for example, the subjectivity of human recognition, comparability of a visual component, and semantic inquiry whole issues. To take care of these issues, intuitive pertinence input, which includes communication among human and framework, was presented. Pertinence input is a directed dynamic learning procedure, which utilizes the positive and negative criticism models from the clients to improve framework execution (Kashyap, R., & Piersson, A. D., 2018). For a given inquiry, the framework initially recovers a rundown of positioned images as indicated by the predefined closeness measurements. Like this, the client denotes the recovered images as relevant or irrelevant to the inquiry. Consequently, the framework will refine the recovery results dependent on the input and present another rundown of pictures to the client. This procedure will experience a few cycles until the client is happy with the recovery result. Even though importance criticism plans to diminish the issues of CBIR, its execution is as yet not attractively attributable to the impediments of the standard pertinence input of CBIR, for example, question refinement band re-weighting. These issues incorporate irregularity of preparing set issue, classification issue, limited data from client issue, and in-adequate preparing set issue. To understand unevenness preparing set issue, we present a short detail of three machine learning procedures, Support Vector Machines (SVMs), additive fuzzy systems, and spectral graph clustering (Saxena & Shefali, 2018).

## SUPPORT VECTOR MACHINES

Support Vector Machines (SVM) belongs to the family of machine-learning Algorithm that utilized for numerical and building issues including for handwriting digit recognition, object recognition, speaker identification, face detection in images and target detection. SVM performs classification by building an N-dimensional hyperplane that ideally isolates the information into two different categories. Among the conceivable hyperplanes, we select the one where the separation of the hyperplane from the nearest data points is as expansive as could reasonably be expected. Instinctive support for this standard is: assume the preparation data are high, as in each conceivable test vector is inside some radius r of a preparation vector. Then, if the picked hyperplane is at any rater from any preparation vector, it will effectively isolate all the test data. By making the hyperplane beyond what many would consider possible from any data, r is permitted to be correspondingly huge. The ideal hyperplane is likewise the bisector of the line between the nearest points on the raised bodies of the two data sets.

Let $\{(x_1,y_1),\ldots\ldots(x_n,y_n)\} \subset R^n \times \{+1, -1\}$ be a training set, and $\langle .,. \rangle$ be an inner product in Rn defined as $\langle x, z \rangle = x^T z$. If the classes are linearly separable, then there exists a hyperplane $\{x \in R^n : \langle w, x \rangle + b = 0\}$ and the induced classification rule, $f$: $R^n \rightarrow \{+1,-1\}$

$$f(x) = \text{sign} \left( \langle w, x \rangle + b \right)$$

Geometrically, this can illustrate. Where the hyperplane (a straight line in the figure) corresponding to $\langle w, x \rangle, +b = 0$ is the decision boundary, and the region $\{x \in R^n : \langle w, x \rangle + b \leq 1\}$ bounded by the hyperplanes above and below the decision boundary. The distance between these two bounding hyperplanes is called the margin between the two classes on the training data under a separating hyperplane. It defined as $\dfrac{2}{\langle w, w \rangle}$. Clearly, defined w's give different margins (Chen, Li, & Wang, 2006).

## Additive Fuzzy Systems

The fuzzy system can effectively connect to an assortment of different sectors, including control and system identification, signal and image processing, pattern classification, and information retrieval. Starting at now, the "smartness" of our fuzzy machines is reliant on the principles are given. The more noteworthy the number of rules, the "smartness" the machine gets. Neural networks, which acts as the eyes and ears of a versatile fuzzy framework whose standard changes with understanding. The versatile fuzzy framework tunes its guidelines as it tests new data (Kashyap, R., & Gautam, P.,2017). At first, the tenets change quick. It gives the fuzzy framework a chance to locate a working arrangement of fuzzy standards. At that point with more examples, the guidelines change and tweak itself, and as the

*Figure 7. Optimal separating hyperplane* $\langle w, x \rangle + b = 0$ *with maximal margin* $\dfrac{2}{\langle w, x \rangle}$ *(Chen et al., 2006)*

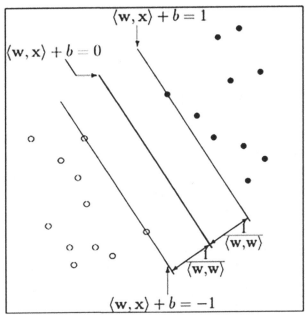

colloquialism goes rigorous discipline brings about promising results. An additive fuzzy system F stores m fuzzy rules of the form "IF X= $A_j$ THEN Y= $B_j$" and computes the output F(x) by defuzzifying the summed and partially fired THEN-part fuzzy sets (Chen et al., 2006).

## Spectral Graph Clustering

Data representation is commonly the initial step to take care of any bunching issue. In the field of PC vision, two sorts of portrayals broadly utilized. One is called geometric depiction, in which data things mapped to some functional normed vector space. The other, alluded to as diagram representation, underlines the astute pair relationship, yet usually is shy of geometric interpretation (Chen et al., 2006). Under graph representation, a collection of n data sample can represent by a weighted undirected graph G= (V; E): the nodes V={1;2;.....;n} represent data samples, the edges E={(i; j): I, j ∈ V} form between every pair of nodes, and the nonnegative weight $w_{ij}$ of an advantage (i; j), indicating the similarity between two nodes, is a function of the distance(or similarity) between nodes i and j (Chen et al., 2006).

Under a chart portrayal, bunching can be a plan as a diagram dividing issue. Among many diagram theoretical calculations, otherworldly chart apportioning strategies have been effectively connected to numerous regions in computer vision, including movement investigation, image segmentation, and item recognition (Chen et al., 2006).

## APPLICATION OF CBIR IN DIFFERENT MEDICAL IMAGE ACQUISITION TECHNIQUE

CBIR is utilized to find restorative images in vast databases. Here we will describe the methodology of a CBIR framework for recovering images from advanced Computed Tomography (CT) image database. A radiologist in a medical clinic takes X-Ray, and Magnetic Resonance Imaging (MRI) scans for patients, which produces many advanced images every day. To encourage simple access later on, one needs to enlist each image in a medicinal image database dependent on the methodology, area, and introduction of the image. In the application perspective, one can counsel the database for a to presume that there is a tumor on the patient's brain as indicated by the brain MRI. Be that as it may, one can only with significant effort judge on the off chance that it is a benign or malign tumor from the MRI filter, and might want to contrast with past cases with choosing if this patient requires a dangerous task. Understanding these sorts of necessities, one can discover comparative looking tumors from the previous MRI images. In the most recent decade, a substantial number of electronic therapeutic copies have been producing in clinics and hospitals. Large scale image databases gather different photos, including X-Ray, CT, MRI, Ultrasound (US), atomic restorative imaging, endoscopy, microscopy, and Scanning Laser Ophthalmoscopy (SLO). The most important part of image database management is how to viably recover the ideal images utilizing a description of image content (Kashyap, R., Gautam P., & Tiwari, V.,2018). This methodology of seeking models is known as CBIR, which refers to the retrieval of images from a database using information directly derived from the content of image as opposed to from going with content or comment Strategies for actualizing therapeutic image recovery frameworks have been determined, which utilize object-oriented queries, semantics by relationship with models, and a nonexclusive plan. Henceforth, medical CBIR classified with three different issues:

1. Which kind of semantics must be modeled by disjunctive semantic layers?
2. Which kind of features should use at each stage of abstraction and which distance or similarity measure should be applied?
3. How can data management and computing be organized efficiently?

The approach for content-based image retrieval in medical applications (IRMA) with specific specialize in its semantic layers of data modeling, its hierarchical concept for feature illustration and distance computation, and its distributed system design for efficient implementation. A low level of medical information set by the imaging modality as well as technical parameters, the orientation of the patient position with relevance the imaging system, the examined body region, and therefore the functional system under investigation. Supported model images, a mid-level of information represented by areas of interest (ROIs) among the images, and a high level obtained from info relating to the spatial or temporal relationships of related objects. Consequently, IRMA splits the retrieval method into seven consecutive steps. Every step represents a better level of image abstraction, reflective associate, increasing level of image content understanding (Pilevar, 2011).

## Information Modelling and Steps of Processing of IRMA (Lehmann Et Al., 2003)

**Step 1:** Categorization in IRMA isn't exclusive. Succeeding steps of processing applied for the first possible classes.

**Step 2:** Registration in geometry (rotation, translation, scaling) and contrast generates a group of transformation parameters that kept for the corresponding image in every one of its possible categories.

**Step 3:** The feature extraction step derives local image descriptions, i.e., a feature value (or a collection of amounts) obtained for every pixel.

**Step 4:** Indexing provides associate degree abstraction of the previously generated and selected image features, leading to the small image description. In action with the chosen feature set, this often done via clustering of similar image elements into regions represented by their second area moment description as ellipses.

**Step 5:** Indexing provides an abstraction of the previously generated and selected image features, resulting in a compact image description. According to the selected feature set, this done via clustering of similar image parts into regions represented by their second area moment description as ellipses

**Step 6:** The identification step provides linking of medical apriori knowledge to individual blobs generated during the indexing step. It relies on the prototypes defined for each category, which are labeled locally by medical experts, and the corresponding parameters for geometry and contrast registration. Thus, identification is the fundamental basis for introducing high-level image understanding by analyzing regional or temporal relationships

**Step 7:** In IRMA, the retrieval itself is processed either on the abstract blob level or referring to identified objects will be the only retrieval step needs on-line computations whereas all alternative measures can be performed automatically in batch mode at entry time of an image into the database.

## Feature Representation and Distance Computation

Image categorization is performed using global features, i.e., a single value or a vector combining several benefits allotted to the whole image. A large variety of full features projected within the literature for content-based image retrieval. Besides major parts from color and grey scale histograms or the moments of dominant regions, global measures obtained from (i) frequency, (ii) texture and (iii) structure analysis is going to be mention. Fourier, discrete cosine or wavelet transforms extract appropriate characteristics of images (Shukla R., Gupta R.K., & Kashyap R.,2019). The feature values obtained for every image combined to a feature vector that used for k-nearest neighbor classification supported, e.g., the geometer or Simard's tangent distance. Local options assigned to every image pixel. In spite of the determined class, local features are extracted uniformly for all images (Kashyap, R., & Rahamatkar, S.,2019). In different words, all ways for local feature extraction applied to every image. Besides the grey value itself, anisotropy, polarity, and distinction are determined in step with the Blobworld approach (Lehmann et al., 2003).

The above figure shows the multi-scale abstraction that is modeled by the IRMA system. The image (left) partitioned into representations with a decreasing number of regions (upper row). While the color-coding of parts initialized randomly; the

*Figure 8. Flowchart of IRMA system (Lehmann et al., 2003)*

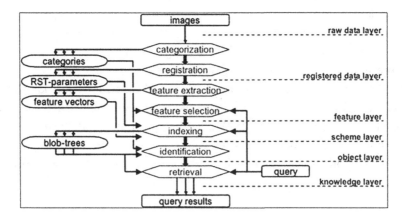

*Figure 9. Initial image (left), hierarchical partitioning and corresponding blobs (middle), and resulting graph representation (right) (Lehmann et al., 2003)*

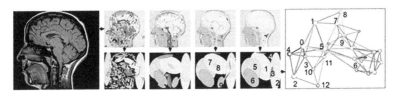

color of the most significant sector maintained during a merge. Dominant areas represented by their best fitting ellipsoids (lower row). These ellipsoids form the nodes of the IRMA blob tree representation of images (right).

## Data Management and Query Processing

Regardless of their semantic layer, all feature extraction and analysis steps of IRMA are considered methodology remodeling options. The strategy joins a program and its parameterization into one. As delineated within the previous section, IRMA provides a general feature model. It solely depends on the policy of whether or not it leads to value, pixel, or tree data. Mainly, value information is numerical values or alphanumeric strings coding global features, pixel data contains images and local features, and tree data holds the hierarchically structured blobs furthermore as their mean feature vector (Lehmann et al., 2003).

## FUTURE SCOPE OF CBIR SYSTEM IN MEDICAL SCIENCE

Initially, the CBIR system for the individual system like either for pattern, color, shape, or texture. But with the evolution of the computing processing technique, the new generation of CBIR can be able to integrate all these four methods. Basically, in medical science for the detection of disease and the disorders of organs can be identified with the help of CBIR technique. The Location of cancer and the type and severity also can be identified with this method. But near future, further, development can also be applied for three-dimensional image based retrieval.

CBIR systems in radiology should, at minimum, capture fine details of the image content, significantly as a result of they are associated with characteristic features utilized by humans in unassisted diagnosing. Additionally, computer-derived features which will not be discerned by humans might also be helpful. The sheer breadth of imaging findings may be a significant challenge, as "diseases" are depicted differently by totally different modalities, they have an effect on several organs and tissues, and

*Figure 10. The schematic diagram of the IRMA system architecture (Lehmann et al., 2003)*

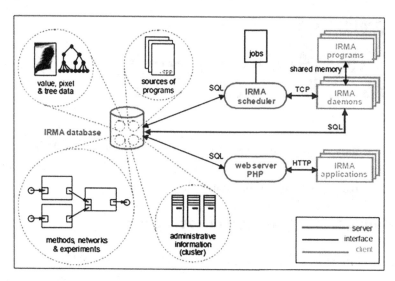

also the findings themselves are incredibly varied. Progress towards clinically helpful CBIR in radiology would require a broad-based and multidisciplinary approach. Following guideline scan a framework for future work

- Focus on clinical importance. The disorders targeted should be those with a significant impact on human health, like oncology, whereby enhancements in imaging diagnosis and monitoring would be expected to enhance treatment outcomes.
- Focus on areas wherever current imaging strategies are imperfect. Whereas imaging technology it can still improve, regions within which imaging results are inaccurate or ambiguous, like early detection of malignant hepatoma, ought to be of high priority.
- Create tools for data collection. Data should be entered consistently and with efficiency to achieve groups with millions of images. Automation of segmentation (if needed) or interactive tools requiring token user input are going to be essential and taking advantage of clinical PACS because the starting point of data assortment also will be crucial for scaling.
- Leverage image processing expertise. The vast amounts of knowledge in existence should be leveraged to optimize pixel level analysis and constructions of mathematical representations of the data. Not only single images, however volumetrically information and temporal information should be described.

- Use composite image features and metadata together whenever possible. The frequent use of visual data within the kind of image descriptors and every one unseeable information to construct medical cases, those area unit composite entities by themselves, is one of the essential directions to follow for CBIR to be useful in medical decision support systems. This integrated data use policy also applies to the selection of image descriptors to use during a medical CBIR system.

## CONCLUSION

The application of CBIR depended upon the features we want to identify in unknown images. So which methods are most appropriate to fire a query is depending upon the request where we use this technique. The scope of that CBIR expertise is presently in routine use is still very limited. Especially, CBIR technology has so far had minimal impact on the more general applications of image searching, like journalism or home amusement. Only in very specialist areas like crime prevention has CBIR technology been adopted to any necessary extent. The dramatic rise within the sizes of images databases has stirred the development of effective and efficient retrieval systems. Systems using CBIR retrieve images based on visual features like color, texture, and shape, as against depending on image descriptions.

CBIR continues to be a developing science the majority of the medical CBIR systems have emerged as diversifications of the multimedia CBIR systems. The medical CBIR approach reflects the continuing efforts of researchers functioning at the crossroads of visual content analysis and medical imaging to adapt existing CBIR techniques and to develop dedicated strategies that take into consideration the unique aspects of the radiology domain. However, because of the variety of medical image content in terms of modalities, human anatomy and diseases furthermore because the challenges specific to the medical field as compared to the multimedia system applications, this diversity is anticipated to extend even more to satisfy the necessities of various subdomains among the Medical Science.

## REFERENCES

Chaudhari, R., & Patil, A. (2012). Content-based image retrieval using color and shape features. *International Journal of Advanced Research in Electrical. Electronics and Instrumentation Engineering, 1*(5), 386–392.

Chen, Y., Li, J., & Wang, J. Z. (2006). *Machine learning and statistical modeling approaches to image retrieval* (Vol. 14). Springer Science & Business Media.

Datta, R., Joshi, D., Li, J., & Wang, J. Z. (2008). Image retrieval: Ideas, influences, and trends of the new age. *ACM Computing Surveys (Csur)*, *40*(2), 5. doi:10.1145/1348246.1348248

Dharani, T., & Aroquiaraj, I. (2017). Pattern-Based Image Retrieval System built with Object Tracking and Segmentation Concepts. *International Journal of Computer & Mathematical Sciences*, *6*(9), 312–319.

Dharani, T., & Laurence Aroquiaraj, I. (2017). *An Essential Image Augmentation Processes for Pattern Based Image Retrieval System*. Academic Press.

Erickson, J. (2009). *Database technologies: Concepts, methodologies, tools, and applications: Concepts, methodologies, tools, and applications*. IGI Global. doi:10.4018/978-1-60566-058-5

Flickner, M., Sawhney, H., Niblack, W., Ashley, J., Qian, H., Dom, B., ... Yanker, P. (1995). Query by image and video content: The QBIC system. *Computer*, *28*(9), 23–32. doi:10.1109/2.410146

Karthikram, G. M. P., & Parthiban, G. (2014). Tag-based image retrieval (TBIR) using automatic image annotation. *International Journal of Research in Engineering and Technology*, *3*(3). doi:10.15623/ijret.2014.0303027

Kashyap, R., & Gautam, P. (2016). Fast level set method for segmentation of medical images. In *Proceedings of the International Conference on Informatics and Analytics (ICIA-16)*. ACM. 10.1145/2980258.2980302

Kashyap, R., & Gautam, P. (2017). Fast Medical Image Segmentation Using Energy-Based Method. In V. Tiwari, B. Tiwari, R. Thakur, & S. Gupta (Eds.), *Pattern and Data Analysis in Healthcare Settings* (pp. 35–60). Hershey, PA: IGI Global. doi:10.4018/978-1-5225-0536-5.ch003

Kashyap, R., Gautam, P., & Tiwari, V. (2018). Management and monitoring patterns and future scope. In Handbook of Research on Pattern Engineering System Development for Big Data Analytics (pp. 230–251). Hershey, PA: IGI Global. doi:10.4018/978-1-5225-3870-7.ch014

Kashyap, R., & Piersson, A. D. (2018). Impact of Big Data on Security. In G. Shrivastava, P. Kumar, B. Gupta, S. Bala, & N. Dey (Eds.), *Handbook of Research on Network Forensics and Analysis Techniques* (pp. 283–299). Hershey, PA: IGI Global. doi:10.4018/978-1-5225-4100-4.ch015

Kashyap, R., & Rahamatkar, S. (2019). Medical Image Segmentation: An Advanced Approach. In S. Paul, P. Bhattacharya, & A. Bit (Eds.), *Early Detection of Neurological Disorders Using Machine Learning Systems* (pp. 292–321). Hershey, PA: IGI Global. doi:10.4018/978-1-5225-8567-1.ch015

Kashyap, R., & Tiwari, V. (2017). Energy-based active contour method for image segmentation. *International Journal of Electronic Healthcare*, 9(2–3), 210–225. doi:10.1504/IJEH.2017.083165

Kaur, D., & Kaur, Y. (2014). Various image segmentation techniques: A review. *International Journal of Computer Science and Mobile Computing*, 3(5), 809–814.

Lehmann, T., Güld, M., Thies, C., Fischer, B., Spitzer, K., Keysers, D., . . . Wein, B. (2003). *The Irma project: A state of the art report on content-based image retrieval in medical applications*. Paper presented at the Korea-Germany Workshop on Advanced Medical Image.

Luo, J., & Crandall, D., (2006). *Color object detection using spatial-color joint probability functions* (Vol. 15). Academic Press.

Marques, O. (2001). *Content-based image retrieval using relevance feedback*. Florida Atlantic University.

Mehta, R., Mishra, N., & Sharma, S. (2011). *Color Texture-based Image Retrieval System* (Vol. 24). Academic Press.

Müller, H., Michoux, N., Bandon, D., & Geissbuhler, A. (2004). A review of content-based image retrieval systems in medical applications—Clinical benefits and future directions. *International Journal of Medical Informatics*, 73(1), 1–23. doi:10.1016/j.ijmedinf.2003.11.024 PMID:15036075

Narwade Manoorkar, J., & Kumar, D. B. (2016). Local and Global Color Histogram Feature for Color Content-Based Image Retrieval System. Academic Press.

Pilevar, A. H. (2011). CBMIR: Content-based Image Retrieval Algorithm for Medical Image Databases. *Journal of Medical Signals and Sensors*, 1(1), 12–18. PMID:22606654

Ramamurthy, B., & Chandran, K. (2011). CBMIR: Shape-based image retrieval using canny edge detection and k-means clustering algorithms for medical images. *International Journal of Engineering Science and Technology*, 3(3).

Regniers, O., Da Costa, J.-P., Grenier, G., Germain, C., & Bombrun, L. (2013). *Texture-based image retrieval and classification of very high-resolution maritime pine forest images.* Paper presented at the 2013 IEEE International Geoscience and Remote Sensing Symposium-IGARSS. 10.1109/IGARSS.2013.6723719

Rubner, Y., & Tomasi, C. (1999). Texture-based image retrieval without segmentation. *Proceedings of the Seventh IEEE International Conference on Computer Vision.* 10.1109/ICCV.1999.790380

Saxena, P., & Shefali. (2018). Content-based image retrieval system by fusion of color, texture, and edge features with SVM classifier and relevance feedback. *International Journal of Research - Granthaalayah, 6*(9), 259-273. doi:10.5281/zenodo.1443433

Shapiro, L., & George, C. (2002). *Stockman g: computer vision.* Prentice Hall.

Shirazi, S. H., Khan, N., Umar, A., Naz, M., & AlHaqbani, B. (2016). Content-based image retrieval using texture color shape and region. *International Journal of Advanced Computer Science and Applications, 7*(1), 418–426.

Shukla, R., Gupta, R. K., & Kashyap, R. (2019). A multiphase pre-copy strategy for the virtual machine migration in cloud. In S. Satapathy, V. Bhateja, & S. Das (Eds.), *Smart Intelligent Computing and Applications. Smart Innovation, Systems and Technologies* (Vol. 104). Singapore: Springer. doi:10.1007/978-981-13-1921-1_43

Tiwari, S., Gupta, R. K., & Kashyap, R. (2019). To enhance web response time using agglomerative clustering technique for web navigation recommendation. In H. Behera, J. Nayak, B. Naik, & A. Abraham (Eds.), *Computational Intelligence in Data Mining. Advances in Intelligent Systems and Computing* (Vol. 711). Singapore: Springer. doi:10.1007/978-981-10-8055-5_59

Varshney, G., & Soni, U. (2011). Color-Based Image Retrieval in Image Database System. *International Journal of Soft Computing and Engineering, 1*(5), 31–35.

Waoo, N., Kashyap, R., & Jaiswal, A. (2010). DNA nanoarray analysis using hierarchical quality threshold clustering. In *Proceedings of 2010 2nd IEEE International Conference on Information Management and Engineering* (pp. 81-85). IEEE. 10.1109/ICIME.2010.5477579

# Chapter 10
# Machine Learning for Health Data Analytics:
## A Few Case Studies of Application of Regression

**Muralikrishna Iyyanki**

iD https://orcid.org/0000-0002-4961-9010
*Independent Researcher, India*

**Prisilla Jayanthi**
*Administrative Staff College of India, India*

## ABSTRACT

*At present, public health and population health are the key areas of major concern, and the current study highlights the significant challenges through a few case studies of application of machine learning for health data with focus on regression. Four types of machine learning methods found to be significant are supervised learning, unsupervised learning, semi-supervised learning, and reinforcement learning. In light of the case studies reported as part of the literature survey and specific exercises carried out for this chapter, it is possible to say that machine learning provides new opportunities for automatic learning in expressive models. Regression models including multiple and multivariate regression are suitable for modeling air pollution and heart disease prediction. The applicability of STATA and R packages for multiple linear regression and predictive modelling for crude birth rate and crude mortality rate is well established in the study as carried out using the data from data.gov.in. Decision tree as a class of very powerful machine learning models*

DOI: 10.4018/978-1-7998-0182-5.ch010

*is applied for brain tumors. In simple terms, machine learning and data mining techniques go hand-in-hand for prediction, data modelling, and decision making. The health analytics and unpredictable growth of health databases require integration of the conventional data analysis to be paired with methods for efficient computer-assisted analysis. In the second case study, confidence interval is evaluated. Here, the statistical parameter CI is used to indicate the true range of the mean of the crude birth rate and crude mortality rate computed from the observed data.*

## 1. INTRODUCTION

Data in digital form is the new oil, as being considered globally. For any developmental activity data are essential and hence data science. According to Bernard (2015) by the end of the year 2025, Forbes estimated that the digital data is quite sure to increase automatically by an order of magnitude from 4.4 ZB. On this planet, every human generates new information of 1.7 MB in every second. Innovative data mining techniques and machine learning techniques are necessary for facilitating related information through data modelling, prediction and prescription. Data mining and Machine learning have a good amount of commonality as the two transect to enhance the collection and usability of large amounts of data for analytics purposes.

According to *"Bio IT World"* statement, the predictive analysis is the future of data mining as it can be seen in advanced analytics across industries like medical applications (Agosta 2004). Arthur Samuel one of the forerunners and developer of machine learning define that "machine learning relates to the study, design and development of the algorithms that give computer's the capability to learn without being explicitly programmed". The process of unstructured data that tries to extract knowledge and/or unknown interesting patterns is defined as data mining. During this process, Machine Learning (ML) algorithms are traditionally used. ML is further associated with the query, how machines can learn, i.e., to the algorithmic part. In ML, an agent learns from rewards (data) in the environment, but not from patterns or pattern-label pairs. In data mining, the question is how to learn from patterns or pattern-label pairs. "ML techniques are fairly generic and can be applied in various settings. Data mining has emphasis on utilizing data from a domain e.g., social media, sensor data, video streams, etc. to understand some questions in that domain". New questions arise that may not be answered in the algorithmically oriented ML perspective including preprocessing of data and the complete data mining process chain (Souhila 2013 and Xavier 2016). From large historical datasets, the data mining intent is to find out unseen patterns and relationships and derive a business value. Its interest is upon uncovering relationships between two or more variables in the dataset and extracting insights. These insights include mapping the data into information and predicting outcomes from incoming events and prescribing actions. Multiple data sorting techniques can be used to achieve this target such as clustering, classification, and sequence analysis. Typically, data mining uses batch-process information to reveal a new insight at any specific point. And DM is not automated process but DM requires human involvement and cannot be implemented without humans.

## 2. MACHINE LEARNING [ML] AND DATA MINING [DM]

ML uses human-based algorithm and works everything without the use of humans' interference; once implemented, the outcome is accurate because the process is automated. Also, ML is capable to take the own decision and resolve the issue. Ever growing ML techniques, overwhelms problems associated with DM techniques as ML techniques are more accurate and less error prone compared to DM. This self-learning technique is not available in DM whereas ML uses self-learning algorithms to improve its performance as an intelligent task with experience over time (Brooks & Dahlke 2017). To summarize the foregoing, it can be stated the following are the definitions and differences or commonalities, if any, between ML and DM:

- "In **Machine learning**, performance is usually evaluated with respect to the ability to reproduce known knowledge, while in knowledge discovery and data mining (KDD) the key task is the discovery of previously unknown knowledge. Evaluated with respect to known knowledge, an uninformed (unsupervised) method will easily be outperformed by other supervised methods, while in a typical KDD task, supervised methods cannot be used due to the unavailability of training data" (Machine_learning, Wikipedia).
- **Data mining** is a cross-disciplinary field that has emphasis on finding out properties of data sets. There are various approaches to discover properties of data sets; among which machine learning is one of them.
- **Machine learning** is a sub-field of data science that focuses on designing algorithms that can learn from and make predictions on the data.
- **Machine learning** and Data Mining often employ similar methods. Machine learning focuses on prediction whereas data mining focuses on the unearthing of unidentified and new properties/ trends in the data. Prediction by ML is based on known properties learned from the training data. Data mining uses many machine learning methods, but with different goals; on the other hand, machine learning also employs data mining methods as unsupervised learning.

In general terms machine learning techniques can be used for data mining. However, data mining can use other techniques besides or with machine learning. As per existing analysis and protocols developed, data mining and machine learning are to be considered as each one inclusive of other and with significant overlap due to commonality of tools and techniques. The reason behind for considering at this stage that data mining and machine learning are mutually inclusive techniques with considerable overlap (supervised, unsupervised and semi-supervised learning) between both. However, there are few ML techniques like reinforcement learning that does not come under data mining which is used more for logical analysis. Further with several examples one can clearly visualize that reinforcement learning belongs to ML, but not to data mining (DM). Machine learning, and/or for that matter, data mining is essentially, the applicable methods for prediction and description of the event or phenomenon of varying dimensions and categories (Data Mining- Machine Learning, doublebyteblog). These differences are depicted in figure 1 as a schematic sketch highlighting the structure of machine learning, comprising of different learning techniques viz. supervised learning, unsupervised learning, semi-supervised learning and reinforced learning.

*Figure 1. Machine learning structure*

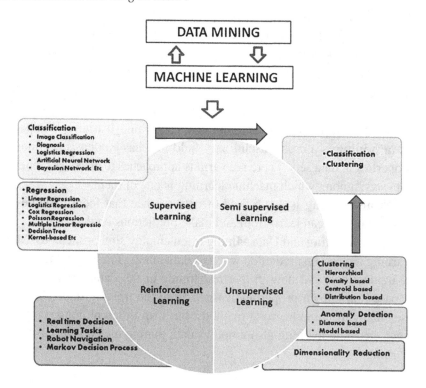

Supervised learning is a case of learning applicable to the efforts in which both input and output are known and thus the system is trained so as to predict output for a given input value. Supervised learning is the task of inferring a function from labeled training data and which is further used for mapping new examples. Supervised learning is one of the methods associated with machine learning which involves allocating labeled data so that a certain pattern or function can be deduced from that data. It is worth noting that supervised learning involves allocating an input object, a vector, while at the same time anticipating the most desired output value, which is referred to as the supervisory signal. The bottom-line property of supervised learning is that the input data is known and labeled appropriately. The algorithm will correctly determine the class labels for unseen instances. This leads the learning algorithm to generalize from the training data to unseen situations in a reasonable way (McNulty 2015). This explanation of supervised learning is applicable to both the tasks of data mining and machine learning.

Data mining is becoming, as discussed in earlier section, essential aspect in the current world due to increased raw data where organizations need to analyze and process so that they can make sound and reliable decisions. Here data mining relates to explaining about the past and predicting the future based on analysis. Data mining helps to extract information from huge datasets. It is the procedure of mining knowledge from data. The techniques of data mining are classification, clustering, regression, association rules, sequential patterns and prediction. R-language and Oracle data mining are prominent data mining tools. The main drawback of data mining is that many analytics software is difficult to operate and requires advanced training to work upon.

The second method is unsupervised learning that determines the hidden patterns from unlabeled data; and used for exploratory data analysis. One main characteristics of unsupervised learning is that both the structures of input and output are unknown. Since the examples that are given during the learning are unlabeled, the scope for assessment of the validation of the output with reference to the real-world situation is not possible. For ex. while, applying clustering technique of unsupervised classification of a digital image, the output essentially gives clusters which represent classes in spectral domain and not feature domain. The techniques used in both the learnings appear to be similar, making the user challenging to differentiate between the two learning methods. However, there exist significant differences between supervised and unsupervised learning. In semi-supervised learning, which is a mix of supervised learning, viz., classification technique and unsupervised learning, viz., clustering technique are used.

Reinforced learning which is basically a type of machine learning and it differs from supervised learning as labelled input / output pairs need not be present, and sub-optimal actions need not be explicitly corrected. Instead, the focus is finding a balance between exploration and exploitation of current knowledge. In this context the regression techniques are very much significant for any sort of learning and modeling.

## 3. REGRESSION MODELS

Regression, as understood from the learning methods discussed in earlier section, is a technique for determining the statistical relationship between two or more variables where a change in a dependent variable is associated with, and depends on, a change in one or more independent variables. The comparison of machine learning algorithms of each learning process with reference to learning type / sub-types and methods is carried out with specific examples related to health data. In simple linear regression, one can use statistics on the training data to estimate the coefficients required by the model to make predictions for new data. Regression techniques mostly differ based on the number of independent variables and the type of relationship between the independent and dependent variables. For health care related application, regression is being used to describe relationships between two variables like gender, age, weight, clinical observations like BP etc. Regression analysis is considered for statistical evaluation which enables three things as given below along with the types as described by Schneider et al (2010).

- Description: The statistically method viz., regression analysis helps to describe the relationships among the dependent variables and the independent variables
- Estimation: The values of the dependent variables can be estimated from the observed values of the independent variables.
- Prognostication: Risk factors that influence the outcome can be identified, and individual prognoses can be determined.

Based on the above factors, the application of regression is given in Table 1 for a typical case study of application to a medical record. Linear regression, polynomial regression, logistic regression, proportional hazard regression, poisons regression and non –linear regression etc. are various types suitable for different types of data modeling and few of which are described below in the Table 1.

The Table 2 describes the divergence with respective to input data, complexity, real time and accuracy between supervised and unsupervised learning.

*Table 1. Machine learning algorithms [doublebyteblog]*

| Learning Type | Sub Type | Method | Sub Method |
|---|---|---|---|
| UNSUPERVISED | Continuous | Clustering | K means SVM PCA |
| | | Dimensionality Reduction | |
| | Categorical | Association analysis | Apriori |
| | | | FP growth |
| | | Hidden Markov Model | Markov Chain |
| SUPERVISED | Continuous | Regression | Linear |
| | | | Polynomial |
| | | Decision Trees | Random Forests |
| | | | Gradient tree |
| | Categorical | Classification | KNN |
| | | | Trees |
| | | | Logistics Regression |
| | | | Naïve-Bayes |
| | | | SVM |

*Table 2. Divergence between supervised and unsupervised learning[ Mujtaba & Irshad (2017)]*

| Factors | Unsupervised Learning | Supervised Learning |
|---|---|---|
| Input data | Unlabeled data and machine must categorize | Labelled data and machine must determine hidden patterns |
| Computational Complexity | Method of learning is less complex | Method of learning is more complex |
| Accuracy | For the method of learning the machine has to define and label the input data before determining the hidden patterns and functions. Hence accuracy is of major concern. | The input data is well known and labelled. The accuracy is high and it analyzes only hidden patterns in a reliable way. |
| Number of classes | No prior knowledge of the classes in unsupervised method is seen. | All the classes used in supervised learning are known. The aim of supervised learning is to determine the unknown cluster. |
| Real time learning | In real time, the learning takes all the input data for analyzing and labeling in the presence of learners which helps them to understand and classification of raw data. Real time data analysis is the most significant of this learning. | The preparing and labeling of input data are carried out off-line while the analysis of the hidden pattern is done online. |

Logistic regression is a regression and / or a binary classification algorithm, producing a continuous or categorical output. Logistic regression is not a classification algorithm on its own. It is a type of classification algorithm in combination with a decision rule. It is a regression model to estimate the probability of class membership as a multilinear function of the features. Unlike in the case of conventional regression which outputs continuous number values, logistic regression transforms its output using the logistic sigmoid function to return a probability value which can be mapped to two or more discrete classes. It may be recollected here that a sigmoid function is a mathematical function having characteristic S-shaped curve or sigmoid curve. The proportional Hazard models are a class of survival models known as Cox Regression for a specific outcome case study which indeed is a method for investigating the effect of several variables on the time a specified event takes to happen. Poisson Regression is used for modeling events where the output is given as counts, to be precise, about count data. It is discrete data with non-negative integer values that counts the number of times an event occurs during a given timeframe. Count data is expressed as rate data, because the number of times an event occurs within a timeframe can be expressed as a raw count (LogisticRegression ufldl.stanford.edu).

*Table 3. Regression models [Schneider et al (2010)]*

| Type | Application | Dependent Variables | Independent variables |
|------|-------------|---------------------|------------------------|
| Linear Regression | Description of a linear relationship | Continuous(weight, blood pressure) | Independent variables can be continuous or categorical |
| Logistic Regression | Prediction of the probability of belonging to groups (outcome: yes / no) | Dichotomous (success of treatment: yes / no) | |
| Cox Regression [Proportional-Hazard Regression] | Modeling of survival data | Survival time (time from diagnosis to event) | |
| Poisson Regression | Modeling of counting processes | Counting data: whole numbers representing events in temporal sequences (e.g. the number of times a woman gave birth over a certain period of time) | |
| Multiple Linear Regression Model | Used to explain the relationship between one continuous dependent variable and two or more independent variables | Continuous (Land use, traffic, etc values) | |
| | | Continuous (chest pain type, blood sugar, ECG etc) | Heart disease prediction |

## 4. MULTIPLE/MULTIVARIATE REGRESSION

Multiple regressions pertain to one dependent variable and multiple independent variables whereas multivariate regression pertains to multiple dependent and multiple independent variables. Multivariate regression (MMR) is used to model the linear relationship between more than one independent variable and more than one dependent variable. MMR with more than one independent variable is referred multiple. MMR is multivariate because there is more than one dependent variable. Few case studies of multiple regressions are discussed in the next section.

## Air Pollution Modeling Using Multiple Regression

In a case of development of a Multiple Linear Regression technique, a study by Mateus et al (2015) is discussed here. The objective of this study is to model air pollution to predict value of $NO_2$ concentration using multiple linear regressions, in which few independent variables were used for bivariate regression analysis. In this study, two independent variables viz., elevation and traffic within 150m radius are used for the multivariate regression coined as Land Use Regression model [LUR] and for the year 2001, it predicted almost 60% of $NO_2$. The results highlight vehicular traffic as important variable responsible to increase air pollutant levels, in the areas where cars are more such as the city center, or close to busy expressways. LUR methods are applied successfully to model annual mean concentrations of $NO_2$, NOx, PM2.5, and VOCs. The LUR model is designed to predict the total concentration of pollutants. The model included key independent co-variables like traffic volume, road type, land use, altitude and demography and their respective coefficients. The bivariate regression and correlation analysis were calculated on SPSS and the multivariate regression was calculated on STATA. The land use data includes nine classifications by type of use (industrial, arable, forests and water) and building patterns (enclosed, low, high, recreational). GIS software MapInfo with buffers 50, 100, 150, 250 and 500 m-radii were used to create the independent variables in 25 locations.

Results of the study by Mateus et al (2015) showed that the geographic characteristics such as altitude and traffic intensity, contribute considerably to the urban air quality. Furthermore, the LUR model is recommended for estimating outdoor concentrations at any specified location. It would support policymaking about the improvement of urban air quality. This study does not include meteorological parameters into the model.

# Heart Disease Prediction Using Multiple Linear Regression Model

Heart disease kills one in three persons every day as per World Health Statistics 2012 worldwide. Researchers have developed various heart disease prediction systems to extract hidden datasets from heart disease databases. They help doctors and other medical professionals by predicting heart diseases more efficiently and accurately and thus make best clinical decisions.

In a study by Polaraju and Durgaprasad (2017), multiple linear regression analysis has been performed to predict the chance of heart disease in a case study, by the training data sets consisting of 3000 instances with 13 different attributes as given in Table 4. In this study a wide range of works have been analyzed related to heart disease prediction system using different data mining algorithms. Based on the study results given in Table 5, it was observed that multiple regression algorithm accuracy is better compared to other techniques. Typically, the methodology includes a procedure to determine whether the patient has heart disease by considering the attributes of patient data set like age, chest pain type, fasting blood sugar, rest ECG, number of major vessels colored by fluoroscopy, blood pressure, serum cholesterol, maximum heart rate achieved etc. The experiment is performed by training data set consists of 3000 instances with 13 different attributes.

*Table 4. Patient's attributes [Mujtaba & Irshad (2017)]*

| Attributes | Description |
|---|---|
| Pid | Patient Identification |
| Gender | Male or Female |
| Age | In years |
| Cp | Chest pain type |
| Thestbps | Resting blood pressure |
| Chol | Serum cholesterol |
| Restecg | Resting Electrographic results |
| Fbs | Fasting blood sugar |
| Thalach | Maximum heart rate achieved |
| Exang | Exercise induced angina |
| Ca | Number of major vessels colored by Fluoroscopy |
| Obes | Obesity |
| Smoke | Smoking |
| Ecg | Electro Cardiogram |

*Table 5. Data set definition [Polaraju & Durgaprasad (2017)]*

| Parameters | Weightage | |
|---|---|---|
| Person | Age < 30 | 0.1 |
| | >30 to <50 | 0.3 |
| | Age>50 and age<70 | 0.7 |
| | Age>70 | 0.8 |
| Smoking | Never | 0.1 |
| | Past | 0.3 |
| | Current | 0.6 |
| Overweight | Yes | 0.8 |
| | No | 0.1 |
| Alcohol Intake | Never | 0.1 |
| | Past | 0.3 |
| | Current | 0.6 |
| High salt diet | Yes | 0.9 |
| | No | 0.1 |
| High saturated fat diet | Yes | 0.9 |
| | No | 0.1 |
| Exercise | Never | 0.6 |
| | Regular | 0.1 |
| | High if age< 30 | 0.1 |
| | High if age> 50 | 0.6 |
| Sedentary Lifestyle/inactivity | Yes | 0.7 |
| | No | 0.1 |
| Hereditary | Yes | 0.7 |
| | No | 0.1 |
| Bad Cholesterol | Very high >200 | 0.9 |
| | High 160 to 200 | 0.8 |
| | Normal < 160 | 0.1 |
| Blood Pressure | Normal (130/89) | 0.1 |
| | Low (<119/79) | 0.8 |
| | High (>200/160) | 0.9 |
| Blood Sugar | High (>129 & <400) | 0.5 |
| | Normal (>90 & <120) | 0.1 |
| | Low (<90) | 0.4 |
| Heart Rate | Low (<60 bpm) | 0.9 |
| | Normal (60 to 100) | 0.1 |
| | High(> 100 bpm) | 0.9 |

The dataset is divided into two parts with 70% of the data used for training and 30% are for testing. Based on the experimental results as shown in Table 5 (Polaraju & DurgaPrasad, 2017), it is clear that the classification accuracy of regression algorithm is better compared to other algorithms. The popular regression technique viz., multiple linear regressions analysis is performed on trained data to build a model on which test data is applied. From the experimental results it is proved that multiple linear regressions are equally appropriate for predicting heart disease chance.

## STATA and R for Multiple Linear Regressions

An example of application the potential of the two software packages for multiple linear regression i.e. Stata and R for Brain Tumor severity assessment is being carried out by the authors. It is initially stated that Stata IC 15.0 is faster in computation, efficient, and has few machine learning algorithms implemented. The analysis of Odd Ratios (OR) and Confidential Interval (CI) calculations using unconditional logistics regression can be performed using Stata, this feature is not available in R. This feature helps the prediction of brain tumor but R provides a definite platform for machine learning algorithms.

## 5. CONFIDENCE INTERVAL: THE PREDICTIVE MODELLING FOR CRUDE BIRTH RATE AND CRUDE MORTALITY RATE

In the next case study, confidence interval is evaluated for crude birth / mortality rate by predictive modelling. Confidence interval is an interval estimate, computed from the observed data, which contain the true value of an unknown population parameter. It is known that in predictive modelling, a prediction is a single outcome value given by some input variable. In other terms, predictive modelling which is the measurement of the uncertain estimated model referred to as confidence interval, CI such as mean or standard deviation. A confidence interval is a bound on the estimate of a population variable. It is an interval statistic used to quantify the uncertainty on an estimate. In machine learning, confidence intervals can be used as a regression predictive model by Jason B (2018). Confidence intervals are a way of quantifying the uncertainty of an estimate. It provides both a lower and upper bound and likelihood on a population parameter, such as a mean, estimated from a sample of independent observations from the population. The 95% confidence interval (CI) is a range of values calculated from the data, including the true value of what one estimates about the population.

For instance, the infant death rate for a particular district, say, a residential area in the year 2000 was 6.5 per 1000 live births = (13 Infant deaths / 1989 births) x 1000 = 6.5.

The following formula is used to calculate a 95% confidence interval:

Upper Limit = (1000/n) (d + (1.96 x square root of d))

Lower Limit = (1000/n) (d - (1.96 x square root of d))

where

d = number of events upon which the rate is based

n = denominator of the rate i.e., area population for crude birth and death rates, live births for infant death rates.

Hence, if a 95% confidence interval was computed for that rate, an upper limit rate of 5.7 and a lower limit rate of 0.75 would be the result.

For example, consider an area which had 20 deaths in 1979, 35 in 1980 and 28 deaths in 1981 (Jason B, 2018). If in the year 1980 population was 10,000, the three-year summary crude death rate can be computed as shown below:

((20 + 35 + 28) / (3 x 10000)) x 1000 = (83 / 30000) x 1000 = 2.77.

This case study deals with the evaluation of confidence interval using crude birth rate and crude mortality rate. The data is taken from www.data.gov.in and analysis was carried out using STATA software. In most of the developing countries, malnutrition is the major cause of child mortality. The areas with better health, hygiene and sanitation facilities help in reduction in mortality rate. Literacy and the economical understanding have blended to lower the birth rate.

The study calculates the confidence interval to understand the crude birth rate and crude mortality rate in India in six different states namely Andhra Pradesh, Assam, Madhya Pradesh, Uttar Pradesh and Dadra & Nagar Haveli and the data was collected from the year 1981 to 2011. The table 8 shows the decrease in crude birth rate and crude mortality rate from 1971 to 2011 with the population rise. The graph in figure 2 shows the decline in crude birth rate (21.8) and crude mortality rate (7.1) in the year 2011.

*Table 6a. Crude birth rate in six different states from the year 1981 to 1995 ["data.gov.in", 2019]*

| Sno. | Name of States for CBR | y-1981 | y-1982 | y-1983 | y-1984 | y-1985 | y-1986 | y-1987 | y-1988 | y-1989 | y-1990 | y-1991 | y-1992 | y-1993 | y-1994 | y-1995 |
|---|---|---|---|---|---|---|---|---|---|---|---|---|---|---|---|---|
| 1 | Andhra Pradesh | 31.7 | 31.2 | 30.8 | 31.2 | 29.9 | 31.6 | 30.3 | 27.4 | 25.9 | 26.3 | 26 | 24.5 | 24.3 | 23.8 | 24.2 |
| 2 | Assam | 33 | 34.2 | 34.7 | 35.3 | 34.3 | 34.7 | 34.2 | 32.9 | 29.4 | 29.7 | 30.9 | 30.8 | 29.5 | 30.8 | 29.3 |
| 3 | Madhya Pradesh | 37.6 | 38.5 | 38.5 | 36.9 | 39.4 | 37.2 | 36.4 | 37 | 35.5 | 37.1 | 35.8 | 34.9 | 34.9 | 33 | 33.2 |
| 4 | Uttar Pradesh | 39.6 | 38.6 | 38.4 | 38.7 | 37.6 | 37.5 | 37.9 | 37.1 | 37 | 35.6 | 35.7 | 36.3 | 36.2 | 35.4 | 34.8 |
| 5 | D&N Haveli | 36.8 | 41.7 | 40.1 | 45.9 | 36.9 | 43.4 | 35.8 | 38.3 | 35.6 | 35.9 | 31.1 | 37.8 | 33.6 | 34.4 | 29.7 |
| 6 | Pondi cherry | 21.7 | 23.8 | 23.5 | 25.3 | 22.1 | 22.5 | 22.4 | 22.5 | 21.1 | 20.4 | 19.2 | 19.8 | 15.5 | 18 | 20.1 |

*Table 6b. Crude birth rate in six different states from the year 1996 to 2011(continuation)*

| Sno | Name of States for CBR | y-1996 | y-1997 | y-1998 | y-1999 | y-2000 | y-2001 | y-2002 | y-2003 | y-2004 | y-2005 | y-2006 | y-2007 | y-2008 | y-2009 | y-2010 | y-2011 |
|---|---|---|---|---|---|---|---|---|---|---|---|---|---|---|---|---|---|
| 1 | Andhra Pradesh | 22.8 | 22.5 | 22.4 | 21.7 | 21.3 | 21 | 20.7 | 20.4 | 19 | 19.1 | 18.9 | 18.7 | 18.4 | 18.3 | 17.9 | 17.5 |
| 2 | Assam | 27.6 | 28.2 | 27.9 | 27 | 26.9 | 27 | 26.6 | 26.3 | 25.1 | 25 | 24.6 | 24.3 | 23.9 | 23.6 | 23.2 | 22.8 |
| 3 | Madhya Pradesh | 32.3 | 31.9 | 30.7 | 31.1 | 31.4 | 31 | 30.4 | 30.2 | 29.8 | 29.4 | 29.1 | 28 | 28.2 | 27.7 | 27.3 | 26.9 |
| 4 | Uttar Pradesh | 34 | 33.5 | 32.4 | 32.8 | 32.8 | 32.1 | 31.6 | 31.3 | 30.8 | 30.4 | 30.1 | 29.5 | 29.1 | 28.7 | 28.3 | 27.8 |
| 5 | D&N Haveli | 28.9 | 28.2 | 34.1 | 34.2 | 34.9 | 29.5 | 30.4 | 30.3 | 28.8 | 29.4 | 28.1 | 27.8 | 27 | 27 | 26.6 | 26.1 |
| 6 | Pondi cherry | 18.1 | 18.4 | 18.2 | 17.7 | 17.8 | 17.9 | 17.9 | 17.5 | 17 | 16.2 | 15.7 | 15.1 | 16.4 | 16.5 | 16.7 | 16.1 |

254

Table 7a. *Crude death rate of six states from the year 1981 to 1995*

| Sno | Names of States for CDR | y-1981 | y-1982 | y-1983 | y-1984 | y-1985 | y-1986 | y-1987 | y-1988 | y-1989 | y-1990 | y-1991 | y-1992 | y-1993 | y-1994 | y-1995 |
|---|---|---|---|---|---|---|---|---|---|---|---|---|---|---|---|---|
| 1 | Andhra Pradesh | 11.1 | 10.6 | 10.4 | 11 | 10.3 | 9.9 | 9.9 | 10.2 | 9.5 | 9.1 | 9.7 | 9.2 | 8.6 | 8.3 | 8.4 |
| 2 | Assam | 12.6 | 12.4 | 12.1 | 13.2 | 13.2 | 12.6 | 11.6 | 11.8 | 10.4 | 10.5 | 11.5 | 10.4 | 10.2 | 9.2 | 9.6 |
| 3 | Madhya Pradesh | 16.6 | 14.9 | 14.5 | 14.2 | 14.2 | 13.6 | 13.3 | 14.3 | 12.9 | 12.6 | 13.8 | 12.9 | 12.6 | 11.6 | 11.2 |
| 4 | Uttar Pradesh | 16.3 | 15.1 | 15.7 | 17.8 | 15.8 | 14.6 | 14.5 | 13.2 | 12.6 | 12 | 11.3 | 12.8 | 11.6 | 11 | 10.3 |
| 5 | D&N Haveli | 14.1 | 13.2 | 14 | 15.5 | 11.9 | 9.4 | 11.3 | 9.8 | 8.7 | 9.6 | 11.4 | 11.4 | 12.2 | 9.4 | 8.2 |
| 6 | Pondi Cherry | 7.3 | 6.5 | 8.5 | 8.3 | 7.2 | 8.3 | 8 | 7.9 | 7.8 | 6.2 | 6.6 | 6.8 | 6.3 | 7.5 | 7.6 |

Table 7b. *Crude death rate of six states from the year 1996 to 2011(continuation)*

| Sno | Names of States for CDR | y-1996 | y-1997 | y-1998 | y-1999 | y-2000 | y-2001 | y-2002 | y-2003 | y-2004 | y-2005 | y-2006 | y-2007 | y-2008 | y-2009 | y-2010 | y-2011 |
|---|---|---|---|---|---|---|---|---|---|---|---|---|---|---|---|---|---|
| 1 | Andhra Pradesh | 8.4 | 8.3 | 8.8 | 8.2 | 8.2 | 8.2 | 8.1 | 8 | 7 | 7.3 | 7.3 | 7.4 | 7.5 | 7.6 | 7.6 | 7.5 |
| 2 | Assam | 9.6 | 9.9 | 10 | 9.7 | 9.6 | 9.6 | 9.2 | 9.1 | 8.8 | 8.7 | 8.7 | 8.6 | 8.6 | 8.4 | 8.2 | 8 |
| 3 | Madhya Pradesh | 11.1 | 11 | 11.2 | 10.4 | 10.3 | 10.1 | 9.8 | 9.8 | 9.2 | 9 | 8.9 | 8.7 | 8.6 | 8.5 | 8.3 | 8.2 |
| 4 | Uttar Pradesh | 10.3 | 10.3 | 10.5 | 10.5 | 10.3 | 10.1 | 9.7 | 9.5 | 8.8 | 8.7 | 8.6 | 8.5 | 8.4 | 8.2 | 8.1 | 7.9 |
| 5 | D&N Haveli | 9.2 | 8.2 | 7.9 | 6.6 | 7.8 | 6.5 | 6.8 | 6.1 | 5.2 | 5.1 | 4.8 | 4.8 | 5.4 | 4.8 | 4.7 | 4.6 |
| 6 | Pondi Cherry | 7.1 | 8 | 7.8 | 6.9 | 6.5 | 7 | 6.7 | 6.3 | 8 | 7.1 | 7.3 | 7.7 | 7.5 | 7 | 7.4 | 7.2 |

*Table 8. Crude birth and mortality rate in India from the year (1971 -2011)*

| Year | Population | Crude Birth Rate | Crude Mortality Rate | Percentage Decadal Variation | Annual Exponential Growth Rate (%) |
|------|-----------|------------------|---------------------|------------------------------|-----------------------------------|
| 1971 | 548.2 | 41.2 | 19 | 24.8 | 2.2 |
| 1981 | 683.3 | 37.2 | 15 | 24.66 | 2.22 |
| 1991 | 846.4 | 32.5 | 11.4 | 23.87 | 2.16 |
| 2001 | 1028.7 | 24.8 | 8.9 | 21.54 | 1.97 |
| 2011 | 1210.9 | 21.8 | 7.1 | 17.7 | 1.63 |

*Table 9. CI of crude birth rate and mortality rate in rural and urban*

| Variable | Mean | Std. err | 95% CI |
|----------|------|----------|--------|
| Crude Birth rate rural | 21.31 | 2.25 | 15.50-27.12 |
| Crude Birth rate urban | 19.13 | 2.17 | 13.5 -24.71 |
| Crude Death rate rural | 7.08 | 0.43 | 5.97 -8.18 |
| Crude Death rate urban | 5.18 | 0.49 | 3.90-6.46 |

From the Table 8,

Population mean = 865.17,
SE = 2.37 with 95% CI = 860.52 to 869.83
and crude birth rate mean = 31.44,
SE = 0.07 and 95% CI = 31.30 to 31.59.
The crude mortality rate mean = 12.24,
SE = 12.16 showed 95% CI = 0.04 to 12.33.
mean = 22.49 and SE = 0.02.
The results of percentage decadal variation 95% CI = 22.44 to 22.54,
mean = 2.034 and SE = 0.002.
The results for annual exponential growth rate were 95% CI = 2.030 to 2.038,

Confidence interval (CI) computes standard errors and confidence intervals for each of the variables.

*Figure 2. Graph representing crude birth rate and crude mortality rate in India*

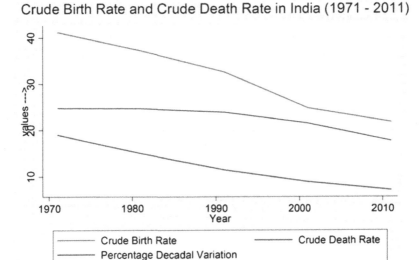

*Figure 3. Normal CI calculation screen shot*

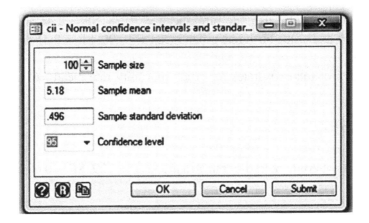

For estimation of CI the following steps are adopted:

- select Statistics > Summaries, tables, and tests > Summary and descriptive statistics > Confidence intervals.
- Enter the mean and std. error in cii dialog box as shown in figure 3 for calculating the normal CI calculation.

Hence, the value of crude birth rate urban is 95% CI = 13.5 to 24.71,

mean = 19.13 and SE = 2.17;

The assessed value of crude birth rate rural - 95% CI = 15.50 to 27.12

mean = 21.31 and SE = 2.25.

The evaluated value of crude mortality rate rural – 95% CI 5.97 to 8.18,

mean = 7.08 and SE = 0.43.

Finally, the calculated value of crude mortality rate urban - 95% CI = 3.90 to 6.46,

mean = 5.18 and SE =0 .49 shown in Table 9.

From the graph in figure 4, the results of total six states for crude birth rate

mean = 21.22, SE = 2.27 and 95% CI = 15.38 to 27.07;

The results of crude birth rate rural mean = 20.78, SE = 2.44 and 95% CI = 14.51 to 27.05 and crude birth rate urban mean = 19.90, SE = 2.41 and 95% CI = 13.69 to 26.11.

The results of total six states for crude mortality rate mean =6.3, SE = 0.58 and 95%

CI= 4.81 to 7.78;

The results of crude mortality rate urban mean = 5.29, SE = 0.60 and 95%

CI = 3.73 to 6.85.

The crude mortality rate rural mean = 6.93, SE = 0.49 with 95%

CI = 5.66 to 8.21.

The peak crude birth rate can be seen in Dadra and Nagar Haveli with 27.7 and lowest total crude mortality rate was found be 4 in Dadra and Nagar Haveli.

*Figure 4. Graph representing crude birth rate and crude mortality rate in urban and rural*

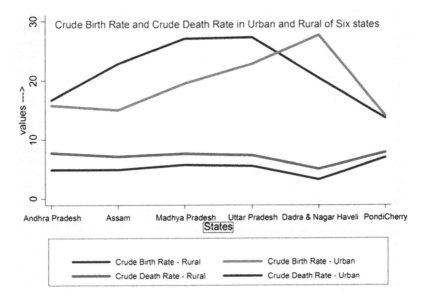

In figure 5, the graph shows the highest crude birth rate in the year 1984 with 45.9 in Dadra and Nagar Haveli and minimum in the year 2007 in Pondicherry.

The spacing between children in the rural and urban areas implies that about half of the birth should have spacing of 36 months and above. Most of rural and urban areas now have 70 percent of births which have birth interval of about 24 months.

*Figure 5. Graph representing crude birth rate in six different states*

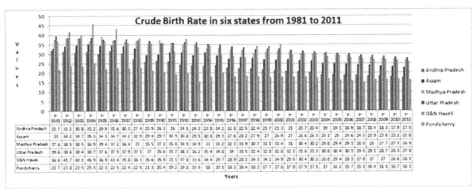

*Table 10. Confidence interval, mean and standard error for crude birth rate in India (1981-2011)*

| Year | Mean | Standard Error | [95% Conf. Interval] |
|------|------|----------------|----------------------|
| 1981 | 32.53 | 1.59 | 29.19 to 35.86 |
| 1982 | 34.32 | 1.59 | 30.99 - 37.65 |
| 1983 | 33.85 | 1.54 | 30.63 - 37.06 |
| 1984 | 35.65 | 1.71 | 32.07 - 39.21 |
| 1985 | 32.58 | 1.54 | 29.35 - 35.80 |
| 1986 | 34.03 | 1.77 | 30.32 – 37.72 |
| 1987 | 32.04 | 1.41 | 29.10 - 34.98 |
| 1988 | 32.34 | 1.49 | 29.21 - 35.45 |
| 1989 | 30.66 | 1.48 | 27.55 - 33.75 |
| 1990 | 30.54 | 1.55 | 27.30 - 33.77 |
| 1991 | 28.98 | 1.49 | 25.87 - 32.09 |
| 1992 | 30.65 | 1.67 | 27.15 - 34.15 |
| 1993 | 28.27 | 1.90 | 24.30 - 32.24 |
| 1994 | 28.86 | 1.63 | 25.45 - 32.25 |
| 1995 | 28.12 | 1.26 | 25.48 - 30.76 |
| 1996 | 26.85 | 1.37 | 23.99 - 29.72 |
| 1997 | 26.66 | 1.30 | 23.94 - 29.38 |
| 1998 | 27.6 | 1.45 | 24.56 - 30.63 |
| 1999 | 27.49 | 1.53 | 24.29 - 30.69 |
| 2000 | 27.70 | 1.56 | 24.43 - 30.97 |
| 2001 | 26.25 | 1.29 | 23.55 - 28.95 |
| 2002 | 26.23 | 1.29 | 23.53 - 28.92 |
| 2003 | 25.96 | 1.31 | 23.23 - 28.70 |
| 2004 | 25.13 | 1.28 | 22.44 - 27.81 |
| 2005 | 24.90 | 1.35 | 22.08 - 27.73 |
| 2006 | 24.30 | 1.33 | 21.52 - 27.09 |
| 2007 | 23.83 | 1.34 | 21.02 - 26.62 |
| 2008 | 23.81 | 1.17 | 21.37 - 26.24 |
| 2009 | 23.68 | 1.14 | 21.31 - 26.05 |
| 2010 | 23.45 | 1.08 | 21.19 - 25.71 |
| 2011 | 22.95 | 1.09 | 20.67 - 25.23 |

*Table 11. Confidence interval, mean and standard error for crude mortality rate in India (1981-2011)*

| Year | Mean | SE | 95% Conf. Interval |
|------|------|-----|--------------------|
| 1981 | 13 | 1.42 | 9.32 to 16.67 |
| 1982 | 12.12 | 1.31 | 8.74 - 15.49 |
| 1983 | 12.53 | 1.11 | 9.67 - 15.39 |
| 1984 | 13.33 | 1.36 | 9.81 - 16.85 |
| 1985 | 12.1 | 1.24 | 8.89 - 15.30 |
| 1986 | 11.4 | 1.03 | 8.72 - 14.07 |
| 1987 | 11.43 | 0.94 | 8.99 - 13.87 |
| 1988 | 11.2 | 0.96 | 8.72 - 13.67 |
| 1989 | 10.31 | 0.84 | 8.14 - 12.49 |
| 1990 | 10 | 0.94 | 7.58 - 12.41 |
| 1991 | 10.71 | 0.98 | 8.19 - 13.24 |
| 1992 | 10.58 | 0.95 | 8.13 - 13.03 |
| 1993 | 10.25 | 0.99 | 7.70 - 12.79 |
| 1994 | 9.5 | 0.64 | 7.86 - 11.13 |
| 1995 | 9.21 | 0.56 | 7.76 - 10.66 |
| 1996 | 9.28 | 0.57 | 7.80 - 10.76 |
| 1997 | 9.28 | 0.52 | 7.94 - 10.62 |
| 1998 | 9.36 | 0.57 | 7.88 - 10.84 |
| 1999 | 8.71 | 0.70 | 6.89 - 10.53 |
| 2000 | 8.78 | 0.62 | 7.17 - 10.39 |
| 2001 | 8.58 | 0.64 | 6.91 - 10.25 |
| 2002 | 8.38 | 0.57 | 6.91 - 9.85 |
| 2003 | 8.13 | 0.66 | 6.43 - 9.83 |
| 2004 | 7.83 | 0.61 | 6.24 - 9.41 |
| 2005 | 7.65 | 0.60 | 6.09 - 9.20 |
| 2006 | 7.6 | 0.63 | 5.97 - 9.22 |
| 2007 | 7.61 | 0.60 | 6.06 - 9.16 |
| 2008 | 7.66 | 0.49 | 6.38 - 8.94 |
| 2009 | 7.41 | 0.57 | 5.94 - 8.88 |
| 2010 | 7.38 | 0.55 | 5.95 - 8.81 |
| 2011 | 7.23 | 0.54 | 5.82 - 8.63 |

## 6. DECISION TREES: A CASE STUDY IN HEALTH CARE

Decision tree is the form of a tree structure which is built on regression or classification models. Decision Tree is a type of very powerful ML model capable of achieving high accuracy in many tasks while being highly interpretable. What makes decision trees special in the realm of ML models is really their clarity of information representation. The "knowledge" learned by a decision tree through training is directly formulated into a hierarchical structure. This structure holds and displays the knowledge in such a way that it can easily be understood, even by non-experts. Decision trees are typically a set of inputs used to create a tree with new cases. It breaks down a dataset into smaller and smaller subsets while at the same time an associated decision tree is incrementally developed. Mujtaba & Irshad (2017) did a Comparative study of existing techniques for heart diseases prediction using data mining approach. On the contrary, decision tree is widely used and practically useful method for reliable inference. For approximating any typical discrete valued target function, learned function is represented by a decision tree.

### Decision Tree for Brain Tumour

For this study data in excel format is taken from Gandhi Hospital and Omega hospital. The decision tree is experimented on the unseen datasets that is highlighted by the prediction and application which decision making does. Decision trees work on huge training set and are built in parallel tractable size training datasets. Decision tree will reduce a set of rules and resolve conflict rules, and the resultant is merged into a single unit. Each case is defined by a set of attributes / features. Each training case is given the class name, and each node of the decision tree contains a conditional test that divides the training cases, and the test has two branches ('Yes' or 'No') which the result has to follow. These properties make decision trees a valuable and standard tool for classification and all it follows is the basic divide and conquer algorithm (Steven, 1994). The construction for a decision tree method adopted is below [Quinlan, 1993]:

If $S$ represents training set and $R$ classes denoted by $\{P_1, P_2 ... P_1\}$, then

- if $S$ has one or more objects where all objects belong to a single class $Pj$, the decision tree is a leaf identifying class $Pj$.
- if $S$ has no objects, the decision tree is a leaf itself ($S$).

- if *S* has objects that belong to a mixture of classes, then a test is chosen, based on single attribute, that has one or more mutually exclusive outcomes {$O_1$, $O_2$,..., $O_n$}. *S* is partitioned into subsets *S1, S2,..., Sn*, where *Si* contains all the objects in *S* that have outcome $O_i$ of the chosen test. The same method is applied recursively to each subset of training objects (Podgorelec V et al, 2002).

With huge number of inputs widely known as features tend the decision trees to overfit. In high-dimensional space, a tree with a few samples is likely to overfit, and the right ratio for samples to the number of features is neccesary. As the number of patient cases increases, the branches in the decision tree increases as shown in figure

*Figure 6. Decision tree diagram on brain tumor obtained through Python Application*
*[ See Appendix 1 and 2]*

6. The figure 6 is an output of the decision tree using python code. The leaf nodes of the tree show that it cannot be divided further and contains an output variable which is used to make a prediction. In this method, from the large training sets the dataset is broken into *n* subsets (Abhishek, R. 2011). A decision tree is generated on each of the subsets, and rules are generated from the decision tree. This rule sets are combined into a single rule set with conflicts among rules resolved. Decision trees are found to be reliable and scalable with its property to handle huge and large datasets in this study as it gave satisfactory result in diagnosing and predicting brain tumors. Decision tree is found to be one of the successful data mining techniques used in the disease diagnosis as per the literature and in the present case of application.

## CONCLUSION

- In the light of the few case studies reported as part of literature survey and specific exercises carried out for this paper, it is possible to say that machine learning provides new opportunities for automatically learning in expressive models.
- The demanding health services by the ever-growing population put the health sector to adopt the computer- based services. This made the entry of machine learning and artificial intelligence, and data mining techniques to unimaginable domain of predictive modelling.
- Regression Models including Multiple and Multivariate Regression techniques are suitable for modeling Air Pollution and heart disease prediction. The applicability of STATA and R packages for multiple linear regression and predictive modelling for Crude Birth Rate and Crude Mortality Rate is well established in the present study carried out using the data from data.gov.in.
- Decision Tree is a class of very powerful Machine Learning model is applied for Brain Tumor. Machine learning is maturing promptly and requires efficient, well-knowledge and skilled persons on supervised as well as on unsupervised machine learning.
- In simple terms, machine learning techniques and data mining techniques go hand-in-hand as the data analytics tools used in the study for prediction, data modelling, and decision making.
- The health analytics and unpredictable growth of health databases require integration of the conventional data analysis to be paired with methods for efficient computer-assisted analysis. There is need for validation of computational models that are composed of multiple processing layers, which form part of deep learning efforts and are not part of this paper. Deep learning

(DL), a technique in artificial neural networks is emerging as a powerful tool for machine learning, promising to reshape the future of artificial intelligence.

- Electronic health records are the source of patient information that include medical history details such as diagnosis, diagnostic exams, medications and treatment plans, immunization records, radiology images, electroencephalogram EEG, laboratory and test lab reports. As such it requires standards for maintenance of these records so as to serve as meaningful and reliable database.

# REFERENCES

Abhishek, R. (2011). Computer aided detection of brain tumor in magnetic resonance images. *IACSIT International Journal of Engineering and Technology*, *3*(5), 523–532. doi:10.7763/IJET.2011.V3.280

Agosta, L. (2004, August). The future of data mining -- predictive analytics. *DM Review*.

Bernard, M. (2015). *Big Data: 20 Mind-Boggling Facts Everyone Must Read*. Retrieved September 30, 2015 from https://www.forbes.com

Brooks, R., & Dahlke, K. (2017). *Artificial Intelligence vs. Machine Learning vs. Data Mining 101 – What's the Big Difference?* Retrieved from October 6, 2017 from https://www.guavus.com

Charles, R. B. (2005). *Predictive analysis is data mining's future*. Retrieved June 5, 2005 from http://www.bio-itworld.com

Data Mining- Machine Learning. (n.d.). Retrieved from August 25, 2014. https://doublebyteblog.wordpress.com

Data Mining Tutorial: Process, Techniques, Tools & Applications. (n.d.). Retrieved from https://www.guru99.com

Jason, B. (2018). *Confidence-intervals-for-machine-learning*. Retrieved from May 28, 2018. https://machinelearningmastery.com

LogisticRegression. (n.d.). Retrieved from http://ufldl.stanford.edu

Machine_learning. Relation_to_data_mining. (n.d.). Retrieved from https://en.wikipedia.org/wiki/

Mateus, H., Monica, B., & Marie, H. (2015). Land use regression as method to model air pollution. Previous results for Gothenburg/Sweden. *ScienceDirect Procedia Engineering, 115*, 21–28. doi:10.1016/j.proeng.2015.07.350

McNulty, E. (2015). *Whats-the-difference-between-supervised-and-unsupervised-learning*. Retrieved from January 8, 2015 http://dataconomy.com

Mujtaba, A. Q., & Irshad, A. M. (2017). Comparative Study of Existing Techniques for Heart Diseases Prediction Using Data Mining Approach. *Asian Journal of Computer Science and Information Technology, 7*(3), 50–56.

Podgorelec, V., Kokol, P., Stiglic, B., & Rozman, I. (2002). Decision trees: An overview and their use in medicine. [PubMed]. *Journal of Medical Systems, 26*(5), 445–463. doi:10.1023/A:1016409317640

Polaraju, K., & Durgaprasad, D. (2017). Prediction of Heart Disease using Multiple Linear Regression Model. *International Journal of Engineering Development and Research, 5*(4), 1419–1425.

Quinlan, R. J. (1993). *C4.5: programs for machine learning*. San Francisco, CA: Morgan Kaufmann Publishers Inc.

Schneider, A., Hommel, G., & Blettner, M. (2010). Linear regression analysis. In a series of part 14 on evaluation of scientific publications. [PubMed]. *Deutsches Ärzteblatt International, 107*(44), 776–782.

Souhila, S. (2013). *What is the difference between machine learning and data mining?* Retrieved October 23, 2013 from https://www.researchgate.net

Steven, L. S. (1994). *Book Review: C4.5: programs for machine learning by Ross Quinlan J., Machine Learning (16)*. Boston: Kluwer Academic Publishers.

Xavier, A. (2016). *What's the relationship between machine learning and data mining?* Retrieved January 14, 2016 from https://medium.com

# APPENDIX 1

## Algorithm for Computation of Information Gain and Entropy of Class Attribute

Understanding which attribute to be placed at the root level from the dataset consisting of '$n$' attributes is a challenging step. Selecting randomly a node to be the root does not solve the problem. Information gain and entropy are the standards which calculate values for every attribute. The attribute with the highest value is placed at the root. Information is the measure of purity, and entropy is the impurity measure. Information gain is the expected reduction in entropy caused by the splitting of attribute. The entropy of class attribute is calculated by the standard rule

Entropy = $-P/(P+N)\log_2(P/(P+N)) - N/(P+N)\log_2(N/(P+N))$

where $P$ and $N$ represent the positive and negative outcome of the class attribute (predicted column). The standard rule for information gain and entropy of an attribute is given below.

$I(P_i, N_i) = -P/(P+N)\log_2(P/(P+N)) - N/(P+N)\log_2(N/(P+N))$

Entropy attribute = $\Sigma(P_i+N_i)/(P+N) \cdot I(P_i, N_i)$

Gain = Entropy class – Entropy attribute

The gain is calculated to find which attribute has the highest value. The one with the highest value will be the root node. The analysis was carried out using python on 101 patients' reports which were collected from Gandhi Hospital (Secunderabad) and Omega Hospital (Hyderabad). Using the standards discussed above the entropy of class attribute (brain tumor) = 2.9736.

Calculating for sex attribute.

$I(P_i, N_i)$ female=0.6235.
$I(P_i, N_i)$ male=0.2076.
Entropy of the sex=0.3929.
Gain of sex=2.5807; similarly, calculate for the age; it can be split into three groups
    1.    Age$\geq$25 and age<40.
    2.    Age$\geq$40 and age<65.
    3.    Age$\geq$65 and above.
$I(Pi, Ni)$ age$\geq$ 25 and age<40=0.738.

*I(Pi,Ni)* age>=40 and age <65=0.6722.
*I(Pi,Ni)* age>=65 and above=0.7219.
Entropy of the age=0.600.
Gain of the age=2.3736,

considering three common and major symptoms, i.e, headache, vomiting, and seizure based on the severity and duration of the symptom on the patient, the values are assigned 0, 1, and 2.

The information gain is calculated as shown in Table 12.

*Table 12.*

| Headache Severity | *I(Pi, Ni)* |
|---|---|
| 0 | 0.937 |
| 1 | 0.175 Entropy of headache=0.5111 |
| 2 | 0 Gain of the headache=2.9736 – 0.5111 = 2.4625 |
| Vomiting Severity | *I(Pi,Ni)* |
| 0 | 0.8058 |
| 1 | 0 Entropy of vomiting=0.582 |
| 2 | 0 Gain of the vomiting=2.9736-0.582=2.3916 |
| Seizure severity | *I(Pi,Ni)* |
| 0 | 0.742 |
| 1 | 0.468 Entropy of seizure=0.651 |
| 2 | 0 Gain of the Seizure=2.9736-0.651=2.3226 |

# APPENDIX 2

## Source Code for Decision Tree Program

**# step 1: import all the required libraries**

```
import numpy as np
import pandas as pd
from sklearn import tree
from IPython.display import Image
from sklearn.externals.six import StringIO
import pydotplus
```

**#step 2: read input data and map each attribute that need to be printed**

```
input_file = "HDetails.csv"
df = pd.read_csv(input_file, header = 0)
d = {'Y': 1, 'N': 0}
df['BrainTumor'] = df['BrainTumor'].map(d)
df['Headache'] = df['Headache'].map(d)
df['Vomiting'] = df['Vomiting'].map(d)
df['Seizure'] = df['Seizure'].map(d)
df['alteredbehaviour'] = df['alteredbehaviour'].map(d)
df['decreasedvision'] = df['decreasedvision'].map(d)
df['difficultyspeech'] = df['difficultyspeech'].map(d)
df['lossofconsciousness'] = df['lossofconsciousness'].map(d)
df['giddiness'] = df['giddiness'].map(d)
df['fever'] = df['fever'].map(d)
```

**#step 3: assigning the types of tumor with a numeric value**

```
d = {'Glioma': 1, 'Meningioma': 2, 'Parietal': 3, 'Recurrent':4}
df['TypeTumor'] = df['TypeTumor'].map(d)
d = {'M': 1,'F': 0}
df['sex'] = df['sex'].map(d)
print(df.head())
```

**# step 4: listing all the columns from the excel/csv datasheet**

```
features = list(df.columns[:13])
features
y = df["BrainTumor"]
X = df[features]
```

**# step5: create the model and create the training data for the classifier / decision tree**

**# install pydotplus and graphviz....Graphviz is a tool for drawing graphics using dot files. Pydotplus is a #module to Graphviz's Dot language**

**# train the classifier (decision tree) with the training data**

```
clf = tree.DecisionTreeClassifier()
clf = clf.fit(X,y)
dot_data = StringIO()
tree.export_graphviz(clf,out_file = dot_data, feature_names = features)
graph = pydotplus.graph_from_dot_data(dot_data.getvalue())
print("Creating graph...")
graph.write_png('tree2.png')
from sklearn.ensemble import RandomForestClassifier
```

**# step 6: random forests algorithm, technically is an ensemble method (based on the divide-and-#conquer approach) of decision trees generated on a randomly split dataset. This collection of #decision tree classifiers is also known as the forest.**

```
clf = RandomForestClassifier(n_estimators=30)
clf = clf.fit(X, y)
```

**# step 7: prints the tree**

```
print (clf.predict([[82, 1, 1, 1, 1, 0, 1, 1, 0, 0, 1, 0, 1]]))
print (clf.predict([[28, 1, 2, 1, 1, 0, 0, 1, 1, 0, 0, 0, 0]]))
```

Output: Decision tree diagram on brain tumor obtained through Python Application [ Fig 6]

# Compilation of References

Abdi, H., & Williams, L. J. (2010). Principal component analysis. *Wiley Interdisciplinary Reviews: Computational Statistics*, *2*(4), 433–459. doi:10.1002/wics.101

Abhishek, R. (2011). Computer aided detection of brain tumor in magnetic resonance images. *IACSIT International Journal of Engineering and Technology*, *3*(5), 523–532. doi:10.7763/IJET.2011.V3.280

Aggarwal, C. C., (2018). Training Deep Neural Networks. *Neural Networks and Deep Learning*, 105-167. doi:10.1007/978-3-319-94463-0_3

Agosta, L. (2004, August). The future of data mining -- predictive analytics. *DM Review*.

Albert, J. R. G., Orbeta, A. C. Jr, Paqueo, V. B., Serafica, R. B., Dadios, E. P., Culaba, A. B., & Bairan, J. C. A. C. (2018). *Harnessing government's role for the Fourth Industrial Revolution*. Academic Press.

Alia, M. A., Tamimi, A. A., & Al-Allaf, O. N. (2013). Integrated system for monitoring and recognizing students during class session. *The International Journal of Multimedia & Its Applications*, *5*(6), 45. doi:10.5121/ijma.2013.5604

Amarapur, B., & Kulkarni, P. (2011). External Force for Deformable Models in Medical Image Segmentation: A Survey. *Signal and Image Processing: an International Journal*, *2*(2), 82–101. doi:10.5121ipij.2011.2208

Anderson, C. W. (1987, January). Strategy learning with multilayer connectionist representations. In *Proceedings of the Fourth International Workshop on Machine Learning* (pp. 103-114). Morgan Kaufmann. 10.1016/B978-0-934613-41-5.50014-3

Avati, A., Jung, K., Harman, S., Downing, L., Ng, A., & Shah, N. H. (2018). Improving palliative care with deep learning. *BMC Medical Informatics and Decision Making*, *18*(4), 122. doi:10.118612911-018-0677-8 PMID:30537977

Awad, M., & Khanna, R. (2015). *Efficient learning machines: theories, concepts, and applications for engineers and system designers*. Apress; doi:10.1007/978-1-4302-5990-9

Awad, W., & Elseuofi, S. (2011). Machine Learning methods for E-mail Classification. *International Journal of Computers and Applications*, *16*(1), 39–45. doi:10.5120/1974-2646

Bailly-Bailliére, E., Bengio, S., Bimbot, F., Hamouz, M., Kittler, J., Mariéthoz, J., . . . Porée, F. (2003). *The BANCA database and evaluation protocol.* Paper presented at the International Conference on Audio-and video-based biometric person authentication. doi:10.1007/3-540-44887-X_74

Balla-Arabe, S., Gao, X., & Wang, B. (2013). A Fast and Robust Level Set Method for Image Segmentation Using Fuzzy Clustering and Lattice Boltzmann Method. *IEEE Transactions on Cybernetics, 43*(3), 910–920. doi:10.1109/TSMCB.2012.2218233 PMID:23076068

Bathaee, Y. (2018). The artificial intelligence black box and the failure of intent and causation. *Harvard Journal of Law & Technology, 31*(2), 889.

Batista, A. P., & DiCarlo, J. J. (2018). Deep learning reaches the motor system. *Nature Methods, 15*(10), 772–773. doi:10.103841592-018-0152-6 PMID:30275586

Baumann, J. (1993, Fall). Voice recognition. *Human Interface Technology Laboratory.*

Benedict, M., Kovács, J., & Czirják, A. (2012). Time dependence of quantum entanglement in the collision of two particles. *Journal of Physics. A, Mathematical and Theoretical, 45*(8), 085304. doi:10.1088/1751-8113/45/8/085304

Beneš, M., & Kučera, P. (2015). Solutions to the Navier-Stokes equations with mixed boundary conditions in two-dimensional bounded domains. *Mathematische Nachrichten, 289*(2-3), 194–212.

Bengio, Y., Boulanger-Lewandowski, N., & Pascanu, R. (2013, May). Advances in optimizing recurrent networks. In *2013 IEEE International Conference on Acoustics, Speech and Signal Processing* (pp. 8624-8628). IEEE. doi:10.1109/ICASSP.2013.6639349

Bennett, K. G., & Vercler, C. J. (2018). When Is Posting about Patients on Social Media Unethical "Medutainment"? [PubMed]. *AMA Journal of Ethics, 20*(4), 328–335. doi:10.1001/journalofethics.2018.20.4.ecas1-1804

Bernard, M. (2015). *Big Data: 20 Mind-Boggling Facts Everyone Must Read.* Retrieved September 30, 2015 from https://www.forbes.com

Bielski, C., Gentilini, S., & Pappalardo, M. (2011). Post-Disaster Image Processing for Damage Analysis Using GENESI-DR, WPS and Grid Computing. *Remote Sensing, 3*(6), 1234–1250. doi:10.3390/rs3061234

Brooks, R., & Dahlke, K. (2017). *Artificial Intelligence vs. Machine Learning vs. Data Mining 101 – What's the Big Difference?* Retrieved from October 6, 2017 from https://www.guavus.com

Buriro, A., Crispo, B., & Conti, M. (2019). AnswerAuth: A bimodal behavioral biometric-based user authentication scheme for smartphones. *Journal of Information Security and Applications, 44*, 89-103.

Buriro, A., Crispo, B., & Conti, M. (2019). AnswerAuth: A bimodal behavioral biometric-based user authentication scheme for smartphones. *Journal of Information Security and Applications, 44*, 89–103.

Cadena, S. A., Denfield, G. H., Walker, E. Y., Gatys, L. A., Tolias, A. S., Bethge, M., & Ecker, A. S. (2019). Deep convolutional models improve predictions of macaque V1 responses to natural images. *PLoS Computational Biology*, *15*(4), e1006897. doi:10.1371/journal.pcbi.1006897 PMID:31013278

Cao, C., Liu, F., Tan, H., Song, D., Shu, W., Li, W., ... Xie, Z. (2018). Deep learning and its applications in biomedicine. [PubMed]. *Genomics, Proteomics & Bioinformatics*, *16*(1), 17–32. doi:10.1016/j.gpb.2017.07.003

Carlos-Roca, L. R., Torres, I. H., & Tena, C. F. (2018, 8-13 July 2018). *Facial recognition application for border control.* Paper presented at the 2018 International Joint Conference on Neural Networks (IJCNN). doi:10.1109/IJCNN.2018.8489113

Charles, R. B. (2005). *Predictive analysis is data mining's future.* Retrieved June 5, 2005 from http://www.bio-itworld.com

Chaudhari, M., Shanta, S., & Vanjare, G. (2015). A review on Face Detection and study of Viola-Jones method. *International Journal of Computer Trends and Technology*, *25*(1), 54–61. doi:10.14445/22312803/IJCTT-V25P110

Chaudhari, R., & Patil, A. (2012). Content-based image retrieval using color and shape features. *International Journal of Advanced Research in Electrical. Electronics and Instrumentation Engineering*, *1*(5), 386–392.

Chen, M., Chen, C., Huang, M., Ciou, J., & Zhang, G. (2015). Design of Unmanned Vehicle System for Disaster Detection. *International Journal of Distributed Sensor Networks*, *11*(4), 784298. doi:10.1155/2015/784298

Chen, Y., Cremers, A., & Cao, Z. (2014). Interactive color image segmentation via iterative evidential labeling. *Information Fusion*, *20*, 292–304. doi:10.1016/j.inffus.2014.03.007

Chen, Y., Li, J., & Wang, J. Z. (2006). *Machine learning and statistical modeling approaches to image retrieval* (Vol. 14). Springer Science & Business Media.

Chintalapati, S., & Raghunadh, M. V. (2013). *Automated attendance management system based on face recognition algorithms.* Paper presented at the 2013 IEEE International Conference on Computational Intelligence and Computing Research. doi:10.1109/ICCIC.2013.6724266

Christopher, M. B. (2016). *Pattern recognition and machine learning.* Springer-Verlag.

Chung, K.-C., Kee, S. C., & Kim, S. R. (1999). Face recognition using principal component analysis of Gabor filter responses. *Proceedings International Workshop on Recognition, Analysis, and Tracking of Faces and Gestures in Real-Time Systems. In Conjunction with ICCV'99 (Cat. No. PR00378).*

Coates, A., Huval, B., Wang, T., Wu, D., Catanzaro, B., & Andrew, N. (2013, February). Deep learning with COTS HPC systems. In *International conference on machine learning* (pp. 1337-1345). Academic Press.

Conduction of Nerve Impulse. (2019). Retrieved from http://simplebiologyy.blogspot.com/2014/08/conduction-of-nerve-impulse.html

Cortes, C., & Vapnik, V. (1995). Support-vector networks. *Machine Learning, 20*(3), 273–297. doi:10.1007/BF00994018

CS231n Convolutional Neural Networks for Visual Recognition. (2019). Retrieved from http://cs231n.github.io/convolutional-networks/

Cui, Z., Yang, J., & Qiao, Y. (2016). Brain MRI segmentation with patch-based CNN approach. *2016 35th Chinese Control Conference (CCC)*. doi:10.1109/chicc.2016.7554465

Das, S., & Das, S. (2017, November 16). *CNN Architectures: LeNet, AlexNet, VGG, GoogLeNet, ResNet, and more...* Retrieved from https://medium.com/@sidereal/cnns-architectures-lenet-alexnet-vgg-googlenet-resnet-and-more-666091488df5

Data Mining- Machine Learning. (n.d.). Retrieved from August 25, 2014. https://doublebyteblog.wordpress.com

Data Mining Tutorial: Process, Techniques, Tools & Applications. (n.d.). Retrieved from https://www.guru99.com

Datta, R., Joshi, D., Li, J., & Wang, J. Z. (2008). Image retrieval: Ideas, influences, and trends of the new age. *ACM Computing Surveys (Csur), 40*(2), 5. doi:10.1145/1348246.1348248

Dean, J., Corrado, G., Monga, R., Chen, K., Devin, M., Mao, M., . . . Ng, A. Y. (2012). Large scale distributed deep networks. In Advances in neural information processing systems (pp. 1223-1231). Academic Press. Coates

Dean, J., Corrado, G., Monga, R., Chen, K., Devin, M., Mao, M., & Ng, A. Y. (2012). Large scale distributed deep networks. In *Advances in neural information processing systems* (pp. 1223–1231). Academic Press.

Deng & Yu. (2013). Deep Learning: Methods and Applications, Foundations and Trends R. *Signal Processing, 7*(3-4), 197–387. doi:10.1561/2000000039

Deng, L., & Yu, D. (2014). Deep learning: methods and applications. *Foundations and Trends® in Signal Processing, 7*(3–4), 197-387.

Deng, J., Dong, W., Socher, R., Li, L., Li, K., & Fei-Fei, L. (2009). ImageNet: A large-scale hierarchical image database. *2009 IEEE Conference on Computer Vision and Pattern Recognition*. 10.1109/CVPR.2009.5206848

Dharani, T., & Laurence Aroquiaraj, I. (2017). *An Essential Image Augmentation Processes for Pattern Based Image Retrieval System*. Academic Press.

Dharani, T., & Aroquiaraj, I. (2017). Pattern-Based Image Retrieval System built with Object Tracking and Segmentation Concepts. *International Journal of Computer & Mathematical Sciences, 6*(9), 312–319.

Diehl, P. U., Neil, D., Binas, J., Cook, M., Liu, S. C., & Pfeiffer, M. (2015, July). Fast-classifying, high-accuracy spiking deep networks through weight and threshold balancing. In *2015 International Joint Conference on Neural Networks (IJCNN)* (pp. 1-8). IEEE. 10.1109/IJCNN.2015.7280696

Du, G., Su, F., & Cai, A. (2009). *Face recognition using SURF features.* Paper presented at the MIPPR 2009: Pattern Recognition and Computer Vision.

Ducournau, A., & Bretto, A. (2014). Random walks in directed hypergraphs and application to semi-supervised image segmentation. *Computer Vision and Image Understanding, 120,* 91–102. doi:10.1016/j.cviu.2013.10.012

Duggal, R., Gupta, A., Gupta, R., Wadhwa, M., & Ahuja, C. (2016). Overlapping cell nuclei segmentation in microscopic images using deep belief networks. *Proceedings of the Tenth Indian Conference on Computer Vision, Graphics and Image Processing - ICVGIP 16.* 10.1145/3009977.3010043

Erickson, J. (2009). *Database technologies: Concepts, methodologies, tools, and applications: Concepts, methodologies, tools, and applications.* IGI Global. doi:10.4018/978-1-60566-058-5

Firozjaei, M., Daryaei, I., Sedighi, A., Weng, Q., & Alavipanah, S. (2019). Homogeneity Distance Classification Algorithm (HDCA): A Novel Algorithm for Satellite Image Classification. *Remote Sensing, 11*(5), 546. doi:10.3390/rs11050546

Flickner, M., Sawhney, H., Niblack, W., Ashley, J., Qian, H., Dom, B., ... Yanker, P. (1995). Query by image and video content: The QBIC system. *Computer, 28*(9), 23–32. doi:10.1109/2.410146

Gallege, L. S., & Raje, R. R. (2017, April). Parallel methods for evidence and trust based selection and recommendation of software apps from online marketplaces. In *Proceedings of the 12th Annual Conference on Cyber and Information Security Research* (p. 4). ACM. 10.1145/3064814.3064819

Gao, W., Cao, B., Shan, S., Zhou, D., Zhang, X., Zhao, D., & Al, S. (2004). *The CAS-PEAL large-scale Chinese face database and evaluation protocols.* Technique Report No. JDL-TR_04_FR_001, Joint Research & Development Laboratory, CAS.

Georgakopoulos, S. V., Iakovidis, D. K., Vasilakakis, M., Plagianakos, V. P., & Koulaouzidis, A. (2016). Weakly-supervised Convolutional learning for detection of inflammatory gastrointestinal lesions. *2016 IEEE International Conference on Imaging Systems and Techniques (IST).* 10.1109/IST.2016.7738279

Ghaffarian, S., Kerle, N., & Filatova, T. (2018). Remote Sensing-Based Proxies for Urban Disaster Risk Management and Resilience: A Review. *Remote Sensing, 10*(11), 1760. doi:10.3390/rs10111760

Goswami, S., Chakraborty, S., Ghosh, S., Chakrabarti, A., & Chakraborty, B. (2018). A review on application of data mining techniques to combat natural disasters. *Ain Shams Engineering Journal, 9*(3), 365–378. doi:10.1016/j.asej.2016.01.012

Grm, K., Štruc, V., Artiges, A., Caron, M., & Ekenel, H. K. (2017). Strengths and weaknesses of deep learning models for face recognition against image degradations. *IET Biometrics*, *7*(1), 81–89. doi:10.1049/iet-bmt.2017.0083

Grósz, T. (2014). Document Classification with Deep Rectifier Neural Networks and Probabilistic Sampling. *Text, Speech, and Dialogue Lecture Notes in Computer Science*. doi:10.1007/978-3-319-10816-2_14

Gruber, L. Z., Haruvi, A., Basri, R., & Irani, M. (2018). Perceptual dominance in brief presentations of mixed images: Human perception versus deep neural networks. *Frontiers in Computational Neuroscience*, *12*, 57. doi:10.3389/fncom.2018.00057 PMID:30087604

Guerguiev, J., Lillicrap, T. P., & Richards, B. A. (2017). Towards deep learning with segregated dendrites. *eLife*, *6*, e22901. doi:10.7554/eLife.22901 PMID:29205151

Guleria, P., & Sood, M. (2014). Data Mining in Education: A review on the knowledge discovery perspective. *International Journal of Data Mining & Knowledge Management Process*, *4*(5), 47–60. doi:10.5121/ijdkp.2014.4504

Gulshan, V., Peng, L., Coram, M., Stumpe, M. C., Wu, D., Narayanaswamy, A., & Webster, D. R. (2016). Development and Validation of a Deep Learning Algorithm for the Detection of Diabetic Retinopathy in Retinal Fundus Photographs. *Journal of the American Medical Association*, *316*(22), 2402. doi:10.1001/jama.2016.17216 PMID:27898976

Guo, W. W., & Xue, H. (2014). Crop Yield Forecasting Using Artificial Neural Networks: A Comparison between Spatial and Temporal Models. *Mathematical Problems in Engineering*, *2014*, 1–7. doi:10.1155/2014/857865

Hagendorff, T. (2019). The Ethics of AI Ethics--An Evaluation of Guidelines. arXiv preprint arXiv:1903.03425

Haines, D. E., & Mihailoff, G. A. (2017). *Fundamental neuroscience for basic and clinical applications*. Elsevier Health Sciences.

Hassabis, D., Kumaran, D., Summerfield, C., & Botvinick, M. (2017). Neuroscience-inspired artificial intelligence. *Neuron*, *95*(2), 245–258. doi:10.1016/j.neuron.2017.06.011 PMID:28728020

Higgins, I., Matthey, L., Glorot, X., Pal, A., Uria, B., Blundell, C., . . . Lerchner, A. (2016). *Early visual concept learning with unsupervised deep learning*. arXiv preprint arXiv:1606.05579

Hinton, G., Deng, L., Yu, D., Dahl, G., Mohamed, A. R., Jaitly, N., ... Sainath, T. (2012). Deep neural networks for acoustic modeling in speech recognition. *IEEE Signal Processing Magazine*, *29*.

Horowitz, M. C. (2018). *Artificial Intelligence, International Competition, and the Balance of Power*. Texas National Security Review.

Huang, P., Lai, Z., Gao, G., Yang, G., & Yang, Z. (2016). Adaptive linear discriminant regression classification for face recognition. *Digital Signal Processing*, *55*, 78–84. doi:10.1016/j.dsp.2016.05.001

Jain, A. K., Flynn, P., & Ross, A. A. (2007). *Handbook of biometrics*. Springer Science & Business Media.

Jain, A. K., Ross, A., & Prabhakar, S. (2004). An introduction to biometric recognition. *IEEE Transactions on Circuits and Systems for Video Technology*, *14*(1), 4–20. doi:10.1109/TCSVT.2003.818349

Jamil, N., & Sa'Dan, S. A. (2014). *Automated face annotation for personal photo management.* Paper presented at the 2014 International Conference on Computational Science and Technology (ICCST). doi:10.1109/ICCST.2014.7045176

Jason, B. (2018). *Confidence-intervals-for-machine-learning*. Retrieved from May 28,2018. https://machinelearningmastery.com

Jingyu, Q. (2018). A Survey on Sentiment Classification in Face Recognition. *Journal of Physics: Conference Series*, *960*(1), 012030.

Jolliffe, I. T. (2002). Principal component analysis and factor analysis. *Principal Component Analysis*, 150-166.

Joseph, J., & Zacharia, K. (2013). Automatic attendance management system using face recognition. *International Journal of Science and Research*, *2*(11), 328–330.

Joyce, K., Belliss, S., Samsonov, S., McNeill, S., & Glassey, P. (2009). A review of the status of satellite remote sensing and image processing techniques for mapping natural hazards and disasters. *Progress In Physical Geography: Earth And Environment*, *33*(2), 183–207. doi:10.1177/0309133309339563

Kang, H., Kim, B., Lee, J., Shin, J., & Shin, Y. (2014). Automatic left and right heart segmentation using power watershed and active contour model without edge. *Biomedical Engineering Letters*, *4*(4), 355–361. doi:10.100713534-014-0164-9

Kar, N., Debbarma, M. K., Saha, A., & Pal, D. R. (2012). Study of implementing automated attendance system using face recognition technique. *International Journal of Computer and Communication Engineering*, *1*(2), 100.

Karthikram, G. M. P., & Parthiban, G. (2014). Tag-based image retrieval (TBIR) using automatic image annotation. *International Journal of Research in Engineering and Technology*, *3*(3). doi:10.15623/ijret.2014.0303027

Kashyap, R. (2019a). Security, Reliability, and Performance Assessment for Healthcare Biometrics. In D. Kisku, P. Gupta, & J. Sing (Eds.), Design and Implementation of Healthcare Biometric Systems (pp. 29-54). Hershey, PA: IGI Global. doi:10.4018/978-1-5225-7525-2.ch002

Kashyap, R. (2019c). *Big Data Analytics Challenges and Solutions*. doi:10.1016/B978-0-12-818146-1.00002-7

Kashyap, R., Gautam, P., & Tiwari, V. (2018). Management and monitoring patterns and future scope. In Handbook of Research on Pattern Engineering System Development for Big Data Analytics (pp. 230–251). Hershey, PA: IGI Global. doi:10.4018/978-1-5225-3870-7.ch014

Kashyap, R. (2019a). Big Data and Global Software Engineering. In M. Rehman, A. Amin, A. Gilal, & M. Hashmani (Eds.), *Human Factors in Global Software Engineering* (pp. 131–163). Hershey, PA: IGI Global; doi:10.4018/978-1-5225-9448-2.ch006

Kashyap, R. (2019b). The sensation of Deep Learning in Image Processing Applications. In A. Hassanien, A. Darwish, & C. Chowdhary (Eds.), *Handbook of Research on Deep Learning Innovations and Trends* (pp. 72–96). Hershey, PA: IGI Global. doi:10.4018/978-1-5225-7862-8. ch005

Kashyap, R. (2019d). Computational Healthcare System With Image Analysis. In C. Chen & S. Cheung (Eds.), *Computational Models for Biomedical Reasoning and Problem Solving* (pp. 89–127). Hershey, PA: IGI Global; doi:10.4018/978-1-5225-7467-5.ch004

Kashyap, R. (2019d). Geospatial Big Data, Analytics and IoT: Challenges, Applications and Potential. In H. Das, R. Barik, H. Dubey, & D. Roy (Eds.), *Cloud Computing for Geospatial Big Data Analytics. Studies in Big Data* (Vol. 49). Cham: Springer. doi:10.1007/978-3-030-03359-0_9

Kashyap, R. (2019e). Systematic Model for Decision Support System. In A. Mukherjee & A. Krishna (Eds.), *Interdisciplinary Approaches to Information Systems and Software Engineering* (pp. 62–98). Hershey, PA: IGI Global; doi:10.4018/978-1-5225-7784-3.ch004

Kashyap, R. (2019f). Miracles of Healthcare With Internet of Things. In J. Rodrigues, A. Gawanmeh, K. Saleem, & S. Parvin (Eds.), *Smart Devices, Applications, and Protocols for the IoT* (pp. 120–164). Hershey, PA: IGI Global; doi:10.4018/978-1-5225-7811-6.ch007

Kashyap, R. (2019g). Deep Learning: An Application in Internet of Things. In H. Purnomo (Ed.), *Computational Intelligence in the Internet of Things* (pp. 130–158). Hershey, PA: IGI Global; doi:10.4018/978-1-5225-7955-7.ch006

Kashyap, R. (2019h). Machine Learning, Data Mining for IoT-Based Systems. In G. Kaur & P. Tomar (Eds.), *Handbook of Research on Big Data and the IoT* (pp. 314–338). Hershey, PA: IGI Global; doi:10.4018/978-1-5225-7432-3.ch018

Kashyap, R. (2019i). Decision Support Systems in Aeronautics and Aerospace Industries. In T. Shmelova, Y. Sikirda, N. Rizun, D. Kucherov, & K. Dergachov (Eds.), *Automated Systems in the Aviation and Aerospace Industries* (pp. 138–165). Hershey, PA: IGI Global; doi:10.4018/978-1-5225-7709-6.ch005

Kashyap, R. (2019j). Medical Image Segmentation and Analysis. In C. Chakraborty (Ed.), *Advanced Classification Techniques for Healthcare Analysis* (pp. 132–160). Hershey, PA: IGI Global; doi:10.4018/978-1-5225-7796-6.ch007

Kashyap, R. (2019k). Big Data and High-Performance Analyses and Processes. In A. Voghera & L. La Riccia (Eds.), *Spatial Planning in the Big Data Revolution* (pp. 45–83). Hershey, PA: IGI Global; doi:10.4018/978-1-5225-7927-4.ch003

Kashyap, R. (2019l). Artificial Intelligence Systems in Aviation. In T. Shmelova, Y. Sikirda, N. Rizun, & D. Kucherov (Eds.), *Cases on Modern Computer Systems in Aviation* (pp. 1–26). Hershey, PA: IGI Global; doi:10.4018/978-1-5225-7588-7.ch001

Kashyap, R. (2020). Applications of Wireless Sensor Networks in Healthcare. In P. Mukherjee, P. Pattnaik, & S. Panda (Eds.), *IoT and WSN Applications for Modern Agricultural Advancements: Emerging Research and Opportunities* (pp. 8–40). Hershey, PA: IGI Global. doi:10.4018/978-1-5225-9004-0.ch002

Kashyap, R., & Gautam, P. (2015, November). Modified region based segmentation of medical images. In *Proceedings of International Conference on Communication Networks* (ICCN) (pp. 209–216). IEEE. 10.1109/ICCN.2015.41

Kashyap, R., & Gautam, P. (2016). Fast level set method for segmentation of medical images. In *Proceedings of the International Conference on Informatics and Analytics*. ACM. 10.1145/2980258.2980302

Kashyap, R., & Gautam, P. (2017). Fast Medical Image Segmentation Using Energy-Based Method. In V. Tiwari, B. Tiwari, R. Thakur, & S. Gupta (Eds.), *Pattern and Data Analysis in Healthcare Settings* (pp. 35–60). Hershey, PA: IGI Global. doi:10.4018/978-1-5225-0536-5.ch003

Kashyap, R., & Piersson, A. D. (2018). Impact of Big Data on Security. In G. Shrivastava, P. Kumar, B. Gupta, S. Bala, & N. Dey (Eds.), *Handbook of Research on Network Forensics and Analysis Techniques* (pp. 283–299). Hershey, PA: IGI Global. doi:10.4018/978-1-5225-4100-4.ch015

Kashyap, R., & Rahamatkar, S. (2019a). Medical Image Segmentation: An Advanced Approach. In S. Paul, P. Bhattacharya, & A. Bit (Eds.), *Early Detection of Neurological Disorders Using Machine Learning Systems* (pp. 292–321). Hershey, PA: IGI Global. doi:10.4018/978-1-5225-8567-1.ch015

Kashyap, R., & Rahamatkar, S. (2019b). Healthcare Informatics Using Modern Image Processing Approaches. In B. Singh, B. Saini, D. Singh, & A. Pandey (Eds.), *Medical Data Security for Bioengineers* (pp. 254–277). Hershey, PA: IGI Global; doi:10.4018/978-1-5225-7952-6.ch013

Kashyap, R., & Tiwari, V. (2017). Energy-based active contour method for image segmentation. *International Journal of Electronic Healthcare*, *9*(2–3), 210–225. doi:10.1504/IJEH.2017.083165

Kaur, D., & Kaur, Y. (2014). Various image segmentation techniques: A review. *International Journal of Computer Science and Mobile Computing*, *3*(5), 809–814.

Klokova, A. (2010). Comparison of various biometric methods. In *Interactive Multimedia Systems*. University of Southampton.

Krithivasan, S., Wahal, S., & Ansumali, S. (2014). Diffused bounce-back condition and refill algorithm for the lattice Boltzmann method. *Physical Review. E, 89*(3), 033313. doi:10.1103/PhysRevE.89.033313 PMID:24730973

Krizhevsky, A., Sutskever, I., & Hinton, G. E. (2017). ImageNet classification with deep convolutional neural networks. *Communications of the ACM, 60*(6), 84–90. doi:10.1145/3065386

Kumar, A., Tyagi, A. K., & Tyagi, S. K. (2014). Data Mining: Various Issues and Challenges for Future A Short discussion on Data Mining issues for future work. *International Journal of Emerging Technology and Advanced Engineering, 4*(1), 1–8.

Kundu, J., & Rajesh, R. (2015). Asymptotic behavior of the isotropic-nematic and nematic-columnar phase boundaries for the system of hard rectangles on a square lattice. *Physical Review. E, 91*(1), 012105. doi:10.1103/PhysRevE.91.012105 PMID:25679568

Le, Q. V., Ngiam, J., Coates, A., Lahiri, A., Prochnow, B., & Ng, A. Y. (2011, June). On optimization methods for deep learning. In Proceedings of the 28th International Conference on International Conference on Machine Learning (pp. 265-272). Omnipress.

LeCun, Y., Bengio, Y., & Hinton, G. (2015). Deep learning. *Nature, 521*(7553), 436–444. doi:10.1038/nature14539 PMID:26017442

Lehmann, T., Güld, M., Thies, C., Fischer, B., Spitzer, K., Keysers, D., . . . Wein, B. (2003). *The Irma project: A state of the art report on content-based image retrieval in medical applications.* Paper presented at the Korea-Germany Workshop on Advanced Medical Image.

Lenti, F., Nunziata, F., Estatico, C., & Migliaccio, M. (2016). Conjugate Gradient Method in Hilbert and Banach Spaces to Enhance the Spatial Resolution of Radiometer Data. *IEEE Transactions on Geoscience and Remote Sensing, 54*(1), 397–406. doi:10.1109/TGRS.2015.2458014

Le, P., & Zuidema, W. (2015). Compositional Distributional Semantics with Long Short Term Memory. *Proceedings of the Fourth Joint Conference on Lexical and Computational Semantics.* 10.18653/v1/S15-1002

Li, C., Huang, R., Ding, Z., Gatenby, J., Metaxas, D., & Gore, J. (2011). A Level Set Method for Image Segmentation in the Presence of Intensity Inhomogeneities With Application to MRI. *IEEE Transactions on Image Processing, 20*(7), 2007–2016. doi:10.1109/TIP.2011.2146190 PMID:21518662

Li, H., Zhou, D., & Wu, Y. (2011). Collision detection algorithm based on mixed bounding box. *Jisuanji Yingyong, 30*(12), 3304–3306. doi:10.3724/SP.J.1087.2010.03304

Litjens, G., Kooi, T., Bejnordi, B. E., Setio, A. A. A., Ciompi, F., Ghafoorian, M., ... Sánchez, C. I. (2017). A survey on deep learning in medical image analysis. [PubMed]. *Medical Image Analysis, 42*, 60–88. doi:10.1016/j.media.2017.07.005

Liu, C., & Wechsler, H. (2003). Independent component analysis of Gabor features for face recognition. [PubMed]. *IEEE Transactions on Neural Networks, 14*(4), 919–928. doi:10.1109/TNN.2006.875987

Li, X.-Y., & Lin, Z.-X. (2018). *Face Recognition Based on HOG and Fast PCA Algorithm.* Academic Press; doi:10.1007/978-3-319-68527-4_2

LogisticRegression. (n.d.). Retrieved from http://ufldl.stanford.edu

Lorenzo, P. R., Nalepa, J., Ramos, L. S., & Pastor, J. R. (2017, July). Hyper-parameter selection in deep neural networks using parallel particle swarm optimization. In *Proceedings of the Genetic and Evolutionary Computation Conference Companion* (pp. 1864-1871). ACM. doi:10.1145/3067695.3084211

Lou, Q., Guo, Z., & Shi, B. (2012). Effects of force discretization on mass conservation in lattice Boltzmann equation for two-phase flows. *EPL*, *99*(6), 64005. doi:10.1209/0295-5075/99/64005

Luo, J., & Crandall, D., (2006). *Color object detection using spatial-color joint probability functions* (Vol. 15). Academic Press.

Machine_learning. Relation_to_data_mining. (n.d.). Retrieved from https://en.wikipedia.org/wiki/

Mahbub, U., Sarkar, S., & Chellappa, R. (2019). Partial face detection in the mobile domain. *Image and Vision Computing*, *82*, 1–17. doi:10.1016/j.imavis.2018.12.003

Manor, R., Mishali, L., & Geva, A. B. (2016). Multimodal neural network for rapid serial visual presentation brain computer interface. [PubMed]. *Frontiers in Computational Neuroscience*, *10*, 130. doi:10.3389/fncom.2016.00130

Marcos-Pablos, S., & García-Peñalvo, F. J. (2019). Technological Ecosystems in Care and Assistance: A Systematic Literature Review. [PubMed]. *Sensors (Basel)*, *19*(3), 708. doi:10.339019030708

Marcus, G. (2018). Deep learning: A critical appraisal. arXiv preprint arXiv:1801.00631

Marques, O. (2001). *Content-based image retrieval using relevance feedback.* Florida Atlantic University.

Martens, J. (2010, June). Deep learning via hessian-free optimization. *ICML*, *27*, 735–742.

Martens, J., & Sutskever, I. (2011). Learning recurrent neural networks with hessian-free optimization. In *Proceedings of the 28th International Conference on Machine Learning (ICML-11)* (pp. 1033-1040). Academic Press.

Martinez, A. M. (1998). *The AR face database.* CVC Technical Report24.

Mateus, H., Monica, B., & Marie, H. (2015). Land use regression as method to model air pollution. Previous results for Gothenburg/Sweden. *ScienceDirect Procedia Engineering*, *115*, 21–28. doi:10.1016/j.proeng.2015.07.350

Ma, Y., Xiang, Z., Du, Q., & Fan, W. (2018). Effects of user-provided photos on hotel review helpfulness: An analytical approach with deep leaning. *International Journal of Hospitality Management*, *71*, 120–131. doi:10.1016/j.ijhm.2017.12.008

McNulty, E. (2015). *Whats-the-difference-between-supervised-and-unsupervised-learning.* Retrieved from January 8, 2015 http://dataconomy.com

Mehta, R., Mishra, N., & Sharma, S. (2011). *Color Texture-based Image Retrieval System* (Vol. 24). Academic Press.

Mohamad & Kuzmin. (2012). The Soret Effect with the D1Q2 and D2Q4 Lattice Boltzmann Model. *International Journal of Nonlinear Sciences and Numerical Simulation, 13*(3-4).

Mraković, I., & Vojinović, R. (2019). Maritime Cyber Security Analysis–How to Reduce Threats? *Transactions on Maritime Science, 8*(1), 132–139.

Mujtaba, A. Q., & Irshad, A. M. (2017). Comparative Study of Existing Techniques for Heart Diseases Prediction Using Data Mining Approach. *Asian Journal of Computer Science and Information Technology, 7*(3), 50–56.

Müller, H., Michoux, N., Bandon, D., & Geissbuhler, A. (2004). A review of content-based image retrieval systems in medical applications—Clinical benefits and future directions. *International Journal of Medical Informatics, 73*(1), 1–23. doi:10.1016/j.ijmedinf.2003.11.024 PMID:15036075

Najafabadi, M. M., Villanustre, F., Khoshgoftaar, T. M., Seliya, N., Wald, R., & Muharemagic, E. (2015). Deep learning applications and challenges in big data analytics. *Journal of Big Data, 2*(1), 1. doi:10.118640537-014-0007-7

Narwade Manoorkar, J., & Kumar, D. B. (2016). Local and Global Color Histogram Feature for Color Content-Based Image Retrieval System. Academic Press.

Neubert, T., Mandea, M., Hulot, G., von Frese, R., Primdahl, F., Jørgensen, J., ... Risbo, T. (2001). Ørsted satellite captures high-precision geomagnetic field data. *Eos (Washington, D.C.), 82*(7), 81–88. doi:10.1029/01EO00043

Neuroscience and its applications through deep learning - Google Search. (2019). Retrieved from https://www.google.com/search?q=Neuroscience+and+its+applications+through+deep +learning&safe

Oh, S. J., Benenson, R., Fritz, M., & Schiele, B. (2018). Person Recognition in Personal Photo Collections. [PubMed]. *IEEE Transactions on Pattern Analysis and Machine Intelligence*, 1–1. doi:10.1109/TPAMI.2018.2877588

Patel, T., & Shah, B. (2017). *A survey on facial feature extraction techniques for automatic face annotation.* Paper presented at the 2017 International Conference on Innovative Mechanisms for Industry Applications (ICIMIA). doi:10.1109/ICIMIA.2017.7975607

Pauplin, O., Caleb-Solly, P., & Smith, J. (2010). User-centric image segmentation using an interactive parameter adaptation tool. *Pattern Recognition, 43*(2), 519–529. doi:10.1016/j.patcog.2009.03.007

Peng, M., Wang, C., Chen, T., & Liu, G. (2016, October 27). *NIRFaceNet: A Convolutional Neural Network for Near-Infrared Face Identification.* Retrieved from https://www.mdpi.com/2078-2489/7/4/61

Phillips, P. J., Moon, H., Rizvi, S. A., & Rauss, P. J. (2000). The FERET evaluation methodology for face-recognition algorithms. *IEEE Transactions on Pattern Analysis and Machine Intelligence, 22*(10), 1090–1104. doi:10.1109/34.879790

Phillips, P. J., Wechsler, H., Huang, J., & Rauss, P. J. (1998). The FERET database and evaluation procedure for face-recognition algorithms. *Image and Vision Computing, 16*(5), 295–306. doi:10.1016/S0262-8856(97)00070-X

Pichuzhkina, A., & Roldugin, D. (2016). Geomagnetic field models for satellite angular motion. *Keldysh Institute Preprints*, (87-e), 1-25. doi:10.20948/prepr-2016-87-e

Pilevar, A. H. (2011). CBMIR: Content-based Image Retrieval Algorithm for Medical Image Databases. *Journal of Medical Signals and Sensors, 1*(1), 12–18. PMID:22606654

Podgorelec, V., Kokol, P., Stiglic, B., & Rozman, I. (2002). Decision trees: An overview and their use in medicine. [PubMed]. *Journal of Medical Systems, 26*(5), 445–463. doi:10.1023/A:1016409317640

Polaraju, K., & Durgaprasad, D. (2017). Prediction of Heart Disease using Multiple Linear Regression Model. *International Journal of Engineering Development and Research, 5*(4), 1419–1425.

Powles, J., & Hodson, H. (2017). Google DeepMind and healthcare in an age of algorithms. [PubMed]. *Health and technology, 7*(4), 351–367. doi:10.100712553-017-0179-1

Purandare, V., & Talele, K. (2014). *Efficient heterogeneous face recognition using scale-invariant feature transform.* Paper presented at the 2014 International Conference on Circuits, Systems, Communication and Information Technology Applications (CSCITA). doi:10.1109/CSCITA.2014.6839277

Quinlan, R. J. (1993). *C4.5: programs for machine learning.* San Francisco, CA: Morgan Kaufmann Publishers Inc.

Raina, R., Madhavan, A., & Ng, A. Y. (2009). Large-scale deep unsupervised learning using graphics processors. *Proceedings of the 26th Annual International Conference on Machine Learning - ICML 09.* 10.1145/1553374.1553486

Ramamurthy, B., & Chandran, K. (2011). CBMIR: Shape-based image retrieval using canny edge detection and k-means clustering algorithms for medical images. *International Journal of Engineering Science and Technology, 3*(3).

Ravì, D., Wong, C., Deligianni, F., Berthelot, M., Andreu-Perez, J., Lo, B., & Yang, G. Z. (2017). Deep learning for health informatics. *IEEE Journal of Biomedical and Health Informatics, 21*(1), 4–21. doi:10.1109/JBHI.2016.2636665 PMID:28055930

Réda, A., & Aoued, B. (2004). *Artificial neural network-based face recognition.* Paper presented at the Control, Communications and Signal Processing, 2004. First International Symposium on. doi:10.1109/ISCCSP.2004.1296323

Regniers, O., Da Costa, J.-P., Grenier, G., Germain, C., & Bombrun, L. (2013). *Texture-based image retrieval and classification of very high-resolution maritime pine forest images.* Paper presented at the 2013 IEEE International Geoscience and Remote Sensing Symposium-IGARSS. 10.1109/IGARSS.2013.6723719

Rubner, Y., & Tomasi, C. (1999). Texture-based image retrieval without segmentation. *Proceedings of the Seventh IEEE International Conference on Computer Vision.* 10.1109/ICCV.1999.790380

Saini, R., & Rana, N. (2014). Comparison of various biometric methods. *International Journal of Advances in Science and Technology, 2*(1), 24–30.

Samuel, A. L. (2000). Some studies in machine learning using the game of checkers. *IBM Journal of Research and Development, 44*(1.2), 206-226.

Saxena, P., & Shefali. (2018). Content-based image retrieval system by fusion of color, texture, and edge features with SVM classifier and relevance feedback. *International Journal of Research - Granthaalayah, 6*(9), 259-273. doi:10.5281/zenodo.1443433

Schneider, A., Hommel, G., & Blettner, M. (2010). Linear regression analysis. In a series of part 14 on evaluation of scientific publications. [PubMed]. *Deutsches Ärzteblatt International, 107*(44), 776–782.

Sergeev, A., & Del Balso, M. (2018). *Horovod: fast and easy distributed deep learning in TensorFlow.* arXiv preprint arXiv:1802.05799

Seymour, V. (2016). The human–nature relationship and its impact on health: A critical review. [PubMed]. *Frontiers in Public Health, 4*, 260. doi:10.3389/fpubh.2016.00260

Shapiro, L., & George, C. (2002). *Stockman g: computer vision.* Prentice Hall.

Shen, D., Wu, G., & Suk, H. I. (2017). Deep learning in medical image analysis. *Annual Review of Biomedical Engineering, 19*(1), 221–248. doi:10.1146/annurev-bioeng-071516-044442 PMID:28301734

Shilwant, D. S., & Karwankar, A. (2012). Student Monitoring By Face Recognition System. *International Journal of Electronics Communication and Soft Computing Science & Engineering, 2*(2), 24.

Shirazi, S. H., Khan, N., Umar, A., Naz, M., & AlHaqbani, B. (2016). Content-based image retrieval using texture color shape and region. *International Journal of Advanced Computer Science and Applications, 7*(1), 418–426.

Shu, C., Ding, X., & Fang, C. (2011). Histogram of the oriented gradient for face recognition. *Tsinghua Science and Technology, 16*(2), 216–224. doi:10.1016/S1007-0214(11)70032-3

Shukla, R., Gupta, R. K., & Kashyap, R. (2019). A multiphase pre-copy strategy for the virtual machine migration in the cloud. In S. Satapathy, V. Bhateja, & S. Das (Eds.), *Smart Intelligent Computing and Applications. Smart Innovation, Systems and Technologies* (Vol. 104). Singapore: Springer. doi:10.1007/978-981-13-1921-1_43

Singh, K., & Nair, J. (2018). A Literature Review On Satellite Image Data Enhancement Using Digital Image Processing. *International Journal on Computer Science and Engineering, 6*(7), 1114–1119. doi:10.26438/ijcse/v6i7.11141119

Souhila, S. (2013). *What is the difference between machine learning and data mining?* Retrieved October 23, 2013 from https://www.researchgate.net

Steven, L. S. (1994). *Book Review: C4.5: programs for machine learning by Ross Quinlan J., Machine Learning (16)*. Boston: Kluwer Academic Publishers.

Suetake, Uchino, & Hirata. (2007). Separability-Based Intelligent Scissors for Interactive Image Segmentation. *IEICE Transactions on Information and Systems, 90*(1), 137-144.

Sun, C., Pérot, F., Zhang, R., Freed, D., & Chen, H. (2013). Impedance Boundary Condition for Lattice Boltzmann Model. *Communications in Computational Physics, 13*(03), 757–768. doi:10.4208/cicp.421011.260112s

Sutskever, I. (2013). *Training recurrent neural networks*. Toronto, Canada: University of Toronto.

Szczuko, P., Czyżewski, A., Hoffmann, P., Bratoszewski, P., & Lech, M. (2019). Validating data acquired with experimental multimodal biometric system installed in bank branches. *Journal of Intelligent Information Systems, 52*(1), 1–31. doi:10.100710844-017-0491-2

Tissera, M. D., & McDonnell, M. D. (2016). Deep extreme learning machines: Supervised autoencoding architecture for classification. *Neurocomputing, 174*, 42–49. doi:10.1016/j.neucom.2015.03.110

Tiwari, S., Gupta, R. K., & Kashyap, R. (2019). To enhance web response time using agglomerative clustering technique for web navigation recommendation. In H. Behera, J. Nayak, B. Naik, & A. Abraham (Eds.), *Computational Intelligence in Data Mining. Advances in Intelligent Systems and Computing* (Vol. 711). Singapore: Springer. doi:10.1007/978-981-10-8055-5_59

Tsutahara, M. (2012). The finite-difference lattice Boltzmann method and its application in computational aero-acoustics. *Fluid Dynamics Research, 44*(4), 045507. doi:10.1088/0169-5983/44/4/045507

Turk, M. A., & Pentland, A. P. (1991). Face recognition using eigenfaces. *1991 IEEE Computer Society Conference on Computer Vision and Pattern Recognition*. doi:10.1109/CVPR.1991.139758

Turner, J. (2019). Controlling the Creators. In *Robot Rules* (pp. 263–318). Cham: Palgrave Macmillan; doi:10.1007/978-3-319-96235-1_7

Tyagi & Rekha. (2019). Machine Learning with Big Data. In *Proceedings of International Conference on Sustainable Computing in Science, Technology and Management (SUSCOM).* Amity University Rajasthan. Available at SSRN: https://ssrn.com/abstract=3356269 or http://dx.doi.org/ doi:10.2139srn.3356269

Tyagi, A. K. (2019). Building a Smart and Sustainable Environment using Internet of Things. In *Proceedings of International Conference on Sustainable Computing in Science, Technology and Management (SUSCOM).* Amity University Rajasthan, Jaipur - India. Available at SSRN: https://ssrn.com/abstract=3356500 or http://dx.doi.org/ doi:10.2139srn.3356500

Tyagi, A. K. (2019). *Machine Learning with Big Data.* Retrieved from https://towardsdatascience.com/why-deep-learning-is-needed-over-traditional-machine-learning-1b6a99177063

Tyagi, A. K., & Reddy, V. K. (2019). *Performance Analysis of Under-Sampling and Over-Sampling Techniques for Solving Class Imbalance Problem.* Retrieved from https://www.edureka.co/blog/what-is-deep-learning

Ullman, S. (2019). Using neuroscience to develop artificial intelligence. *Science, 363*(6428), 692–693. doi:10.1126cience.aau6595 PMID:30765552

Urabe, K., & Saji, H. (2009). Detection of Road Blockage Areas after Earthquake Disaster in Mountainous Districts Using Aerial Images. *Journal Of Japan Association For Earthquake Engineering, 9*(4), 26–38. doi:10.5610/jaee.9.4_26

Utyuzh, O., Wilk, G., & Wodarczyk, Z. (2007). Numerical symmetrization of state of identical particles. *Brazilian Journal of Physics, 37*(2).

Varshney, G., & Soni, U. (2011). Color-Based Image Retrieval in Image Database System. *International Journal of Soft Computing and Engineering, 1*(5), 31–35.

Vinay, A., Shekhar, V. S., Rituparna, J., Aggrawal, T., Murthy, K. B., & Natarajan, S. (2015). Cloud-based big data analytics framework for face recognition in social networks using machine learning. *Procedia Computer Science, 50,* 623–630. doi:10.1016/j.procs.2015.04.095

Viola, P., & Jones, M. (2001). Rapid object detection using a boosted cascade of simple features. *Computer Vision and Pattern Recognition, 2001. CVPR 2001. Proceedings of the 2001 IEEE Computer Society Conference on.* doi:10.1109/CVPR.2001.990517

Viola, P., & Jones, M. J. (2004). Robust real-time face detection. *International Journal of Computer Vision, 57*(2), 137–154. doi:10.1023/B:VISI.0000013087.49260.fb

Wang, L., He, L., Mishra, A., & Li, C. (2009). Active contours driven by local Gaussian distribution fitting energy. *Signal Processing, 89*(12), 2435–2447. doi:10.1016/j.sigpro.2009.03.014

Wang, Y., Shu, C., & Yang, L. (2016). Boundary condition-enforced immersed boundary-lattice Boltzmann flux solver for thermal flows with Neumann boundary conditions. *Journal of Computational Physics, 306,* 237–252. doi:10.1016/j.jcp.2015.11.046

Waoo, N., Kashyap, R., & Jaiswal, A. (2010). DNA nanoarray analysis using hierarchical quality threshold clustering. In *Proceedings of 2010 2nd IEEE International Conference on Information Management and Engineering* (pp. 81-85). IEEE. 10.1109/ICIME.2010.5477579

Wei, W. A. N. G. (2018). *Prediction of protein-ligand binding affinity via deep learning.* Academic Press.

Win, S., & Aung, T. (2018). Automated Text Annotation for Social Media Data during Natural Disasters. *Advances In Science. Technology And Engineering Systems Journal, 3*(2), 119–127. doi:10.25046/aj030214

Worsey, J. N. (2016). *Face recognition in an unconstrained environment for monitoring student attendance.* Academic Press.

Wu, J., & Guo, H. (2014). Sonar Image Segmentation Based on an Improved Selection of Initial Contour of Active Contour Model. *AMM, 709,* 447–450. doi:10.4028/www.scientific.net/AMM.709.447

Xavier, A. (2016). *What's the relationship between machine learning and data mining?* Retrieved January 14, 2016 from https://medium.com

Yang, G., & Fang, S. (2016). Improving remote sensing image classification by exploiting adaptive features and hierarchical hybrid decision trees. *Remote Sensing Letters, 8*(2), 156–164. doi:10.1080/2150704X.2016.1239282

Zafar, U., Ghafoor, M., Zia, T., Ahmed, G., Latif, A., Malik, K. R., & Sharif, A. M. (2019). Face recognition with Bayesian convolutional networks for robust surveillance systems. *Eurasip Journal on Image and Video Processing, 2019*(1). doi:10.118613640-019-0406-y

Zhang. (2013). *Automated biometrics: Technologies and systems* (Vol. 7). Springer Science & Business Media.

Zhang, K., Song, H., & Zhang, L. (2010). Active contours driven by local image fitting energy. *Pattern Recognition, 43*(4), 1199–1206. doi:10.1016/j.patcog.2009.10.010

Zhuang, X., Ji, X., & Wei, Z. (2013). A Novel Deformable Grid Method for Image Segmentation. *AMM, 310,* 624–628. doi:10.4028/www.scientific.net/AMM.310.624

Zhu, Y., Zhu, C., & Li, X. (2018). Improved principal component analysis and linear regression classification for face recognition. *Signal Processing, 145,* 175–182. doi:10.1016/j.sigpro.2017.11.018

# About the Contributors

**Ramgopal Kashyap** has areas of interest in image processing, pattern recognition, and machine learning. He has published many research papers in international journals and conferences like Springer, Inderscience, Elsevier, ACM, and IGI-Global indexed by Science Citation Index (SCI) and Scopus (Elsevier) and many book chapters. He has Reviewed Research Papers in the Science Citation Index Expanded, Springer Journals and Editorial Board Member and conferences programme committee member of the IEEE, Springer international conferences and journals held in countries: Czech Republic, Switzerland, UAE, Australia, Hungary, Poland, Taiwan, Denmark, India, USA, UK, Austria, and Turkey. He has written many book chapters published by Springer, Elsevier and IGI Global, USA.

**A. V. Senthil Kumar** obtained his BSc Degree (Physics) in 1987, P.G.Diploma in Computer Applications in 1988, MCA in 1991 from Bharathiar University. He obtained his Master of Philosophy in Computer Science from Bharathidasan University, Trichy during 2005 and his Ph.D in Computer Science from Vinayaka Missions University during 2009. To his credit he has industrial experience for five years as System Analyst in a Garment Export Company. Later he took up teaching and attached to CMS College of Science and Commerce, Coimbatore and now he is working as a Director & Professor in the Department of Research and PG in Computer Applications, Hindusthan College of Arts and Science, Coimbatore since 05/03/2010. He has to his credit 6 Book Chapters, 85 papers in International Journals, 2 papers in National Journals, 23 papers in International Conferences, 5 papers in National Conferences, and edited four books in Data Mining, Mobile Computing, Fuzzy Expert Systems and one more book in Web Usage Mining by process (IGI Global, USA).. Key Member for India, Machine Intelligence Research Lab (MIR Labs).

\* \* \*

**Muralikrishna Iyyanki** Iyyanki is the Chief Advisor, UC Berkeley Andhra Smart Village Program. Former Raja Ramanna DRDO Distinguished Fellow, RCI, Ministry of Defence, Govt of India (2014-17). Professor of Excellence, Chiba University, Chiba, Japan. Adjunct Professor, Asian Institute of Technology -Bangkok, Thailand. Member, GIS Academia Council of India. Professor and Head Spatial Information Tech. & Director [R&D] & Head, Centre for Atmospheric Sciences and Weather Modification Technologies, JNTUH, India. FIE, FIS, FAPAS, FISG, FIGU www.linkedin.com/in/iyyanki-v-muralikrishna.

**Prisilla Jayanthi** is a Assistant Professor and doing an independent research on brain tumors using deep learning. She has published 7 Springer papers, 2 IEEE papers, and 1 ACM paper.

**Vinayak Majhi** is a Research Scholars in the Department of Biomedical Engineering, School of Technology, North-Eastern Hill University, Shillong, India under the guidance of Dr. Sudip Paul. He completed his M.Tech Degree in Computer Science and Engineering from University of Calcutta in 2013. Presently he is working on Automatic Diagnosis of Neurological Disorder.

**Pauline Ong** is Associate Professor in the Department of Mechanics Engineering, Universiti Tun Hussein Onn Malaysia. She has a first degree in Pure Mathematics from Universiti Sains Malaysia, Malaysia. After receiving her PhD from the Universiti Sains Malaysia in 2011, she worked for some time as post-doctoral fellow at School of Mathematical Sciences, Universiti Sains Malaysia before joining Universiti Tun Hussein Onn Malaysia where she has had a permanent post since 2013. She has authored more than 60 publications in artificial intelligence. Her research interest concerns neural networks and evolutionary computation over large scale of applications.

**Hiral Patel** has completed their Doctor of Philosophy under Faculty of Computer Applications in 2017. He has published 18 International papers which are differently recommended by Springer, ACM, IEEE, Americal Society, Google Scholar, UGC Approval Journal, ProQuest etc. He has presented more than ten research papers in various conferences. He was awarded as "Young Scientist in 2016" by Indian Science Congress Association. He was also achieve the Presidential Award from our University in the form of amount 1 lakh rupees. His research work is purly focus on financial domain and machine learning.

**Sudip Paul** is currently Assistant Professor in Department of Biomedical Engineering, North-Eastern Hill University, Shillong, India. It is Central University located in the northeast part of the country. He received his Ph.D degree from Indian Institute of Technology (Banaras Hindu University), Varanasi with specialization in Electrophysiology and brain signal analysis. He was selected as Post Doc Fellow under Biotechnology Overseas Associateship for the Scientists working in North Eastern States of India: 2017-18 supported by DBT, Government of India. He has many credentials in his credit out of which his First Prize in Sushruta Innovation Award 2011 sponsored by Department of Science and Technology, Govt. of India and also he also organized many workshops and conferences out of which most significant are the 29th Annual meeting of the SNCI, India and IRBO/APRC Associate School 2017. Dr. Sudip published more than 90 International journal and conference papers and also filled four patents. He is member of APSN, ISN, IBRO, SNCI, SfN, IEEE. He received many awards specially WFN travelling fellowship, Young Investigator Award, IBRO Travel Awardee and ISN Travel Awardee.

**Surendra Rahamatkar** has enormous Teaching, Research and Administrative experience in the field of Technical & Engineering Education, worked at various capacities as Principal/Director, Dean–Research & Development, Dean–Academics, Head of Department with academic positions as a Professor, Associate Professor & Assistant Professor/ Lecturer in Computer Science & Engineering. Prof. Rahamatkar has been conferred, Hon. D.Litt. (Doctor of Letters) by the University of South America (USA) for his outstanding research contribution in the field of Wireless Sensor Networks and also for his distinct participation to promote technical education in the State of Goa. He has been also honored with Life Time Achievement Award by REST Society for Research International, on 28th September 2018 He has published 40+ Research Papers along with 02 International Research Books including one listed in ACM Digital Library. Most of his research work published in Scopus Indexed, Internationally renowned Journals, ISI listed Chapters and conference proceedings.

**Angana Saikia** is currently pursuing her PhD in the Department of Biomedical Engineering, NEHU, Shillong. Previously she was working as a Junior Research Fellow (JRF) and followed by Senior Research Fellow (SRF) in the Department of Biomedical Engineering, NEHU, Shillong. She completed her B.E in Applied Electronics and Instrumentation from Guwahati University, Assam, in 2011 and her M-Tech in Bioelectronics from Tezpur Central University, Assam, India in 2014.

Presently she is pursuing her PhD from Department of Biomedical Engineering, NEHU, Shillong. She is specialized in Electrophysiology, Neurorehabilitation, Biomedical Signal Processing and Instrumentation. Recently she wrote a book on "Overview of Parkinson's disease and its Relevance" published by LAP LAMBERT Academic Publishing, Germany.

**Sanjay Saxena** has research interests in the field of Medical Image Processing, High Performance Computing, Deep Learning. Dr. Saxena teaches Image Processing, Java Programming, Computer Vision and Parallel Computing. Dr. Saxena has published almost 27 research articles in various peer reviewed international & national journals and conferences. Dr. Saxena is the member of various international societies such as IEEE, SCIEI, ACM, IAENG, ISOC. Dr. Saxena has visited several national institutes for the presentation and invited talk on significant research areas of parallel medical image processing. He has also visited numerous international technically recognized institutes like Imperial College London, United Kingdom, Vienna university of Technology, Austria, Stony brook university, New York, USA.

**Amit Tyagi** received his Ph.D degree in 2018 from Pondicherry Central University, Puducherry, India, in area of "Vehicular Ad-hoc Networks". His research interests include Formal Language Theory and Unconventional Models of Computing like DNA Computing, Natural Computing, Cloud Computing, Smart and Secure Computing, Privacy (including Genomic Privacy), Machine Learning with Big data, etc. He has completed his M.Tech degree from the Pondicherry Central University, Puducherry, India. He joined the Lord Krishna College of Engineering, Ghaziabad (LKCE) for the periods of 2009-2010, and 2012-2013. With more than 08 (Eight) years of teaching and research experience across India, currently he is working as an Assistant Professor in Vellore Institute of Technology, Vellore, 632014 Tamilnadu, India. Additionally, He is also the recipient/ awarded of the GATE and NPwD-JRF fellowship in 2009, 2016 and 2013. He has been published one major book titled "Know Your Technical (IT) Skills". Also he is a member of various Computer/ Research Communities like IEEE, ISOC, CSI, ISTE, DataScience, MIRLab, etc.

# Index

Ensure Quality Research is Introduced to the Academic Community

# Become an IGI Global Reviewer for Authored Book Projects

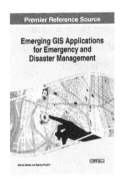

Premier Reference Source

Emerging GIS Applications for Emergency and Disaster Management

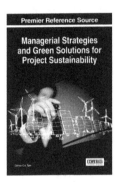

Premier Reference Source

Managerial Strategies and Green Solutions for Project Sustainability

Premier Reference Source

Comparative Approaches to Using R and Python for Statistical Data Analysis

Premier Reference Source

Solutions for High-Touch Communications in a High-Tech World

## The overall success of an authored book project is dependent on quality and timely reviews.

In this competitive age of scholarly publishing, constructive and timely feedback significantly expedites the turnaround time of manuscripts from submission to acceptance, allowing the publication and discovery of forward-thinking research at a much more expeditious rate. Several IGI Global authored book projects are currently seeking highly-qualified experts in the field to fill vacancies on their respective editorial review boards:

## Applications and Inquiries may be sent to:
development@igi-global.com

Applicants must have a doctorate (or an equivalent degree) as well as publishing and reviewing experience. Reviewers are asked to complete the open-ended evaluation questions with as much detail as possible in a timely, collegial, and constructive manner. All reviewers' tenures run for one-year terms on the editorial review boards and are expected to complete at least three reviews per term. Upon successful completion of this term, reviewers can be considered for an additional term.

If you have a colleague that may be interested in this opportunity, we encourage you to share this information with them.

# IGI Global Proudly Partners With eContent Pro International

## Receive a 25% Discount on all Editorial Services

## Editorial Services

IGI Global expects all final manuscripts submitted for publication to be in their final form. This means they must be reviewed, revised, and professionally copy edited prior to their final submission. Not only does this support with accelerating the publication process, but it also ensures that the highest quality scholarly work can be disseminated.

### English Language Copy Editing

Let eContent Pro International's expert copy editors perform edits on your manuscript to resolve spelling, punctuaion, grammar, syntax, flow, formatting issues and more.

### Scientific and Scholarly Editing

Allow colleagues in your research area to examine the content of your manuscript and provide you with valuable feedback and suggestions before submission.

### Figure, Table, Chart & Equation Conversions

Do you have poor quality figures? Do you need visual elements in your manuscript created or converted? A design expert can help!

### Translation

Need your documjent translated into English? eContent Pro International's expert translators are fluent in English and more than 40 different languages.

Printed in the United States
By Bookmasters